# FAITH DAILY

# 365 DAILY DEVOTIONS TO BUILD YOUR FAITH

# (VOLUME 4)

ANDRÉ & JENNY ROEBERT

## Copyright © 2023
## Faith Broadcasting Network

### Notice of Copyright

No part of this book may be reproduced, or stored in a retrieval system, or transmitted in any form or by any means, electronic, mechanical, photocopying, recording, or otherwise, without express written permission of the publisher.

ISBN: 9-7988578891-0-7

Faith Broadcasting Network | 1845 San Marco Rd | Marco Island FL 34145

mediadirector@myriver.com

Printed in the United States of America

**DEVOTIONS:**
Contributed by the pastoral teams and staff of Faith Broadcasting Network and Faith Church

**Edited by:**
Jenny Roebert, Waldo Malan

**Cover Design:**
Waldo Malan

# PREFACE

*The Word of God is alive and powerful! It's filled with a rich treasury of practical wisdom that remains vitally relevant to every area of life. This devotional is for your spiritual growth and enrichment; and as you choose to pour your attention on its pearls, we are certain you will be greatly rewarded for doing so. That's because applying God's priceless wisdom to our lives brings peace, joy, and favor into each day. Every devotion has been carefully written by a small team of people who have waited on the Lord for a specific word that would bring you sure hope, build your faith, and guide you to a life of freedom and victory in Christ Jesus. We are fully confident that each truth has been hand-picked and inspired by the Holy Spirit just for you.*

*André, Jenny & the Faith Family*

# CONTENTS

PREFACE ........................................................................... 3

JANUARY ........................................................................... 1

FEBRUARY ...................................................................... 33

MARCH ............................................................................ 62

APRIL ............................................................................... 94

MAY ............................................................................... 125

JUNE .............................................................................. 157

JULY .............................................................................. 188

AUGUST ........................................................................ 220

SEPTEMBER ................................................................. 252

OCTOBER ..................................................................... 283

NOVEMBER .................................................................. 315

DECEMBER .................................................................. 346

# JANUARY

# Day 01

## The Golden New Year's Resolution

*Proverbs 20:27 (AMPC), "The spirit of man [that factor in human personality which proceeds immediately from God] is the lamp of the Lord, searching all his innermost parts."*

There is a New Year's Resolution that will cause us to walk in Divine favor, protection, and provision this year, and bring us great success in everything we put our hands to. It is to set aside time, every single day, to meditate on the Word of God. The born-again spirit of man is where the Spirit of God resides. It's what the Bible calls the inner-man, and it's the place from where God's Spirit speaks to us. If we could develop and strengthen the voice of our spirit-man, so that it speaks louder than our own thoughts, or the thoughts the enemy puts into our minds, we would be able to recognize and follow God's perfect will for every detail of our lives. We would become people that are truly *led* by the Spirit of God. The only way to develop and strengthen the voice of our spirit-man is by us meditating on God's written word. That's because the written word sounds just like God! It's full of His own thoughts and wisdom! As we meditate on it, the Holy Spirit makes it alive and a supernatural flow of wisdom to rise inside us. Walking in this Godly wisdom will pave a way for daily prosperity and success, where goodness and mercy follow every step! Victory is yours this year as you meditate on the word of God to recognize His voice and walk in the way He has planned for you to walk in!

# Day 02

## Stay in the Fight

*1 Timothy 1:18 (NKJV), "This charge I commit to you, son Timothy, according to the prophecies previously made concerning you, that by them you may wage the good warfare."*

As children of God, we are called to press forward into all God has for us! The finished work of the cross has made the glorious, good life God prepared for us to walk in completely accessible! While it's true we have an enemy who is devoted to keep us from walking in God's glorious plan for our lives, we must constantly be aware of his defeat and the authority we have been given over him. That's why Paul says we are to wage the good warfare! It's a fight that has already been won - a victory that is already secured for those who are in Christ Jesus (1 Corinthians 15:57)! The Word of God clearly tells us that our victory is wrapped up in our faith (1 John 5:4). We don't wrestle against flesh and blood, but against adversaries in the spirit realm, and what sets us apart as children of God is that Jesus attained the victory and we as heirs are assigned to enforce it - by faith!

We are not struggling to become victorious in this life, Jesus has already done that for us. We are called to overcome and walk in that victory by maintaining the correct mindset, the right confessions, and acting on our God-given authority. (John 16:33). So, refuse to grow weary! Refuse to draw back! Keep fighting the good fight of faith and enforce the finished work of the cross in every area of your life. Stay focused on your victory and you will stay in the fight!

# Day 03

## Strong in Him

***Psalm 28:7 (NLT) "The Lord is my strength and shield I trust Him with all my heart. He helps me, and my heart is filled with joy. I burst out in songs of thanksgiving."***

Your Heavenly Father loves you so much. His desire is to be intricately involved in every detail of your life, so you never have to be alone, or unaware of His Presence being with you. He does this through the indwelling of His Holy Spirit, who is His precious gift to us. The Holy Spirit pours the most powerful force that exists into our hearts - the unconquerable love of God (Romans 5:5)! It's power never, ever fails (1 Corinthians 13:8). In Ephesians 1:19 we are told that the Holy Spirit fills us with an exceedingly great power that is demonstrated in our lives as a mighty inner strength! Philippians 2:13 says that the Holy Spirit is continuously working within us, creating a desire to do God's will, and giving us the ability to do it! Hallelujah! All we need to do is acknowledge Him, turn our affection towards Him, and spend time with Him in the Word!

Look at what Jesus promised the Holy Spirit will do for us: *"But the Helper, the Holy Spirit, whom the Father will send in My name, He will teach you all things, and bring to your remembrance all things that I said to you."* (John 14:26). It's time to make the greatest investment we could ever make this side of heaven! Invest time in your relationship with the Holy Spirit. Place all hope and trust in Him and draw from His never-ending supply of wisdom and strength as He teaches you truth - making God's word come alive inside of you!

# Day 04

## Prosper in Every Way

*Isaiah 33:6 (AMPC), "And there shall be stability in your times, an abundance of salvation, wisdom, and knowledge; the reverent fear and worship of the Lord is your treasure and His."*

The truth of God's Word is never affected or altered by the circumstances around us. No matter how evil the days seem to be, God's Word will always be the stabilizing truth that offers a sure hope to whoever fastens their hold onto it (Philippians 2:15-16). It is the anchor of our souls, keeping our minds in perfect peace, regardless of the trouble around us (Hebrews 6:19).

Acts 20:32 says the Word of God can build us up and give us our rightful inheritance as God's set-apart ones (those consecrated, purified, and transformed of soul)! That means there is no limit to what the Word of God can and will do for us when we commit to meditating on its truth and allow it to transform us. Our greatest way to success in all areas of life is to make God's Word the ultimate authority for our lives.

Choose to make its wisdom your first and only source of reference and it will guard and fortify your mind and heart and cause you to prosper in every way!

# Day 05

## Incomparable God!

*1 Corinthians 1:31 (AMPC), "So then, as it is written, 'Let him who boasts and proudly rejoices and glories, boast and proudly rejoice and glory in the Lord.'"*

The prophet Isaiah asked, *"To whom then will you liken God? Or with what likeness will you compare Him?"* (Isaiah 40:18). He described God as being able to measure the waters in the hollow of His hands! There is absolutely no-one like Him. His greatness is incomparable, and His wisdom infallible. The Bible describes Him as being completely good and true! It says His faithfulness is immeasurable and that He desires to show us the exceeding richness of His kindness throughout the ages. No wonder scripture tells us to boast and proudly rejoice in Him alone! If our God is so awesome in His stature and nature, how could we possibly please Him? Hebrews 11:6 answers this for us. It says, *"But without faith it is impossible to please Him, for he who comes to God must believe that He is, and that He is a rewarder of those who diligently seek Him."*

Choosing to believe in God, to seek Him out, and to trust in His good nature towards us is what pleases Him. What delights His heart is that even when we can't see Him with our physical eyes, we still believe He is exactly who His Word says He is, and we desire to know Him more deeply. Spend time seeking the Lord today, trusting Him to reveal His good, wonderful nature to you. Delight yourself in Him, and He will satisfy the desires of your heart! How great is our incomparable God!

# Day 06

## Give Your Way into Abundance

*Proverbs 11:24-25 (AMPC), "There are those who [generously] scatter abroad, and yet increase more; there are those who withhold more than is fitting (appropriate) or what is justly due, but it results only in want. The liberal person shall be enriched, and he who waters shall himself be watered."*

The Bible tells us that the person who is generous in their giving will always be provided for, and through their generosity will increase even more! That means the level of generosity they reached in their giving immediately increased their capacity to give again! In other words, their generosity made way for more provision to come into their lives. The same verse that gives this promise of increase through generous giving, mentions what happens when we give without generosity in our hearts. Notice, it doesn't say anything about those who don't give. In fact, it speaks of two different kinds of givers: Those who give generously, and those who withhold more than is appropriate, or due. In other words, those who knew in their hearts what they should give yet chose to withhold the full amount. This lack of generosity only results in want. For the most part, people hold back on their giving when times are financially tough, out of fear that their giving will result in lack. However, lack doesn't come from money we don't have - it comes from money we do have that we should not be keeping to ourselves (Mark Hankins). In the kingdom of God, His way to bring increase to us is through our generosity! Our generous giving, even in tough times, will open the door for God's abundance in our lives. It will get us out of debt and release a flow of supernatural resources into our lives that will enrich ourselves, as we enrich His kingdom!

# Day 07

## Misplaced Trust

*Psalms 33:17 (ESV), "The war horse is a false hope for salvation, and by its great might it cannot rescue."*

In the time the Israelites exited out of Egypt, the Egyptian war horses and chariots were formidable and potent instruments of war. Despite their usefulness and potency in combat, in this Psalm, David reminds his readers that even these magnificent warhorses offer false hope for rescue, if the Lord is not on our side. Of course, he was alluding to the Egyptian Calvary that were in hot pursuit after the just-liberated Hebrew slaves. In the natural, those powerful animals would carry their masters with speed and accuracy into certain victory every time. However, this time they were no match to the power of the Israelite God!

It would do us well to understand that placing our trust in anyone, or anything other than the Lord for deliverance in battle is futile. We can't afford to lean on our own understanding to see the victory. While God may give us tools and resources to aid and assist us, our trust must never rest in them. No earthly object or advantage, by itself, can guarantee victory. Our help comes from the Lord! Misplaced trust will only lead to disappointment, but those who choose to trust in the Lord will never be ashamed for doing so!

# Day 08

## Delivered Promises

*Isaiah 48:3 (AMPC), "I have declared from the beginning the former things [which happened in times past to Israel]; they went forth from My mouth and I made them known; then suddenly I did them, and they came to pass [says the Lord]."*

The same God who promised Israel's freedom from captivity - delivered on His promise. We serve a God who is true to His Word, despite what skeptical on-lookers may report, or temporary circumstances may indicate. Scripture has many records of people who declared promises the Lord had placed on their hearts to speak, even when those promises seemed foolish. Without fail every promise came to pass: Noah and the flood (Genesis 6-9); the Prophet Elijah and the rain (1 Kings 18); John the Baptist and the coming Messiah (Matthew 3). All were logically invalid – until they happened.

Whatever the Lord has spoken to you (that is in line with the spirit of His written word) concerning who He is, who you are in Him, and what He will do in and through you – believe it, profess it, and expect to see it come to pass. God will always watch over His Word to see it accomplish exactly what He sent it to do (Isaiah 55:11). Praise God! He delivers on every promise He makes.

*Isaiah 55:11 "So shall My word be that goes forth from My mouth; It shall not return to Me void, but it shall accomplish what I please, and it shall prosper in the thing for which I sent it."*

# Day 09

## Stand Firm

*Ephesians 6:13 (NLT), "Therefore, put on every piece of God's armour so you will be able to resist the enemy in the time of evil. Then after the battle you will still be standing firm."*

The Bible tells us that if we faint in the day of adversity our strength is small (Proverbs 24:10). The good news is - that won't be said of us! As people of faith, we must recognize that our enemy, the devil, while being a very real adversary, is in truth a defeated foe! His assignment is threefold, he seeks to kill, steal, and destroy every good thing the Lord has placed in our lives - if we give him the grounds to do it. Paul instructs us to not be ignorant of the devil's devices lest he gains an advantage over us. Understanding his schemes gives us a sure advantage over his advances. The Bible clearly tells us to guard our hearts from any offence or unforgiveness. It says to refuse fearful thoughts or being anxious. It teaches us to keep our eyes fixed on the truth of God's Word, and our thoughts on things that are good, pure, and true.

All these principles, amongst others found in the word will give the devil no room in our lives and keep us strong and confident in our faith. Despite every threat he boasts, we can walk in a confident boldness and exercise our legal authority over him - keeping him in the place Jesus put him - under our feet. As we pursue knowing God and His ways more, we will become so supernaturally strong in the Lord, that in the end, we will be found standing firm.

# Day 10

## Follow His Voice

*Isaiah 49:10 (AMPC), "They shall neither hunger nor thirst, neither heat nor sun shall strike them. For He who has mercy on them will lead them, even by the springs of water He will guide them."*

The Bible calls Jesus our 'Good Shepherd'. Something interesting about the oriental shepherd is that for the most part, he goes before his flock, leading them along the path that's best for them. He guides them away from danger and into places where they will be well nourished, and watered. Before Jesus left the earth, He told His disciples that He was not going to abandon them but send them a helper who would remain with them forever. This is what He said the Holy Spirit would do: *"...when He, the Spirit of truth, has come, He will guide you into all truth; for He will not speak on His own authority, but whatever He hears He will speak; and He will tell you things to come. He will glorify Me, for He will take of what is Mine and declare it to you. All things that the Father has are Mine. Therefore I said that He will take of Mine and declare it to you."* (John 16:13-15). Whatever decisions we need to make in this life, no matter how insignificant they may seem, we will find their answers when we consult the Spirit of God. He will lead us along the right path that is best for us. He leads us through the wisdom in His Word and His voice in our inner-man, and it always comes with a supernatural peace. A life lived in submission to and under the direction of the Spirit of God will always draw us to a place of endless victory, abundance and blessing! Trust in your Good Shepherd as you follow His voice today.

# Day 11

## No God Like Our God

*1 Samuel 2:2 (NKJV), "No one is holy like the Lord, for there is none besides You, nor is there any rock like our God."*

This verse is Hannah's song of praise to the Lord after she delivers her son, Samuel to Eli, the priest, to fulfil her vow to God. She describes God in three distinct phrases, each attributing a quality in which He is unequalled. First, she calls Him holy. This means He is set apart from any other being. He is completely unique, free of impurity, selfishness, and wrongdoing. But this quality doesn't make Him cold or distant. He is, in truth, the exact opposite. He literally moved heaven and earth to make a way for us to be reconciled to Himself. He sacrificed His only Son so we could live in an inseparable relationship with Him - for eternity. Then Hannah affirms that there simply is no one like our God. In a world where diverse cultures call on numerous gods, He is the only true, living God, incomparable to any other. The Creator of the universe is faithful to those who trust Him. Finally, Hannah refers to God as a place of safety and refuge, especially in times of trouble. He was her rock. He alone had the love and power to reverse her barrenness and pain by giving her a beautiful son. Hannah's song of praise was from the depth of her heart to God, and it rings true in our hearts towards Him too.

There truly is no God like our God!

# Day 12

## Live Like Your New Nature

*Colossians 2:6 (AMPC), "As you have therefore received Christ, [even] Jesus the Lord, [so] walk (regulate your lives and conduct yourselves) in union with and conformity to Him."*

I have heard many people say that the Gospel is free. In truth, following Christ, costs us everything. That's the greatest miracle of salvation. We get to lay down our old, sinful, selfish natures that were enslaved to sin; and take on a brand-new nature in Christ Jesus! Our old self has been nailed to the cross with Christ, it died with Him and was buried with Him. Then, the very same Spirit that raised Jesus to life, raised us IN Him too! Now we get to live with His nature inside our spirit-man! His own Holy Spirit dwells inside us! If this is truly our reality, then our lives must reflect His nature. There's simply no other option. We aren't saved in degrees or measures. We are either completely saved, or not saved at all. And if we are completely saved then it's impossible for us to live like the world. Sin has absolutely no appeal to us! We hate wickedness and love righteousness - because this is our new nature! Paul explained this miracle the best when he said, *"I have been crucified with Christ; it is no longer I who live, but Christ lives in me; and the life which I now live in the flesh I live by the faith of the Son of God, who loved me and gave Himself for me."* (Galatians 2:20). If we started our new life in faith, being totally reliant on God and His power to set us free from the kingdom of darkness; why have some of us abandoned that way, or not learned to continue in it? Paul goes on to warn us to not frustrate the grace of God by refusing to live this new life of faith we have been given! It's time to live like the new nature of Christ that's living inside you today!

# Day 13

## Overwhelming Joy

***Psalm 4:7 (ESV), "You have put more joy in my heart than they have when their grain and wine abound."***

David wrote that God put more joy in his heart than the joy people had when their grain and wine abounded after a great harvest. There are many ways people attempt to find joy and satisfaction. Some try find it in other people, or in places they visit. Some try finding joy in material things. While all these things make us happy, true, and lasting joy can only come from knowing the Lord. The Bible says that in His presence there is fullness of joy. Nothing can fill our hearts with joy as the Holy Spirit can. His joy is our strength. It sustains and empowers us. That's because He created us to be filled with Himself! No wonder nothing else can satisfy us or bring us true joy outside of Him. The Word says, *"... the God of hope will fill us with joy and peace IN BELIEVING"!* (Romans 15:13). This means the condition to being filled with God's joy is *believing*.

As we believe in the Lord and the promises of His Word, our hearts fill up with joy. Though circumstances might be tough, our hearts will overflow with joy because of our faith in Him. Even when faced with challenging circumstances, the Church at Macedonia – as Paul writes – still had an abundance of joy. In the same way, we can abound with joy regardless of what we may be facing, as we choose to believe steadfastly in the Lord.

# Day 14

## Words that Bring Life

*Ephesians 4:29 (NLT), "Don't use foul or abusive language. Let everything you say be good and helpful, so that your words will be an encouragement to those who hear them."*

Paul wrote this letter to teach believers how to live as "Children of Light" by the words we speak. We are to *build* one another up by using words intended for good. Jesus said, *"...the words that I speak to you are spirit, and they are life."* (John 6:63). As children of God and heirs to the Kingdom of Light, it's expected of us to speak like people belonging to the culture of heaven. Even when we bring correction, it must be done in love and the sincere intention of bringing someone back into line with their purpose. Harsh words that cut and break down are destructive in nature and will produce destruction in the hearer.

Beware of speaking words that mask jealousy or insecurity, they will only ensnare you deeper in bitterness. When our words carry faith and love, they can connect us to a limitless reality, where nothing is impossible. God's order of design has always been to use words to create and bring every life-giving promise from His word into our natural word. Speaking life that brings change to every impossible circumstance becomes second nature to us when we fill our hearts and minds with the truth of God's word. As we fill our lives with His words, they begin to flow through us like a river of life - bringing light, love, joy, and peace whenever we speak.

# Day 15

## Kindness that Positions for Blessing

*2 Samuel 9:7 (AMPC), "David said to him, Fear not, for I will surely show you kindness for Jonathan your father's sake, and will restore to you all the land of Saul your father [grandfather], and you shall eat at my table always."*

King David had a noteworthy quality to honor those who had been loyal and helpful to him in times of trouble. Jonathan, King Saul's son was one of those people. When his father tried to kill David, Jonathan remained loyal to David, helping him escape. After Jonathan's death, David made a vow to care for the needs of Jonathan's family. He learnt that Jonathan had a disabled son called Mephibosheth and summoned him to come to the palace. On hearing that King David, the enemy of his late grandfather King Saul, wanted to see him - Mephibosheth was extremely apprehensive. He had already gone through so much in his life, when he was a baby, he suffered a fall that caused him to be lame. This brought shame on the Royal Family, so he was isolated, and hidden from public scrutiny. He had just, suddenly lost his father and grandfather in battle, and now he certainly wasn't hopeful for meeting his grandfather's enemy, who just happened to be king! But King David was gracious! He not only gave Mephibosheth the land his grandfather owned, and caretakers to keep it for him, he made him a permanent guest at his table!

Jonathan's loyalty and kindness produced great fruit for his offspring. King David became a vessel of blessing to Jonathan's family when he was un-able to take care of them himself. Understand, every act of kindness positions us to receive the blessing of the Lord, even for generations to come.

# Day 16

## A Fearless Security

*Isaiah 43:1 (NKJ), "But now, thus says the LORD, who created you, O Jacob, and He who formed you, O Israel: 'Fear not, for I have redeemed you; I have called you by your name; You are Mine.'"*

One of the greatest sources of fear common to man is founded on deep-seated insecurity. When the Word of the Lord came through the prophet Isaiah, a strong sense of confident trust was instilled in his listeners. Knowing that the God who created heaven and earth had willingly, and lovingly taken full responsibility for His people, had given them an identity amongst the nations of the world, and had declared them as His very Own gave them a true sense of belonging and purpose. It placed deep within them a security that cast out all fear. We know from scripture, that this covenant promise extends to and stands sure and true for every born-again child of God. Only, now it's even better for us than it was for the children of Israel (Hebrews 7:6). Their experience of being secure in God came from outward demonstrations only; and when their hearts began to fail them, they were dependent on the voice of the prophets to guide and encourage them. Today, we can experience the presence of God living inside us to comfort, guide and strengthen us; but also, we are able to carry His presence into every place we go! It's the reality of carrying His presence that sets us apart from everybody else. It instils a confident trust and purpose that casts out all fear and is a powerful tool to attract others to know and experience a relationship with the Living God for themselves. You can be fearless as you choose to embrace, host, and carry the presence of God, starting today.

# Day 17

## Keep Building

*Proverbs 14:1 (AMP), "The wise woman builds her house [on a foundation of godly precepts, and her household thrives], But the foolish one [who lacks spiritual insight] tears it down with her own hands [by ignoring godly principles]."*

As Covenant Believers, we are called to a lifestyle of constantly building and moving forward in the things of God. The Word of God doesn't call for us to stagnate or be unfruitful, and it certainly doesn't tell us to draw back! Even when we are waiting for a promise from the Lord to be fulfilled, we don't sit around doing nothing. We press on, building ourselves up in faith and constantly obeying what the Word teaches us to do. The life of faith always leads to growth and success, in all areas of life. Just as the wise man built his house upon the solid rock, we are to daily build ours on the truth of God's Word. As a result, when trouble comes that foundation, we built our hope on will not fail under the pressure! It will keep us anchored and full of confident peace! As we build ourselves firmly in God and on His Word, supernatural stability and soundness will infiltrate our families and relationships too. This is how we build the kingdom of God together! When we continue to steadfastly build ourselves up and stand firm in the word, people in this world will recognize and be drawn to the inner strength and stability we have in God. Be diligent to press into the things of God and build yourself up in His word today.

# Day 18

## Faith in The Name!

**Colossians 3:17 (NKJV), "And whatever you do in word or deed, do all in the name of the Lord Jesus, giving thanks to God the Father through Him."**

Do you want to do things God's way or the world's way? God's ways might seem strange sometimes, but they always work irrespective of times or seasons. Psalm 18:30 says, *"As for God, His way is perfect; The word of the LORD is proven; He is a shield to all who trust in Him."* It works to trust God. It works to live by faith. Since the Word is the source of faith and God is always watching over His Word to perform it, the outcome is *always* sure. Paul says to live this life of faith in the Name of the Lord Jesus. Now, when we understand the power and authority that backs that Name, and we have knowledge of everything that is invested in it - we will confidently know that every power or circumstance opposing God's perfect will must and will bow to the power of that Name! This is why we are told to do everything in the Name of Jesus - whatever we do in word or deed - we do in His Name, proclaiming His Lordship over it, with thankful hearts!

We are thankful because the battle has already been won! The victory has already been secured! All we need to do is get our level of faith in that Name to match the level of obedience that all things have when they are subject to it! Then, when we truly believe - nothing will remain the same as we declare the Name of Jesus!

# Day 19

## The Goodness of God

*2 Kings 6:6 (AMPC), "The man of God said, 'Where did it fall?'. When shown the place, Elisha cut off a stick and threw it in there, and the iron floated."*

The Prophet Elisha and his students were working together on a building project when one of the students ax-head broke off and fell into the river. He cried out in dismay because the ax had been borrowed, it wasn't his. Elisha, fully persuaded of his covenant with God, threw a stick into the water and the impossible happened - the iron ax-head floated to the surface to be retrieved!

This miraculous account certainly stirs our hearts when we see how God's intervention can suddenly turn any bad situation around. What is even more impressive is the truth that our supernatural God is willing to care about all the details in our lives, both the significant and insignificant ones.

This story emphasizes a quality of God that showcases His tender, watchful care over His children. Learning to depend completely on the Lord and His kindness towards us instils a desire to walk closer to Him. It also causes us to delight to walk in His ways, because we know they are as good and perfect as He is!

As we do, we see how He graciously causes His manifest glory to be displayed in every area of our lives.

# Day 20

## Eyes of Faith

*Hebrews 11:23 (NLT), "It was by faith that Moses' parents hid him for three months when he was born. They saw that God had given them an unusual child, and they were not afraid to disobey the king's command."*

We are all called to follow the Lord Jesus with eyes of faith, being careful to not be dissuaded by any circumstances that oppose the path He has chosen for us to walk in. It would have been easy for Moses' parents to opt to preserve and protect themselves rather than disobey Pharaoh when he ordered all Hebrew baby boys to be taken from their parents. There's no doubt such a cruel ruler had brutal consequences in store for anyone who disobeyed him. By faith, Moses' parents chose their purpose to preserve the life of their son above their own safety. Their decision to act in faith opened their hearts to receive divine wisdom from the Lord to act with haste and skill.

The Bible says they recognized God had given them an unusual child with a significant destiny. They understood their responsibility to refuse fear and act in faith, trusting the Lord to work out every detail following each step of obedience. *Because* of their faith and obedience, Moses lived to be one of the greatest instruments of God's grace and deliverance in the history of mankind. He was used by God to liberate the entire nation of Israel. Today, recognize you have been called by God for a higher purpose than just existing. You are called as His own representative, to walk in His authority over the devil and release His goodness here on earth. With joy and relentless faith, engage in your assignment and let God live in and through you to advance His kingdom each day, in a significant way.

# Day 21

## Refreshing Humility

*Philippians 2:3-4 (ESV), "Do nothing from selfish ambition or conceit, but in humility count others more significant than yourselves. Let each of you look only to his own interests, but also to the interests of others."*

Humility in the kingdom of God is abandoning our own selfish desires or plans in exchange for God's perfect ones. In truth, God's ways are always better than our own! His ways continuously lead to abundant blessing for everyone! While our needs and interests are important, finding God's heart for those around us and being mindful and considerate to them before meeting our own needs, paves a way for His blessing to flow in our lives. In fact, being mindful of others is a Biblical principle that teaches us to be generous. Proverbs 11:24-25 explains how our generosity towards others immediately enlarges the capacity in our hearts for more acts of generosity.

The result is not just the benefit of others, but we become enriched by our generous ways too! Getting on board with the Lord in being a blessing to others significantly demonstrates His character in us. Jesus came to serve the needs of others, not to be served. He clothed Himself with humility and took on the form of a bond servant even though He was the Son of God.

So, we choose to clothe ourselves with humility and serve the needs of others too, and while we refresh others, we become refreshed too.

# Day 22

## Trust and Obey

*Deuteronomy 28:1 (NKJV), "Now it shall come to pass, if you diligently obey the voice of the Lord your God, to observe carefully all His commandments which I command you today, that the Lord your God will set you high above all nations of the earth."*

Faith-filled obedience to the will of God always results in the fulfilment of His promises! Faith is not just believing; it's applying the appropriate action to our belief that activates its rewards! Every person recorded in the Bible who saw the hand of God supernaturally intervene in their lives, had to first act in obedience to God's instruction before they saw anything happen. They could all testify that their faith in God was evidenced by their obedience. It literally authenticated their absolute trust and belief in God and His Word. When God spoke, they had full confidence in His trustworthy nature and immediately acted on His instructions.

Our reluctance to step out in faith, after clearly hearing God's voice, demonstrates our lack of trust in one of two areas. Either we don't really believe He spoke, or we don't really believe He will take care of every detail once we step out and obey Him. If you find yourself in a place of stagnation with God - seek Him out and listen to His voice. Then, step out and obey Him - trusting Him to take care of every detail along the way. Obedience is the catalyst that makes things happen in the life of every believer, it's the highway His blessing travels upon.

Today, determine to hear and obey the voice of the Lord and see His blessing of provision flow!

# Day 23

## Faith is Not Blind

*Proverbs 4:20 – 22 (NLT), "My child, pay attention to what I say. Listen carefully to my words. Don't lose sight of them. Let them penetrate deep into your heart, for they bring life to those who find them, and healing to their whole body."*

There are great benefits and rewards for those who are led by the Spirit of God! To see the manifestation of God's Word, take place in our lives, we must be intentional when it comes to hearing His voice, so we can be led by His Spirit. The Holy Spirit will never lead us astray, He will only lead us in the direction of God's very best for our lives. Jesus did nothing without first hearing from His Heavenly Father, as a result His life was filled with great works of faith and significant, lasting fruit! As we are led by His Spirit, we do have certainty, because faith is never *blind* - it always attaches itself to the Word of God. Hebrews 11:1 says faith is the title-deed, or the evidence of things God has spoken, even before they are manifest in the natural world.

For that reason, faith is never a walk in the dark. It is a purposeful walk towards God's promises regardless of what is happening in the world around us. The God that we serve is not a God of confusion and chaos, instead He enables us to build our lives and families on His never changing Word, and He is a never changing God! He never changes His mind concerning what He has said and promised us. There will always be a confidence and certainty in following Him! As we pay attention to God's Word, listen carefully to what He is saying to us, and purposing to do what He says - our lives will overflow with the richness of His manifest promises!

# Day 24

## Rely on His Strength

*2 Corinthians 12:9 (NKJ), "And He said to me, 'My grace is sufficient for you, for My strength is made perfect in weakness.' Therefore most gladly I will rather boast in my infirmities, that the power of Christ may rest upon me."*

There's no better time to be strong in the Lord than in these last days. The believer's walk of faith calls for a complete dependence on the power of God's might, and absolutely no confidence in the flesh. The AMPC version of this verse says God's grace, which is His supernatural empowerment, is *"...sufficient against any danger and enables you to bear the trouble manfully."*

There's no question our faith will be tested, and it's in the testing that we must know what it means to remain in Christ. The devil will do his best to distract you from spending time in the Presence of the Lord and in His Word. That's because in God's presence there is fullness of joy - which is supernatural strength to overcome the devil. While we are in the Word, our faith is built, and we can recognize His voice and be led by His Holy Spirit. 2 Corinthians 2:14 tells us that He always leads us in triumph! Keeping God's Word in our hearts, minds and in our mouths will cause us to continually walk in victory and dominion. Remember that while you are not focused on the Presence of God, or His Word, you will begin to rely on your own strength and wisdom, making you easy prey for the enemy. Rather, give yourself completely to fellowshipping with the Lord in His Word so that Paul's testimony will be yours too! *"...that the strength and power of Christ (the Messiah) may rest (yes, may pitch a tent over and dwell) upon me!"*

# Day 25

## Joyful, Reverential Respect

*Psalm 2:11 (AMPC), "Serve the Lord with reverent awe and worshipful fear; rejoice and be in high spirits with trembling."*

The author of this psalm, King David, was calling upon the rebellious kings and rulers to serve the Lord with reverential fear and joy, instead of opposing Him. The Bible makes it abundantly clear that while born-again believers will not be judged for our sin, we will give an account for the way in which we served the Lord here on earth. Serving Him is not to be taken lightly. We are to dedicate our lives to fulfilling His perfect will for us. Every thought, every word, and every deed will be judged to see if it was in harmony with His will or not. Since God's Own Spirit lives within us, and we can hear and heed His voice, only thinking, speaking, and doing what is in line with His leading is certainly possible! In truth, it is a joy to *think* as He does, to *speak* His words of faith, and to *act* in kindness towards others, with excellence in all we do, and to use our authority over the devil!

Being led by the Holy Spirit in all things will cause us to live in a way that is truly pleasing to the Lord. His power in us gives us both the desire to think, speak, and do His will, and the supernatural ability to carry it out too. Joyful, reverential respect for the Lord is only accomplished through us yielding to the Holy Spirit and obeying the leading of His voice. The results of doing this will be pure joy, peace, and overwhelming victory, carrying through from this life into eternity!

# Day 26

## A Foolish Exchange

***Genesis 25:32 (NLT), "'Look, I'm dying of starvation!' said Esau. 'What good is my birthright to me now?'"***

In a moment of weakness, Esau overlooked the most important privilege he could have - his birthright! He literally gave up his inheritance for a bowl of stew! His lack of self-control caused him to make the most foolish mistake of his life. Proverbs 25:28 says, *"He who has no rule over his own spirit is like a city that is broken down and without walls."* If Esau was able to control his flesh, he wouldn't have traded something so significant for something of no value at all.

Paul teaches us the importance of training our senses so that we can discern and act wisely (Hebrews 5:14). The only way to do this is by exposing our thoughts to as much of the truth of God's word as possible. The Holy Spirit reveals God's wisdom as we give His word the attention it deserves. When we apply its principles to our lives, it transforms the way we perceive things in life. We begin to see circumstances and people from God's perspective, instead of our own limited, selfish one. It's not that difficult to act as foolishly as Esau did when the pressure is on, and the influence of our spirit-man is weak. Make a concerted effort to embolden the voice of your spirit-man and weaken the voice of your flesh by spending quality time with the Holy Spirit in God's Word. Instead of being victim to the pressure of circumstances, you will learn how to discern correctly and reign in life in the wisdom of Christ Jesus!

# Day 27

## Turn a Deaf Ear

*Psalm 38:13 (NLT), "But I am deaf to all their threats. I am silent before them as one who cannot speak."*

David records that his enemies insulted him and sent false accusations his way. They actively sought to harm him. Yet the Word of the Lord says he turned a deaf ear to all their threats and accusations. Instead of retaliating, he became silent. Why? Because he knew his God would fight for him. He knew the Lord would deliver him out of the hand of his enemies. Instead of avenging himself, he waited upon the Lord. The Bible tells us that we are to wait upon the Lord and He will exalt us, while we see the wicked cut off (Psalm 37:34).

In other words, we shouldn't take matters into our own hands to vindicate ourselves, but rather roll our concerns onto the Lord, because He cares for us. He will comfort, encourage, and strengthen us with His joy, and flood our minds with His peace. Then, while we are focused on His goodness, our enemies will set a trap for themselves to fall into.

Just as David turned a deaf ear to the threats of those seeking his life and he remained silent before them, we too should turn a deaf ear and keep silent when we are insulted or wrongly accused or receive threats while standing for righteousness. As we do, the God of peace will establish us and protect us from every plot and plan of the enemy.

# Day 28

## Treasure the Word

***Job 23:12 (NKJV), "I have not departed from the commandment of His lips; I have treasured the words of His mouth more than my necessary food."***

Your attitude towards the Word of God determines the position God holds in your life. No person can say they truly love God and display a low regard for his Word. We simply can't separate God from His Word; they are one.

When we understand the value of the Word and see the evidence of what it produces in us, we develop a deep passion for it. We desire it more than the natural food we need for survival. Ask yourself this question, "What position does God's Word hold in my life?" Is it the first thing you turn to and meditate on in the morning, or is it the last thing on your list to do? Do you love the Word of God enough to abandon your own preferences and do what it teaches with a willing and grateful heart?

The truth is, nobody puts God's Word first and lives to regret it, and whoever believes in and follows it with their whole heart, will never be ashamed of doing so.

Today, allow the Holy Spirit to reignite your passion for the Word of God. As you prioritize His Word, He will prioritize your advancement.

# Day 29

## No Turning Back

*Exodus 14:13 – 14 (NLT), "But Moses told the people, 'Don't be afraid. Just stand still and watch the Lord rescue you today. The Egyptians you see today will never be seen again. The Lord Himself will fight for you. Just stay calm.'"*

Many men and women in the Bible had to make a choice to either continue pressing on doing what God had said to do or turn back and live apart from His direction. The same is true for us today, we need to choose to press on, keep walking in faith and look forward to what He has promised us, or make the choice to turn away and follow what seems to be the easy way, or the path of least resistance. Moses had to make a very serious decision when he was staring at the red sea. The nation God had told him to lead out of slavery was trapped between their quickly advancing pursuers and an ocean. If Moses had chosen to step down, and away from what God had originally instructed him to do at that moment, God's people would have been taken right back into slavery. Instead, Moses chose to stay in the fight, he chose to believe God and continue looking forward to their destiny. In that impossible moment, he told the people to stay calm and listened for the Lord's instruction. As soon as he acted on the Word the Lord gave him, the miraculous happened and God's people were saved while their enemies were destroyed - just as the Lord had promised. When we are faced with impossible situations, as we wait on the Lord, He will give us a Word to act upon. Our immediate obedience will open the way for our deliverance and silence the enemy, destroying his plan for our destruction. Refuse to fear, wait on the Lord and as you do what He says to do - you will walk in the way He has personally carved out for you!

# Day 30

## A Trustworthy Partnership

*Jeremiah 17:7-8 (NLT), "But blessed are those who trust in the Lord and have made the Lord their hope and confidence. They are like trees planted along a riverbank, with roots that reach deep into the water. Such trees are not bothered by the heat or worried by long months of drought. Their leaves stay green, and they never stop producing fruit."*

Placing our full trust and confidence in people will only lead to disappointment. Psalm 118:8 says, *"It is better to trust in the LORD than to put confidence in man."* The only One we can place all our trust in is the Lord. Psalms 111:7 says, *"... all His decrees and precepts are sure (fixed, established, and trustworthy)."* This means that no matter what trials, challenges, or hardships we endure here on earth, we have a faithful, trustworthy God to depend upon. As we are faithful to spend time in fellowship with Him while we meditate on His Word, He will comfort, strengthen, and release a flow of His peace - giving wisdom for us to apply to every situation. Without fail, He will lead us through every difficulty as we refuse to fear and hold fast to His truth. 1 Corinthians 1:9 says, *"God is faithful (reliable, trustworthy, and therefore ever true to His promise, and He can be depended on); by Him you were called into companionship and participation with His Son, Jesus Christ our Lord."* We must remember that this life of faith is all about responding to the call of partnership with Jesus, through His Holy Spirit. As we learn to hear His voice, closely follow His lead, and rely completely on Him, we will not be bothered by the pressures or seasons this world is subject to. Instead, we will flourish and be fruitful because we are drawing from the giver of life Who is wisdom Himself.

# Day 31

## An Endless Supply of God's Love

*John 13:34 (AMPC), "I give you a new commandment: that you should love one another. Just as I have loved you, so you too should love one another."*

What a great commandment. Love one another – your spouse, your children, your brother, or sister in Christ, the one who hurt you, the mocker, the beggar, the persecutor, the unjust and the wicked - just as Christ has loved you! Jesus loved us so dearly that He gave us His life. He gave everything!

1 John tells us we love because He first loved us. Christ poured into us so lavishly that we are enabled to pour into others. The more we allow Jesus to pour into us, the more we are empowered to love unconditionally, without growing weary. There is enough love in Christ's reservoir for us to draw from to satisfy our own need to be loved, and to pour out to others. Romans 5:5 says that the Holy Spirit pours the love of God into our hearts. Each time we enter His Presence with open hearts to receive, and spend time with Him in His Word, His endless supply of love and power begins to flow.

When we find ourselves in situations that trouble us, and we know that if we open our mouths our words will not be seasoned with peace and love, we must learn to keep silent, separate ourselves and tap into that reservoir of love and wisdom. Then, as we yield to the Holy Spirit and the wisdom of God's Word, His peace and understanding will overpower the troubling thoughts and give us the right spirit and appropriate words to release at the proper time. This is how we walk in love, and display righteous character, just as Jesus showed us to do.

# FEBRUARY

# Day 01

## The Power of Humility

*1 Peter 5:6 (NKJV), "Therefore humble yourselves under the mighty hand of God, that He may exalt you in due time."*

In the Kingdom of God there is something that causes the mighty Hand of God to come upon us in a powerful way. It's a Kingdom character trait called humility, and it attracts God's protection and favor upon a person's life. This is why the devil actively tries to make people prideful. Pride not only makes you an enemy of God, but it also effectively repels the hand of God from your life and limits your destiny. There is a fruit of the Spirt every child of God possess. It's called meekness. Of course, the devil does everything he can to make this quality seem like weakness, when in truth, it's supernatural power under perfect control.

Jesus demonstrates this powerfully throughout the gospels. There was no pride in Him, and His complete submission to the Holy Spirit within Him caused the power of God to flow unhindered. Jesus always chose His Father's will above His own - in every situation. His humility resulted in Him being exalted to the highest position in heaven and gave Him the Name above every name to which every knee must bow and every tongue confess that He is Lord! In the Kingdom of God, lifting up is always a result of laying down. Humility is our portion, and it not only attracts the favor of God, but it also causes us to walk in the fullness of His power to display His glory through our lives!

# Day 02

## Living on the Altar

*Romans 12:1 (NLT), "And so, dear brothers and sisters, I plead with you to give your bodies to God because of all He has done for you. Let them be a living and holy sacrifice—the kind He will find acceptable. This is truly the way to worship Him."*

Paul explained that just as a sacrifice is laid upon an altar to be burned up, we are to do the same with our lives! We are to become living and holy sacrifices to God. Deciding to follow Jesus means a daily choice to lay down our own intents, thoughts, words, and actions for His Own. As a fire consumes what is on the altar, our surrendered lives become consumed by the fire of God. It burns up everything that is not of Him so we can represent Him well. Then that same fire burns within us a passion to live boldly for Him.

What a glorious privilege to be fully filled with the power of God like this! It's a power that is explosive and demonstrative, but it's only fueled by a life that is surrendered to the transforming power of the Holy Ghost. We are transformed into the image of Jesus when we become living sacrifices, fully laid down and surrendered to Him. The scripture calls this true worship that is pleasing and fully acceptable to the Lord. It's how we position ourselves to become just like Him, and to be used by Him. The ultimate privilege we were destined to fulfil.

# Day 03

## Living Close

*James 4:8 (AMPC), "Come close to God and He will come close to you..."*

When we understand that we were born to know and experience an inseparable relationship with God in this life, living full of Him and for Him, life as we know it changes. So, we start drawing close to the Lord, spending time in His Presence to receive His love and wisdom, before setting out to do what is required of us for the day. There is more than enough pressure and pull from the demands of the worlds system to keep us distracted and focused on personal plans, aspirations, and ambitions.

But the time spent touching His heart, and having His Presence fill us with Himself alerts our senses to be sensitive to His purpose instead of our own. Now, instead of just going through the motion of fulfilling responsibilities and doing what is required to keep us functioning in this world - we live with a purpose burning in our hearts. We begin to see people through His eyes of love and compassion, and are drawn to meet their needs, more than the demands of our day's agenda. We live for Him, responding to His nudges and pulls on our hearts for others.

Miraculously, by the end of the day - we see the results of living close to Him, as He enabled us to accomplish more than what was required, while touching the lives of those around us with His love.

# Day 04

## His Personal Care

*John 10:27-30 (NLT), "27My sheep listen to my voice; I know them, and they follow Me. I give them eternal life, and they will never perish. No one can snatch them away from Me, for My Father has given them to Me, and He is more powerful than anyone else. No one can snatch them from the Father's hand. The Father and I are one."*

Jesus promised to personally take care of us. There is an undeniable comfort that comes with the knowledge that we are deeply loved, and our lives personally accounted for. Jesus expressed such confidence in the above scripture regarding those who *truly* follow Him. He said no-one will be able to snatch them away from Him. Nothing, and no-one can separate us from the love God has for us – *except us*. Matthew 22:14 declares that many are called but few are chosen. The context of this scripture reveals that there was no limit to the calling, only a condition to fully partake. When we choose to not fully partake in all that God has for us – we choose to not be chosen. Through Jesus, God extends the invitation to all to enter an all-inclusive relationship with Him. And yet, even those who accept the call to come to Him, must believe and fully engage in the benefits of the finished work of the cross, by their own choice. Only those who choose to sincerely and deeply *obey* the call to know God and follow wholeheartedly after Him, are the chosen ones. Sheep are completely dependent on their shepherd; they know Him and follow His voice alone.

To be under our Good Shepherd's personal care is the result of a personal choice to fully engage in a life of undivided devotion to Him.

# Day 05

## Advance at Any Cost

*Acts 13:50 (TPT), "The Jewish leaders stirred up a violent mob against Paul and Barnabas, including many prominent and wealthy people of the city. They persecuted them and ran them out of town."*

Paul and Barnabas were on a mission to declare the Gospel of Christ, and in so doing, many Jews and Gentiles believed the message and became disciples. The mockers and angry religious leaders were never far off. They constantly tried to silence the Christians with the intent to kill the faith. Even amid violent persecution, and after being driven out of the city, the followers of Jesus refused to succumb to a spirit of fear or take offence against those who hated them. They merely dusted off their feet and moved on. In our passion to bring people into the Kingdom and see them set free to live in the fullness of life Jesus died for them to have, it's not surprising to encounter opposition. The rejection is aimed at Christ who overcame the devil and has empowered us to seek and save the lost and snatch them out of the hands of the evil one!

Don't take it personally - rejoice that you are being persecuted for Christ's sake. If the unbelief of others causes you to hold back on your passion for Christ, repent today! The world is crying out for a Savior, they desperately need what you are carrying! Shake off the critical remarks and move on in compassion and determination to see God's kingdom advance, at the devil's expense!

# Day 06

## A Personal Pursuit

*Acts 17:30 (TPT), "In the past, God tolerated our ignorance of these things, but now the time of deception has passed away. He commands us all to repent and turn to God."*

The message of Christ has been widely spread, and there are very few who can say they have never heard about Him. Our dilemma today is not that people have never heard; it's that they hear but refuse to listen. Just because we can pick the Bible up at any time and read a few portions of scripture, doesn't mean we have a relationship with the Lord. It is those who willingly, and eagerly choose to pursue knowing God wholeheartedly, who enter a relationship with Him, and feast with Him. We have the responsibility to get to know God for ourselves.

Those who seek will indeed find. The Lord longs for an intimate relationship, and He has given us His Word and His Holy Spirit to accomplish this. Ephesians 3:9 describes how the mysteries of knowing God are not hidden from us, but for us. The book of Proverbs tells us we receive life when we choose to find God in His Word. When we choose to seek a meaningful relationship with the Lord, we will walk in the fullness of peace, joy, and un-conquerable love it brings.

Ignorance is no longer a viable excuse - victory in this life is fully obtainable through a personal pursuit to live in Christ.

# Day 07

## Pledge Allegiance

*Hebrews 13:15 (NLT), "Therefore, let us offer through Jesus a continual sacrifice of praise to God, proclaiming our allegiance to His name."*

The word "allegiance" is defined as "loyalty or commitment to something". When we praise the Lord from sincere hearts, we are proclaiming, announcing, declaring, and affirming our loyalty and commitment to Him, and everything His Word says He is.

In John 14:6, Jesus makes it very clear that the only way to the Father is through Him. We have been reconciled to God, through Jesus, by the finished work of the cross. Hebrews 13:15 says because of Jesus - we can *continually* praise God!

Since our words of faith and praise carry tremendous power, our continual praise causes our lives to become powerful beacons, sending out a never-ending declaration of our allegiance to the Name that is above every other name!

So, while negative opinions oppose the perfect will of God for our lives - we can choose to lift the Name of Jesus instead of repeating their negative reports. This sends out our declaration of allegiance to God's Name and the full victory it has already won! Every knee will bow to that Name as our praise causes God's perfect will to triumph over every ploy of the enemy!

# Day 08

## Cultivating a Lifestyle of Praise

*Psalm 22:3 (AMPC), "But You are holy, O You Who dwell in [the holy place where] the praises of Israel [are offered]."*

Do you know that praise carries such power that the devil will do everything he can to convince Christians that praise is only a couple songs we sing on a Sunday. Praise is not a segment of a service, it's a divine weapon against our enemy, the devil, and a most effective tool to empower the life of every believer!

Our praise is an expression and declaration of our faith in God. It provokes the power of God in the life of a believer because God inhabits and is enthroned in our praise. When we cultivate a lifestyle of praise, we never have to wonder if we have God's attention, we know we have it!

Praise secures God's attention for divine intervention in our lives! Be intentional throughout your day, whether it's in the form of a song or a confession, to let praise flow from you perpetually! Then get ready to see the hand of God move mightily in and through your life.

As your praise declares His greatness and faithfulness, you will witness every opposing force move out the way, and every chain of bondage broken off as you lift the name of Jesus high!

# Day 09

## Carriers of God's Presence

*Deuteronomy 10:8 (NKJV), "At that time the Lord separated the tribe of Levi to bear the ark of the covenant of the Lord, to stand before the Lord to minister to Him and to bless in His name, to this day."*

As a carrier of God's divine presence, we respond to life's situations differently from the world around us. We have been set apart to reflect God's consistently good character and nature even in the most challenging of times. Instead of responding from our flesh in fright, panic, anger, resentment, offence, or fear - we respond from our spirit-man with faith, peace, love, kindness, and joy. Which is wonderful because we get to change the very atmosphere around us and then speak the will of God right into the situation. In essence, we take whatever the enemy intended for evil, and turn it around for good! In the Old Testament, the tribe of Levi were set apart to do just this. They literally changed the atmosphere for a nation that faced certain defeat on the battlefield. When they carried the ark of the covenant which held the presence of God, they were able to praise and worship Him, and with hearts full of faith - declare victory in His Name! As a result - God's people only had to stand and watch the enemy's camp be thrown into confusion as they destroyed themselves. Today, become more aware of God's indwelling presence than what is going on around you. Speak from your spirit and watch how God supernaturally causes you to triumph over every trial - gloriously showing off the powerful nature of God!

# Day 10

## One with God

*John 5:19, "So Jesus answered them by saying, I assure you, most solemnly I tell you, the Son is able to do nothing of Himself (of His own accord); but He is able to do only what He sees the Father doing, for whatever the Father does is what the Son does in the same way [in His turn]."*

Walking this earth, Jesus was completely in tune with, and dependent on His Father. He chose to do nothing apart from His Father's approval or instruction. He beautifully demonstrated a unity that every born-again believer has been given the privilege to walk in. John 15:5 expresses that we can do nothing apart from Christ. In the same manner Jesus was divinely connected to God, in that He didn't do or say anything He didn't see the Father already doing or saying – we likewise must be divinely connected to Christ! We have already been joined to Him by the Spirit (1 Corinthians 6:17). Jesus kept His humanity parallel to His divinity. He came from God, and was the Living Word on earth, and still depended on and obeyed every word from His Father. We are called to do the same. We must maintain constant communion with the Lord, in prayer and in His Word. We must constantly and progressively desire to know everything there is to know about Him, and how to live inseparably connected to Him. As our dependency increases, our unity deepens, and we get to operate in the fullness of compassion, power, and authority Jesus operated in.

# Day 11

## Let Your Spirit-Man Dominate

*Galatians 5:17 (AMPC), "For the desires of the flesh are opposed to the [Holy] Spirit, and the [desires of the] Spirit are opposed to the flesh (godless human nature); for these are antagonistic to each other [continually withstanding and in conflict with each other], so that you are not free but are prevented from doing what you desire to do."*

The Passion Translation of this verse says, *"For your self-life craves the things that offend the Holy Spirit and hinder Him from living free within you! And the Holy Spirit's intense cravings hinder your old self - life from dominating you! So then, the two incompatible and conflicting forces within you are your self-life of the flesh and the new creation life of the Spirit."*

There is a conflict between our born-again spirit and our old nature of the flesh. The reality is the one we feed the most is the one that's going to dominate our lives! When we give ourselves to meditating on the Word of God; spending time in biblical prayer and worshiping the Lord - our spirit-man is given the place to dominate the way we think, speak, and live! Suddenly, the old sinful cravings and pull to the things of the world completely subside in comparison to the life and joy and peace we are experiencing from our spirit-man being in charge. We can bring our flesh into subjection to the life of the Spirit every day by continually turning our affection and attention to things that relate to the kingdom of God. Practice being sensitive to the Spirit of God within you, He will remind you of the Word you have placed in your heart and guide you to establish His kingdom way of life everywhere you go!

# Day 12

## Store Up a Bountiful Supply!

*Genesis 2:15 (NLT), "The Lord God placed the man in the Garden of Eden to tend and watch over it."*

In 1 Timothy 6:17-19, Paul instructs Timothy to command the believers who were wealthy to not put their trust in their uncertain riches but to trust God, Who ultimately is the source of their wealth. God has nothing against His children being wealthy, in fact there are over 300 scriptures from Genesis through Revelations attesting to the fact that He delights in the prosperity of His children. What He does require however, is the right attitude towards material riches. We are to be rich in good works, ready to give, and willing to share. God entrusts all things to us to steward well, for His purpose. Adam and Eve never owned the garden; they were given the responsibility to tend and watch over it, and they were allowed to enjoy all the benefits that garden produced.

God's Kingdom operates by the principle of sowing and reaping. At any time, He can call on us to give of what He has blessed us with, and when we give or sow it with a willing, grateful heart, we are guaranteed a bountiful harvest in return. That's because there is no such thing as lack in His kingdom. In 1 Timothy 6:19, the wealthy believers were told their good stewardship would store up for them a good supply for the time to come! Be ready at any time to give into God's kingdom - it will store up for you a bountiful supply in your future too.

# Day 13

## Never Changing

*Hebrews 13:8 (NLT) "Jesus Christ is the same yesterday, today, and forever."*

The Bible says Jesus is seated at the right hand of the Father - far above all rule and authority and power and dominion and every name that is named, or title that can be granted (Ephesians 1:21).

He is seated there for the benefit of His Church here on earth! It's a benefit of great power and authority for us to operate in, enabling us to walk in His fullness and to stand up boldly against any attack of the enemy. Just as He did His Father's will and spoke His Father's words - representing Him and His kingdom way of living here on earth through the power of the Holy Spirit - He has made a way for us to do the same. His plan has never wavered or changed.

His deep love and compassion for mankind to be reconciled to Himself, and restored to fullness of life and victory over the devil remains and is completely attainable through the victory of the cross. The resurrected Jesus is our sure foundation, our constant truth, and the solid rock we can build our lives upon. He is truth and He will never fail or change. We can confidently place all our hope, trust, and life in Him who never changes! As you decide to root yourself in Him, have His Word planted in your heart, and live in partnership with His Holy Spirit - you will enjoy the surety of knowing Him, His perfect will, and live out His never changing, glorious purpose for your life.

# Day 14

## Stay in Faith

*Romans 1:17 (KJV), "For therein is the righteousness of God revealed from faith to faith: as it is written, The just shall live by faith."*

Faith is vital to effectively live out God's Kingdom way of life here and now! It is the very substance that causes the will of God to operate in our lives. From walking in our authority over the devil to enjoying every promise recorded in His Word - faith is the catalyst that brings the realm of the supernatural into our natural reality. Not having faith causes a believer to become ineffective in his walk with God and secures a life that is not pleasing to Him. Every time we open the scriptures faith is required to trust the Holy Spirit to use them to transform us into the image of Jesus.

When we pray without faith - the Bible says we can expect NO results. Even hearing and obeying the voice of God requires faith. That's why we must choose to fill our hearts and minds with the truth of God's word so we can increase our faith and cause it to dominate our everyday lives; instead of allowing our natural senses to override and dictate the way we respond to circumstances. Living by faith not only empowers us for effectiveness, but it also gives us overwhelming victory!

Choose to stay in the realm of faith today and watch what God will do!

# Day 15

## Be Fruitful and Multiply

*Genesis 1:28 (NKJV), "Then God blessed them, and God said to them, 'Be fruitful and multiply; fill the earth and subdue it; have dominion over the fish of the sea, over the birds of the air, and over every living thing that moves on the earth.'"*

It is God's desire is to see His children live a daily life of fruitfulness and increase. It brings Him no pleasure when we don't live in divine prosperity. God is not only interested in our spiritual fruitfulness, but our physical and material fruitfulness too. From Genesis to Revelations there are over 300 recorded scriptures revealing the truth that God delights in His children prospering. He is certainly not glorified in our misfortune, or our bodies suffering under sickness, or our families living in lack. Through the finished work of the cross the curse of poverty was broken over our lives and the blessing of the Lord released to all who choose a life in Christ Jesus!

Proverbs 10:22 says the blessing of the Lord makes rich and adds no sorrow with it! The last time I checked, suffering and lack amounts to sorrow - which is not the will of God for us!

3 John 1:2 says God's will is for us to prosper in every way so that our bodies may keep well, even as our souls keep well and prosper. Worry over lack and sickness destroys the wellbeing of our souls which leads to the destruction of every other area of our lives. This is not God's will for us!

So, determine to have God's Word dominate your heart and mind today, producing a life of increase and fruitfulness for His glory!

# Day 16

## As Good as His Word

*Psalm 138:2, "I will worship toward Your holy temple and praise Your name for Your loving-kindness and for Your truth and faithfulness; for You have exalted above all else Your name and Your word and You have magnified Your word above all Your name!"*

The Name of Jesus Christ is powerful; and when we declare it from a heart full of faith, we release that power right into the situation we're praying over. Salvation can be found in no other name, everyone who calls upon it will be cleansed and made holy. At the Name of Jesus, every knee will bow, and every tongue will confess His Lordship. At His Name, demons tremble and flee. His Name is high above every other name, giving it the power to override and overcome all things that oppose God's perfect will.

There simply is nothing more powerful than the Name of Jesus! Yet - understand this: God has exalted His Word *above* His Name – wow! A person's name is only as good as his word. God's Word is Yes and Amen in Christ Jesus. It is alive, powerful, active, sharp and an incorruptible seed! It is true and its integrity infallible. We can have absolute confidence in the truth that God's Word and His Name will NEVER fail; and with the confirmation the Holy Spirit gives through inner witness – we can never go wrong when taking God at His Word.

Make God's word the final authority of your life - and you will see the overwhelming victory it produces.

# Day 17

## Co-laborer with Christ

*1 Corinthians 3:9 (NLT), "For we are both God's workers. And you are God's field. You are God's building."*

Paul calls the children of God, *God's workers*. Other translations use the word *co-laborers*. Both imply that we work together with Him, so His work essentially becomes our work too.

While on earth, Jesus did the work of His Father, and instructed us to do the same. We are to go out, in the power of the Holy Spirit, preach the good news of the Gospel, lay hands on the sick, and see them healed. God created man to live from his spirit-man - the part that is connected to the Spirit of God. Since the fall of man, sin changed this, and man started living from the flesh instead. Jesus, through the finished work of the cross, restored what was once lost - and once again we are reconciled with God, our spirits one with His. Now we can live in Him! In Him we live and move and have our being (Acts 17:28).

This is how we become a co-laborer with Him. We see as He sees, feel as He feels, and act as He acts! As God's workers, we are His representatives, not only representing who He is, but also doing the works Jesus did while on earth – all through the power of His Holy Spirit living in us. Yield to His Spirit today and be the extension of His compassion and power to those around you.

# Day 18

## Written on Our Hearts

*Isaiah 35:8 (NKJV), "A highway shall be there, and a road, and it shall be called the Highway of Holiness. The unclean shall not pass over it, but it shall be for others. Whoever walks the road, although a fool, shall not go astray."*

Some people complain of there being too many rules in the Word of God. They reason that they are unrealistic and too demanding for any person to faithfully follow. The children of Israel felt the same way when they were commanded to follow all the laws of Moses. However, they lived under the old covenant. We have a new covenant through the finished work of the cross. Because of Jesus, we can live in the reality of the prophecy recorded in the book of Isaiah 59:2, that says God's Spirit has written the law of God inwardly on the heart. Since the Holy Spirit lives within us, He empowers us to do God's will.

Philippians 2:13 says, *"[Not in your own strength] for it is God Who is all the while effectually at work in you [energizing and creating in you the power and desire], both to will and to work for His good pleasure and satisfaction and delight."*

As we choose to surrender to the leading of God's Spirit each day - being careful to fill our hearts with His Word - He will teach us, lead us, and empower us to do His will in a way that becomes so natural and joyful. His yoke is easy, and His burden is light when we delight in Him and His way of living; and it always results in more blessing than we could ever contain!

# Day 19

## Choose Him and be Loved!

*Proverbs 8:17 (NLT), "I love all who love Me. Those who search will surely find Me."*

When we seek, call out and desire to encounter our God – He promises to make Himself known to us (John 14:21). Many people desperately seek affirmation and encouragement. They look to and rely on man or possessions to make them feel accepted, admired, or respected by others. As children of God, we have been divinely chosen and recognized by God Himself! We don't need to look anywhere else for acceptance and affirmation - we already please God by believing in Him and accepting His redeeming love. This is the starting point of our fulfilled and satisfied life in Him. As we continue to respond to His love and diligently seek Him first in our lives - He rewards us far greater than the world ever could (Hebrews 11:6, Matthew 6:33).

While popularity, and opinions constantly fluctuate according to the standards of a rapidly declining world - make a choice to only see yourself through the mirror of God's Word. You are loved and cherished. You are righteous and pure, and you will never be abandoned or left without while your heart is fixed on loving your God. We were never created to live separately and out of fellowship with the Father, and yet, because He loves us so much, He has given us the ability to choose – so choose Him and be loved completely and unconditionally every day.

# Day 20

## The Greatest Reward

*Genesis 12:1-2 (ESV): "Now the Lord said to Abram, 'Go from your country and your kindred and your father's house to the land that I will show you. And I will make of you a great nation, and I will bless you and make your name great, so that you will be a blessing.'"*

When God called Abram, not only did He call him *out* of the familiar, but He called him to a covenant relationship with Himself and *to* purpose. Moreover, Abram's obedience had a promise attached to it: blessing for Abram, a great name, and empowerment for him to be a blessing. Every promise of God is already settled and approved by Him. They become our sure reality through obedience to His ways and refusing to waver in our faith - trusting in His faithfulness to honor His Word. The sacrifice of forsaking what we once put our security in, for a life of faith in Christ, is something Jesus promised we would be rewarded a hundred-fold for (Mark 10:29-30).

Cheerfully embrace the call of Christ today – the call to live in Him, and for Him. Forsaking your old way of life to embrace a life of trust and obedience, that will bring the greatest joy and blessing you could ever imagine.

# Day 21

## Pray!

**Acts 2:42 (NKJV), "And they continued steadfastly in the apostles' doctrine and fellowship, in the breaking of bread, and in prayers".**

As children of God, spending time with the Lord in prayer is significant for our life here and now. Jesus called us to a *life* of prayer, marking it as vital for our personal walk with God. He said, "*when* you pray" not "*if* you pray"! The early church had the most effective attitude towards prayer. They continued steadfastly in it. Another translation says they "devoted themselves" to prayer. The Hebrew word for the phrase "devoted themselves" means to persist and to persevere in.

To see signs, wonders and miracles the early church walked in, there must be a private dedication to prayer. God promises to demonstrate His power through His children when we diligently align ourselves with His heart and walk sensitive and obedient to His leading. Our time in private prayer with Him positions us for this.

Today, seek the Lord and He will reveal His heart to you - when you search for Him with all your heart.

# Day 22

## Speak Life!

*Ezekiel 37:3-4 (AMPC), "And He said to me, Son of man, can these bones live? And I answered, O Lord God, You know! Again He said to me, Prophesy to these bones and say to them, O you dry bones, hear the word of the Lord."*

In your journey of faith, there will be challenging times. During these times, don't complain about what you're going through, refuse to be discouraged. Don't make the mistake of running helter-skelter, looking for help from man. Instead, find God's word on it, and declare His truth until you come right out of it - victoriously! This was what the Lord told Ezekiel to do in the valley of dry bones. The Lord asked Ezekiel if dry bones could live again. He was emphasizing that even the impossible could be changed by declaring faith-filled words.

God told Ezekiel to *"prophesy to the bones."*. As he prophesied, a great miracle took place, and they came together and lived again! Instead of being overwhelmed in the hour of crisis, speak God's word over your health, your finances, your family, and your future. The Word in your mouth is a creative force, empowered to bring forth miracles. Use faith-filled words to frame your world, and align your thoughts, emotions and will for victory.

Remember, God's Word in your mouth is just as powerful as His Word in His own mouth - so speak and live!

# Day 23

## Transformed by His Kindness

*John 1:14 (TPT), "And so the Living Expression became a man and lived among us! And we gazed upon the splendor of His glory, the glory of the One and Only who came from the Father overflowing with tender mercy and truth!"*

We have glorious opportunities to encounter God daily! Even though we don't get to experience Jesus in the physical like the disciples did - we get to experience His tangible presence by His Holy Spirit, who lives within us. The Holy Spirit is the living expression of Jesus Christ, who is the living expression of God the Father! John 1:1 says Jesus is the Word, so the more we gaze upon the word - we gaze upon who Jesus is. The Holy Spirit reveals Jesus to us and causes His mercy and truth to be the reality that we enjoy. We have not been called to only encounter the goodness, tenderness, mercy, and truth of God once-in-a-while.

We are to encounter the Person of Jesus daily, by beholding Him in the light of His Word. Seeing and experiencing Jesus this way is what transforms us, one degree at a time, into His very image and nature! That's because the truth of who He is so impresses and influences our hearts and minds - it literally changes us from the inside out! His influence on us becomes reflected in the way we see ourselves and others, and act according to the kindness and love we've personally received from Him.

Be changed by His kindness today.

# Day 24

## His Word Brings Fullness

*Psalm 1:2 (AMPC), "But his delight and desire are in the law of the Lord, and on His law (the precepts, the instructions, the teachings of God) he habitually meditates (ponders and studies) by day and by night."*

Have you ever struggled to find a scripture that's relevant to stand upon for victory over your problem? The Bible is far more than stories showcasing the trials and victories of people from ages past. It is alive and active, carefully designed to contain principles, prophecies and promises for us to hold onto and live by to overcome in this life. The Lord wants you to delve into His Word and discover the answers that are there for your victory. We have the gift of the Holy Spirit as our helper, mediator, and advisor.

So, when we ponder over scripture, the Holy Spirit brings understanding, and customizes the truth to our own personal lives and circumstances. He ensures that when we apply the written Word, by faith, we will experience the power of God and the victory of the cross in every specific area we apply His word to. According to Revelation 4:1, God invites us to come up higher and delve deeper into His Word, to where we see our lives from His perspective. Ask and trust the Holy Spirit to give you wisdom and understanding as you spend time in His Word. Expect Him to speak and reveal the specifics of His truth into your spirit.

This marks a beautiful journey of intimacy with the Lord, as He leads you into the fullness of life, through His word being made alive in your heart - every day of your life.

# Day 25

## God is Faithful

*Romans 16:25 (NLT), "Now all glory to God, who is able to make you strong, just as my Good News says. This message about Jesus Christ has revealed His plan for you Gentiles; a plan kept secret from the beginning of time."*

How wonderful and Glorious is our God! He had a redemptive plan for us through His only Son Jesus. His integrity and ability to be faithful will stand steadfast and true forever. These are character traits of God that set Him apart. They are the reason we have faith and confidence in His character and His promises. There are wonderful people who have integrity. They are well-meaning when making promises to help or provide. But circumstances in their personal lives may change, resulting in them not being able to fulfil their promises. On the other hand, God has both the integrity and ability to consistently follow through on every promise concerning us. Let that sink in for a moment.

The Word says His faithfulness extends to the heavens - there is no end to it. Let this truth cause peace and joy to flood your being. God Almighty is on your side, and He has promised to perfect all things concerning you.

As you lean on Him and trust in His faithful character today, watch how He makes you strong and able to overcome all things!

# Day 26

## Complete in Him

*Romans 6:11 (NLT), "So you also should consider yourselves to be dead to the power of sin and alive to God through Christ Jesus."*

God has created us to find our wholeness in Him. He perfectly designed us to fulfil our purpose, and to bring glory to His Name. Many look to the things of this world, or other people to complete them. But anything short of knowing God Himself, will result in disappointment. When we turn to God, accept Him, and follow Him wholeheartedly – we are made complete in Him - and sin has no power over us. Nothing compares to the wholeness we find when we come to fully know the One who created us. Paul said we can pray for the spirit of wisdom and revelation to know Jesus as He really is. This will cause us to be firmly rooted in the security of His love for us.

His love never fails and casts out all fear of rejection. It always believes in our best and when we allow it to flood our hearts, we will be filled with all the confidence we will ever need to know who we belong to, and how wonderful it is to be filled to overflowing with Him. He has made you; He has placed purpose inside of you, and He has chosen you to bring glory to His Name.

You are made complete in Him, and to remain in this place you simply must learn to abide in Him and let His love make you whole!

# Day 27

## Blessed Beyond Belief

*Proverbs 16:20 (TPT), "One skilled in business discovers prosperity, but the one who trusts in God is blessed beyond belief!"*

God instructs us through His Word, and not through pain and calamity. Yet, *even if* we encounter either of those, if we remain in His love and set our hearts on loving Him and doing His will – all things will work together for our good (Romans 8:28). We can absolutely expect to see God's goodness in the land of the living, because trusting in the LORD singles us out for blessing. The Word says the eyes of the Lord search out those whose hearts are devoted to Him, so He can act on their behalf (2 Chronicles 16:9).

The book of Proverbs teaches that the blessing of the LORD makes one *truly* rich – it brings great gain – and it brings no grievances with it. It brings favor and accomplishes far beyond what any human effort could. Walking and working with God ensures that "*even the hard pathways overflow with abundance*" (Psalm 65:11, NLT).

Make the choice today to put your trust in God; entrust your life to Him – there's no being put to shame for doing so, instead there's a life of abundance to enjoy!

# Day 28

## Know Him

*Daniel 11:32 (NKJV), "...but the people who know their God shall be strong and carry out great exploits."*

The life of a believer is to be a life of impact, because of the Greater One who dwells within us. We aren't called to conform to what's taking place in the world, instead we are anointed to bring about a transformation through the Power of God that rests on us and resides inside us. We are the ones that carry the solution to every problem - the Presence of God! This is the way we need to begin to see ourselves, because this is how God sees us. The key ingredient for dynamic impact, supernatural strength and exploits for the Kingdom is knowing God. The Word "know" in the original Hebrew is the word "yada". This is the same word used in Genesis 4 when the Bible says that Adam knew Eve. It speaks of intimately knowing someone through personal experience, and not just knowing of them.

It's the people that intimately know God that are empowered for strength and exploits. The factors that cultivate intimacy with God in the life of a believer are devotion to dwelling in His Presence through the Word, worship, and prayer. The Bible promises that when we draw near to God, He will draw near to us - so step out today and choose to get to know your God and you will see Him do great things through you!

# MARCH

# Day 01

## Redemption

*Hebrews 10:19-20 (NKJV), "Therefore, brethren, having boldness to enter the Holiest by the blood of Jesus, by a new and living way which He consecrated for us, through the veil, that is, His flesh,"*

A reality we must wholeheartedly treasure is that intimacy with God is available to every person who receives Jesus as their Savior. He is our redeemer and has gained us access to a very real, intimate relationship with God - a privilege that was initially lost through sin. Many Christians feel they're not good enough to enjoy an intimate relationship with the Father, or that they must first earn the privilege to do so. The truth is our acceptance into experiencing this relationship has everything to do with the redemptive nature of the blood of Jesus - not through any good works or personal merit. The Bible says the first Adam sinned and brought eternal separation between man and God. As a result, we became slaves to sin and victims to the struggles, shame, and harassment it brings. But Jesus, the second Adam, gave His Own blood to pay in full for the penalty of sin. Now we are no longer slaves to sin - we are victorious over it! We are restored to our original position of being called and recognized as sons and daughters of God (Galatians 4:7)!

Today, boldly approach the Throne of Grace and be welcomed by the joyful love of our Heavenly Father, all because of Jesus!

# Day 02

## Restoration

***Psalm 23:3a (NKJV), "He restores my soul"***

The knocks and challenges of life in this world can leave us feeling shaken and unnerved. However, 1 Corinthians 6:17 says that the person who is united to the Lord becomes one spirit with Him!

When we choose to live in Christ, we have the source of life flowing from His Spirit in and through us. His Spirit makes us alive, energizes us, empowers us, and infuses us with inner strength to restore our bodies and souls! The quickest way to activate this process is to build yourself up in faith as you pray God's perfect will over your life, by praying in the Holy Ghost; and by keeping yourself in the love of God (Jude 1:20-21).

Keeping yourself in God's love means spending quality time in His Presence - opening your heart to be filled and flooded with His love (Romans 5:5). It also means spending quality time in His Word where your faith is built, and hope is restored - while all fear and dread is expelled. Today, be unwilling to do without the constant regeneration and energizing work of God's Spirit.

Allow His divine influence on you to restore and recharge you to walk in the fullness of life and purpose He planned for you to enjoy.

# Day 03

## From Slavery to Royalty

*Galatians 4:7 (NLT) "Now you are no longer a slave but God's own child. And since you are His child, God has made you His heir."*

When a born-again believer has a revelation of his identity in Christ, all past insecurities and inadequacies are washed under the blood of Jesus, and no longer have a hold on him. Instead, there is a confidence that stems from a very grateful heart, understanding everything that is good, noble, and praiseworthy in him - comes from Christ alone! This confidence comes with an authority that terrifies the kingdom of darkness. That's because it can never be shaken. When we grasp the value of our freedom in Christ, we become passionate about our commitment and devotion to Him. We delight in His Word and His ways, and love to be in His Presence and do His will.

Every day we are reminded of the new life of grace He has given us. Instead of being enslaved to sin and death - we have been redeemed, set free, and given a position of sonship - where God Himself has made us His heirs! Now we can walk with a true sense of belonging, knowing how much we are loved. We can follow His voice every day, walk in His wisdom and peace, and know His joy as every promise He has made becomes our reality - and we did nothing to deserve it. Everything we are and ever will be is attributed to Christ alone. He took us from slavery and transformed us into royalty!

# Day 04

## Bountiful Provision

*Philippians 4:19, "And this same God who takes care of me will supply all your needs from His glorious riches, which have been given to us in Christ Jesus."*

A beautiful benefit of our covenant relationship with Christ is being under His watchful care, where all our needs are supplied. What's more, they aren't supplied according to the standard of the present economy, they are supplied according to His standard of riches in glory! That kind of abundance is exceptional! Now, for a covenant relationship to work, there is an expectation placed on both parties. Jesus has already met His expectation by securing every benefit through the finished work of the cross. Our part is to obey the conditions of these benefits. We call these conditions - kingdom of God principles. When these principles are applied by faith, they cause us to be recipients of His abundant provision.

The church of Philippi was well practiced in the principle of sowing and reaping. They generously sowed financial seed into the work of the ministry, and as a result, received an abundant harvest back into their personal lives. Likewise, when we give generously into the kingdom of God, our covenant of provision is secured. Every financial seed sown into His kingdom causes a bountiful supply of provision to come back into our lives - by His standard of glorious riches!

# Day 05

## Empowered for Purpose

*Acts 9:18 (NLT), "Instantly something like scales fell from Saul's eyes, and he regained his sight. Then he got up and was baptized."*

Proverbs 19:21 says, *"Many plans are in a man's mind, but it is the Lord's purpose for him that will stand."* This certainly rang true for Saul's life. He was extremely diligent and determined to rid the world of the Christian faith until he had a supernatural encounter with Jesus. Then everything, including his name, dramatically changed! Throughout scripture and history, God encountered men and women, changed their perspectives, and set them on course for His purpose for their lives. When Saul met Jesus, he was introduced to the very Person he was bent on persecuting. Talk about a drastic change of perspective. The Bible says Paul was instantly blinded for three days. In that time, Jesus not only manifested Himself to Paul, but He also revealed His plan for his life, and let him know how much he would need to endure and suffer for His sake. That's why God sent Ananias to Paul, to lay hands on him, not only to have his sight returned, but to baptize Him in the Holy Spirit! Like Paul, and so many men and women who did great exploits for God - we are never equipped to successfully achieve God's purpose for our lives without the baptism of the Holy Spirit. He authorizes and empowers us to significantly impact this world as we yield to His leading and flow in His supernatural power.

Yield yourself to the fresh infilling of His power today and walk in the fullness of His purpose for you.

# Day 06

## Come Eat and Drink

*John 6:35 (TPT), "Jesus said to them, 'I am the Bread of Life. Come every day to Me and you will never be hungry. Believe in Me and you will never be thirsty.'"*

We need the Word more than we need daily food. In the times we live in, it's not good enough to just be alive - we must be alive in Christ! We must be filled with the Word and led by His Holy Spirit! Jesus said that He is the bread of life, that partaking of Him will never leave us hungry. Since Jesus is the Living Word (John 1:1,14), the Bread of Life we are to consume involves us reading, meditating, and applying God's Word to our lives. When Jesus said we would never thirst if we believed in Him, He was referring to the encounter He had with the woman at the well in John 4. He told her that if she'd ask of Him, He will give her living water that would satisfy her for eternity. The Holy Spirit is that living water.

The more Word we consume, the more the Holy Spirit reveals Jesus to us, influencing and transforming our lives to be more like Him in the process. The Holy Spirit quickens the word within us, bringing it to remembrance in times of need. The life and power that flows from the Word (Jesus), and the Living Water of the Holy Spirit keeps us satisfied, fruitful, and prosperous in every area of our lives. Come to Jesus, eat and drink deeply of His Word and Spirit - and you will never hunger or thirst again!

# Day 07

## Against All Odds

*Genesis 39:21 (AMPC), "But the Lord was with Joseph, and showed him mercy and loving-kindness and gave him favour in the sight of the warden of the prison."*

No matter what hardships or desperate challenges Joseph found himself in, the Lord always gave him favor and made a way, against all odds, for him to prosper. When we constantly remind ourselves of who we are in Christ, and how God Himself lives within us, there is nothing we will ever face without having the power and blessing of God to make a way for us to prosper. Becoming God-inside minded is what activates the reality of our covenant relationship with Him. We understand that He has blessed us with every spiritual blessing in Christ Jesus (Ephesians 1:3). That same blessing continuously works by His Spirit within us, for our favor! It makes us rich and adds no sorrow with it (Proverbs 10:22). God has already promised us everything we will ever need to succeed in this life, during trouble and calamity. He has sworn every promise to be ours by His Word and His blood. He has given us the very keys of His kingdom to experience days of heaven on earth. Our part of the covenant is to think like God and speak like God. He doesn't perform in our lives what *He* says in His word - He performs in our lives what *we* say that's in line with His word. When we say what He says - He'll do it - in its fullness! No matter what life or the devil throws your way - you must remember you are a covenant child of God. He lives within you and is greater than anyone or anything that opposes you in this world. And He is faithful to honor His word concerning you!

# Day 08

## The Journey of Faith: Part I

***Psalm 37:23, "The** steps **of a good man are ordered by the LORD, And He delights in his way".***

Often, we read a portion of Scripture, only to read over the depth of revelation just beneath the surface. Today's Scripture is one of those gems. Unfortunately, our English language is not able to truly convey the bountiful riches of this Scripture as it was originally written – in Hebrew. The Hebrew word, "step" within this context refers to "companionship". When it comes to our faith walk, we will never walk alone for the Lord Himself will be our traveling companion. His Spirit lives within the born-again child of God, and He promises to remain in us forever, and never leave us (John 14:16).

We were created for fellowship, and He longs to fellowship with us. On the Road to Emmaus, we read about Jesus catching up with some of His followers. He travelled the entire journey alongside them, and yet, they were completely unaware that it was Him.

If you currently feel alone – or even isolated – we pray that you will become so aware of His presence that *is* within you. That in every step, you will draw strength from the truth that He *is with you*, that He is for you and that He will never let you go!

# Day 09

## The Journey of Faith: Part II

**Psalm 37:23, "The steps of a good man are ordered by the LORD, And He delights in his way".**

This Scripture reveals that "the steps of a good man are ordered by the Lord" ... First, remember that Jesus said: "*No one is good, except God alone*" (Mark 10:18). The word, "good", refers to "righteousness". We are not perfect, we're not even "good"; however, we have become the righteousness of God through Christ Jesus!

In this verse, the word, "man" refers to a "warrior" or a "valiant man" – someone possessing or showing courage or determination. You may not feel courageous or determined right now, but in Christ Jesus - this is your *true* identity. When God called on Gideon, the Angel of the Lord referred to him as a "mighty man of valor", even though he was hiding in fear at the time. God speaks from the perspective of your identity in Him, and not the way you feel about yourself at that moment. He is the Spirit of Truth, and He will lead you into the truth of who you truly are in Him.

Today, know that you are called, chosen, accepted, and loved. Remember that you are who He says you are - a warrior, powerful and victorious in Him.

# Day 10

## The Journey of Faith: Part III

***Psalm 37:23, "The steps of a good man are*** ordered by the LORD, ***And He delights in his way".***

Have you ever considered what it means to have your steps ordered by the Lord? The word "ordered" has two specific meanings, each applicable to this verse. The first meaning is directly linked to faith. God didn't just speak the universe into existence, He gave the order or command, and it was immediately executed. In the New Testament we read about the Roman Centurion, a man whom Jesus said had 'great faith'. This military officer understood the significance of an order or command. He said to Jesus, "*Just give the order, and my servant will get well.*" (Matthew 8:8 CEV).

The Lord has a wonderful plan and purpose for your life. The Bible clearly reveals that His sole intention is to see you succeed and prosper. The question is whether you will come into agreement over what the Lord has already 'ordered' with regards to your life? Which brings us to the next meaning of the word "ordered". It is the state in which everything is arranged in its correct place. When we come into agreement with God's plan for our lives - according to His Word - we can trust Him to order our steps and cause us to walk in His exact plan as we trust and obey His leading. You can be sure that if you walk with Him, your life will be marked by the prosperity and peace He has already ordered for you to walk in.

# Day 11

## The Journey of Faith: Part IV

**_Psalm 37:23, "The steps of a good man are ordered by the LORD, And He delights in his way"._**

Yesterday, we discovered the significance of our steps being ordered by the Lord. Today, we'll look at the latter part of our Scripture: "_He delights in His way_". The word, "delight", refers to "incline or to bend" as well as "to be pleased with". What is fascinating is that the Psalmist is painting a powerful picture where the Lord inclines Himself with anticipation, expecting us to discover our divine purpose in Him, and as we do, it brings Him great pleasure.

Have you ever planned a surprise, where you asked the person to close their eyes as you escort them towards that surprise? The moment they are about to open their eyes to see it, you are overjoyed and can hardly contain yourself, knowing that what you are about to reveal will bless them out of their socks. When we deliberately choose to come into agreement with God's way of living, and we pay careful attention to listen to His voice and follow in His ways - He takes great pleasure in seeing us walk in the blessing and prosperity it leads us into. Each day is full of His mercy and goodness. It is not just pleasant; it is fruitful and full of joy.

Step in order with the Lord today, so you can live the good life He has prearranged and made ready for you to walk in with Him (Ephesians 2:10).

# Day 12

## Put on Your Glory Garments

*Isaiah 52:1(AMPC), "Awake, awake, put on your strength, O Zion; put on your beautiful garments, O Jerusalem, the holy city; for henceforth there shall no more come into you the uncircumcised and the unclean."*

The Passion Translation says, *"...Beautiful Zion, put on your majestic strength! Jerusalem, the sacred city, put on your glory garments!"* When Jesus rose from the dead, He arose victoriously! He conquered death, hell, and the grave for us! He didn't just conquer and retain victory; He gave us that same authority and power over *all* things.

In 1 Peter 2:9, God calls us His royal priesthood. The word priesthood here has two meanings: Firstly, it refers to the power and authority of God. Secondly, in mortality, priesthood is the power and authority that God gives to man to act in all things necessary for the salvation of God's children. God called us to this assignment, long before we had the sense to respond to Him, and He has given us everything we need to fulfil the purpose He has called us to. We are to influence this world with His kingdom ways, and push back the kingdom of darkness, enforcing the devil's defeat. The call has gone out and whenever God commands us to do something, He authorizes and empowers us to do it. He literally transfers His power in and on us to accomplish what He says we are to do.

Choose this day to put on your glory clothes! Put on your royal robes of strength, as you walk in the power and authority He has given you to call those things that are permissible in heaven to be here on the earth; and to forbid on earth what is forbidden in heaven! This is your purpose.

# Day 13

## What's in Your Heart?

***Proverbs 27:19 (NLT), "As a face is reflected in water, so the heart reflects the real person."***

It's remarkable how revealing the heart of a man is. As much as a person tries to conceal the true nature of his heart by portraying an image he is not - the truth will always come to light. Jeremiah 17:9 says the heart is deceitful above all things and that the Lord Himself searches the mind and tries the heart. That's why it's imperative for us to fix our hearts on the Lord and keep it full of His truth and love. Psalm 112:7 says that when our hearts are firmly fixed, trusting, leaning on and being confident in the Lord - we never have to be afraid of evil tidings. We don't risk having our hearts being led astray and swayed by every opinion or circumstance. We are to give the Lord the exclusivity of our hearts and let our eyes delight in His ways. This is how we reflect His light in every situation. Let's not be of those who say one thing and reflect something completely different. The abundance of our hearts should be the Word - we are called to reflect Jesus.

As our face is reflected in water, may our hearts reflect Christ within us, as we radiate His love, kindness, compassion, peace, and joy always.

# Day 14

## Faith and Love Conquers All

*Romans 8:37 (NKJV), "Yet in all these things we are more than conquerors through Him who loved us."*

In Christ, being an over-comer is the heritage of every believer, irrespective of circumstances and difficulties. Our victory is never dependent on the seriousness of our situation, its dependent on the victory Jesus has already won for us. God is mightier than any problem we will ever encounter in this life, and He has transferred His victory power to us. Having this understanding certainly gives us a confidence to stand our ground in faith, doesn't it? What's important is to stand in faith, while being rooted soundly in God's love for us. This is where the power really is!

Ephesians 3:17 says, *"May Christ through your faith [actually] dwell (settle down, abide, make His permanent home) in your hearts! May you be rooted deep in love and founded securely on love."* Verse 18 goes on to say this is the only way we will be able to experience love's power! Remember it's the love of God that conquers all! We can have all the faith in the world, but if we're not rooted in God's love - it's pretty much useless (1 Corinthians 13:2). The language of faith is love and thanksgiving. So, respond to fearful and conflicting situations with this kind of language, and the devil will have no power to use against you. When you're tempted to moan or fear at the sight of trouble - STOP! Remember how much you are loved, and let your words express that instead. That will release love's power to activate your faith, and victory will be your portion!

# Day 15

## On Purpose

**Luke 19:10 (NKJV), "for the Son of Man has come to seek and to save that which was lost."**

Everything about God is intentional! Jesus came to live amongst us, he died, and was raised again - victoriously, for a specific purpose, and we were that purpose! The Bible tells us everything Jesus did for us was out of God's love for us. He came, out of love, to seek and save the lost. He came to rescue us from a hopeless state, to restore all the devil stole from us, to reconcile us to the Father, and to reveal His true nature to us. Then, before He left to return to heaven, He told us to do the same! And He gave us all the power and authority to do it! The same purpose of rescue, restoration, reconciliation and revealing has become our own.

The wonderful truth is we don't do it in our own strength or wisdom, we do it the same way Jesus did! We stay vitally connected to the heart of our Heavenly Father. We keep His Word alive in our hearts and we rely completely on the leading and empowering of the Holy Spirit - Who lives in us! Hallelujah!

This is our time to arise and shine, because the glory of the Lord is upon us, ready and able to draw all men to experience His goodness.

# Day 16

## Freely Receive - Freely Give

*Luke 15:32 (NLT), "We had to celebrate this happy day. For your brother was dead and has come back to life! He was lost, but now he is found!"*

The parable of the prodigal son sheds light on the heart of an earthly father, but even more so, we see a glimpse of the heart of our Heavenly Father. Jesus came to earth to reveal the character of His Father and demonstrate how His kingdom operates. Our motives, attitudes, and actions must always reflect the reality of the Father's compassionate, loving character and generous, righteous kingdom ways! We do this effectively when we spend quality time with the Father, drawing from His wisdom and heart for each situation we face.

Psalms 40:6 (TPT) says, *"It's not sacrifices that really move Your heart. Burnt offerings, sin offerings—that's not what brings You joy. But when You open my ears and speak deeply to me, I become Your willing servant, Your prisoner of love for life."* When we allow our personal experiences of encountering the Presence of God, and our understanding of His true character and ways to influence the way we relate to others - we represent Him well. Bringing hope and joy to the broken hearted, always being ready to forgive and extend unconditional love and compassion is the heart of the Father to us. And just as we have freely received, we freely give - this is what we have been redeemed to do.

# Day 17

## Take the Step and See the Promise!

*2 Kings 7:4 (NKJV), "If we say, 'We will enter the city,' the famine is in the city, and we shall die there. And if we sit here, we die also. Now therefore, come, let us surrender to the army of the Syrians. If they keep us alive, we shall live; and if they kill us, we shall only die."*

This verse of scripture gives the account of the four lepers that decided to rise and do something about their situation. These men had been banished to live outside the city gates to fend for themselves, but they refused to give up, sit still, and die. As they rose and took a bold step forward, they found that God had moved on their behalf and in favor of the entire nation of Israel! He had scattered their enemies, leaving riches and plenty of much needed food in their wake! Perhaps you haven't seen God move because He hasn't seen you move. He has already provided your miracle and breakthrough, it's time for you to take a step of faith and make a move towards the promise. Taking the first step means doing what He has instructed you to do, no matter how small or insignificant it seems. If it's a financial breakthrough you need - sow a financial seed by faith. If it's employment you need - get out there and offer your services wherever the Lord leads you. If it's healing you're believing for - start thanking Him for the healing, speak to your body, command it to be healed and start doing what you couldn't do before.

You don't need to know all the details when you trust God's direction and take that first step of faith. Move now and watch how He has already moved on your behalf. Remember, He is the author and the finisher of *our* faith - so take the step and walk in the promise!

# Day 18

## The Light that Pierces

*John 9:5 (TPT), "As long as I am with you My life is the light that pierces the world's darkness."*

As much as this world is wrapped up in darkness and confusion - while there are born-again children of God living here - there will be light! Jesus declared He is the light of the world. We also know from scripture that He is the Living Word of God (1 John 1:1). He is the light, and He is the Word!

In Matthew 5:14, he calls us, who belong to Him, the light of the world too. Not just because His Spirit lives in us, but because His Word lives in us too! Psalm 119:109 says God's Word is a lamp to our feet and a light to our path. When we meditate on its principles and truth, the Holy Spirit causes it to come alive inside our hearts and influence the way we think, speak, and behave. We begin to walk in the practical wisdom of God's ways and as a result, favor, success, and prosperity become a very visible part of our lives (Joshua 1:8; Psalm 1:2-3, John 15:7).

When the Word is allowed the chance to flourish in our hearts, darkness will never be able to overwhelm or overcome us. Instead, the wisdom, peace, and joy the Living Word produces inside us, equips us with more than enough to stand our ground in faith with great confidence - in the face of any trouble. That same glorious, victorious light that shines in Jesus - shines brightly in us as His word produces faith and life in our hearts. While you abide in Jesus and keep His Word alive in your heart - His light will pierce the darkness wherever you go.

# Day 19

## Keep Moving Forward

***Isaiah 58:11 (NLT), "The Lord will guide you continually, giving you water when you are dry and restoring your strength."***

The most dangerous place for us to be is stagnant in our spiritual growth. When we celebrate a victory or a breakthrough, it's vital to not set up camp, and refuse to move forward from that point. God is ever moving and has so much more for us to experience and do for His kingdom through our faith in Him.

His Holy Spirit is constantly moving, empowering, and leading us to do exploits in the name of the Lord Jesus Christ! Even if we don't have all the answers or details to get things done, as long as we remain thankful, speak according to His Word, and obey what He has clearly told us to do, His word will go to work for us.

Instead of trying to figure out how God will bring you through the current trial, spend time in His Word, listen intently to His Spirit, and you will see He is ready and waiting to guide you. Your swift and faithful obedience, coupled with your grateful, expectant heart will see you refreshed, strengthened, and moving forward into His perfect will for you!

# Day 20

## Same Works as Jesus did

*John 14:12 (NLT), "I tell you the truth, anyone who believes in Me will do the same works I have done, and even greater works, because I am going to be with the Father."*

It might seem daunting to think that Jesus expects us to do the same and even greater works than He did while He was on the earth. Especially when we only think of our humanity compared to the supernatural power that flowed in and from Him. The beautiful revelation is that Jesus was fully human while on earth. He grew in wisdom, stature, and favor with God and man. He obtained power and insight from spending time with His Father. He was completely dependent on Him for instruction, direction, and power! Being filled with the Holy Spirit is what led Him to be at the right place, at the right time, every time.

Since His ministry was very practical, it makes it easy to imitate Him. He ensured that we would be successful in following Him and yield the same results He had. He was subject to the same struggles, trials, and temptations that we face so that we can never say He can't relate to our humanity. Since He made fellowship with His Father and total dependency on the power of the Holy Spirit the key to success in ministry - we can too!

The New covenant we have through the finished work of the cross secures this for us! Just as He is now - the resurrected, victorious Jesus - so are we in this world (1 John 4:17)! It's time to imitate Jesus and see Him do the same work through us!

# Day 21

## Prove by the Way We Live

**Matthew 3:8 (NLT), "Prove by the way you live that you have repented of your sins and turned to God."**

The Bible refers to John the Baptist as the man who prepared the way for Jesus to walk on this earth. Many people would travel to hear the message John shared. Their hearts would be pierced with the truth, and they would repent and be baptized. True repentance means to turn away from what you once did, and wholeheartedly live your life surrendered to the Lordship of Jesus Christ.

In this scripture, John was responding to the religious leaders who assumed they were in right standing with God because they were descendants of Abraham. They believed that since Abraham and Moses knew God and was in covenant with Him - they automatically were too. John was telling them their assumption was wrong - they had to know God for themselves to receive salvation! We can't rely on our family's, spouse's, or friends' relationship with God for our salvation.

What Jesus accomplished on the cross was done for everyone, so we need to individually choose to turn away from all that is part of our old, sinful natures, and follow Jesus ourselves (Hebrews 2:9). We must choose to remain in close fellowship with Him and allow Him to change us through His Word. This is how we prove, by the way we live, that we have repented of our sins and turned to God.

Let your life reflect the measure to which you have allowed His love and power to influence and dominate you.

# Day 22

## God In You for Victory

*Ephesians 6:12 (NKJV), "For we do not wrestle against flesh and blood, but against principalities, against powers, against the rulers of the darkness of this age, against spiritual hosts of wickedness in the heavenly places."*

An exposed enemy is a defeated one!

As believers, we have the high ground – a vantage point – where we can overcome the enemy as he attempts to attack us. We are seated in heavenly places with Christ Jesus – victorious!

God has placed His Own Holy Spirit within us, He has given us His Word, and His Name to use with authority! If we are going to live in the full-time victory Jesus won for us on the cross - we need to acknowledge and act on the truth of our covenant relationship with Him - every day! This is the high calling to which we're called. This way, regardless of whatever cunning deceptions the enemy of our souls tries to trip us up with – we are found fully aware of the reality that we carry the power and authority of God in us to withstand him, and release God's blessing in the earth!

So, our true battlefield takes place in our minds where we must constantly be aware of our identity and purpose.

Today, and every day, live out the truth that God is IN you - you cannot fail!

# Day 23

## God's Word is Life

***Psalm 119:37 (NLT), "Turn my eyes from worthless things, and give me life through Your Word."***

Did you know the position God's Word holds in our lives is a direct reflection of how much of our lives He has a hold of?

According to the gospel of John, God is His Word, the two can never be separated from each other. The Word of God is not a 'side thing' in the life of a believer, it's EVERYTHING! When we realize this truth, it will drastically alter the way we approach the Word, and its priority in our lives. Inquiring of God and His ways must become the vital necessity in our lives, over and above all of life's pressing demands. This life will pass, and its values will fade away, but God's Word holds truth that holds value for us - for eternity.

David recognized this; he knew God's Word would instill eternal life in him when He gave it his full attention. Today, recognize that the Word of God that's alive in your heart will empower you to operate in supernatural wisdom, and walk in unprecedented favor. When it becomes your priority, it will cause you to prosper and have good success - you have His Word on it.

# Day 24

## God is My Strength

*2 Samuel 22:33-34 (NKJV), "God is my strength and power, And He makes my way perfect. He makes my feet like the feet of deer and sets me on my high places."*

Strength of character must never be underestimated - and yet we are about to see things in this world that even the strongest of people will be tempted to waver in their faith. But remember this: as children of God, regardless of what is thrown against us, if we have resolved to remain steadfast and securely rooted in - the truth of God's Word, and our belief in His good character and sincere love for us - we will not be shaken.

Our strength comes from knowing God, and not being a stranger to His covenant promises in this world. Anything we choose to draw strength from to overcome outside of this is superficial and inconsistent. God is supernatural and unchanging. He supersedes all our natural strength and ability, and desires to give us strength for every situation we face. He doesn't only want to give you strength though; He wants to *be* your strength.

The Bible says, *"... the people who know their God will be strong and do mighty exploits."* (Daniel 11:32). Today be empowered by the supernatural strength that comes from knowing God and trusting in His Word.

# Day 25

## He Satisfies My Soul

*John 10:9 (TPT), "I am the Gateway. To enter through Me is to experience life, freedom, and satisfaction."*

In times of uncertainty and unrest, no matter the cause - we must remember our source of life, freedom and satisfaction is Christ alone. Jesus declared that He is our gateway to fullness of life where there is freedom from fear, lack, sickness, and every bondage. He also said that in Him we will experience satisfaction.

Have you ever hungered after God and experiencing the fullness of His Presence?

Anyone who has ever experienced the tangible, manifest Presence of God knows what it is to feel so complete and fully satisfied, to the point where your cup runs over with the pleasure and joy of experiencing Him. Psalm 100:4 tells us to enter God's Presence with thanksgiving and praise! Choosing to exalt Jesus, our faithful Savior, in thankful praise, attracts His manifest Presence, like a magnet to steel.

The Bible also says He inhabits and is enthroned in our sincere praise of Him. It creates an atmosphere that is exclusively for His Presence! A place where no opposing force can co-exist with His Presence. If our gaze is fixed on Jesus, we can enter in and enjoy being energized, healed, restored, and empowered by His Presence. If you long to be refreshed and empowered by Him today, then come to Him, step through the gateway and be satisfied.

# Day 26

## When Trouble Comes

*2 Chronicles 20:2 (MSG), "Jehoshaphat received this intelligence report: "A huge force is on its way from beyond the Dead Sea to fight you. There's no time to waste—they're already at Hazazon Tamar, the oasis of En Gedi."*

Being a born-again child of God, does not exempt us from experiencing troubling times, or from receiving disturbing news. Jesus said we would have trouble in this world, but since He has overcome it, and deprived it of its power to harm us - we can joyfully be partakers of that victory too (John 16:33). In times of trouble, there are vital steps to take that lead to triumph.

When Jehoshaphat heard their enemies were about to attack them, he immediately asked God for guidance. This is the first step! Since the Lord is not caught by surprise, He knows the exact actions we should take to secure our victory. So, before anything else, seek Him and get His Word on the matter. Get His perspective so you can take authority over the spiritual realm before you make your move in the natural one.

The next step is to praise God and recall all the former victories He has already brought you through. By doing this, our spirit man is stirred up to stand in faith with confidence - knowing God will surely deliver us again. This approach to trouble ensures us receiving a clear strategy from the Lord so we can remain in victory as the Lord goes with us. We are more than over-comers when we lean on and yield to the Spirit of Victory that lives within us!

# Day 27

## When Jesus Speaks

*John 21:6 (NLT), "Then He said, 'Throw out your net on the right-hand side of the boat, and you'll get some!' So they did, and they couldn't haul in the net because there were so many fish in it."*

Sometimes the disappointments of the past keep us from moving forward in faith. They can steal our joy, dampen our hope for the future, and keep us stuck and fruitless. The disciples found themselves in this predicament when after doing all they knew to do - still yielded no results. When Jesus approached them and told them to cast their nets yet again, everything changed. It was the same nets, in the same body of water, but this time with the power of the spoken Word! And the results were astounding.

Jesus is saying the same thing to you today: "Trust Me and try again." Yesterday's set back doesn't define your future. Don't allow disappointments from the past to influence your faith today. God's mercies are new every morning. One word from God, spoken into your spirit, changes everything.

Draw near to the Lord, pay attention to His Words, and let your faith arise as you trust Him to bring the increase and blessing, He has already promised you.

Only do what He tells you to do, and your willing obedience will bring your breakthrough.

# Day 28

## Keep the Faith

*2 Timothy 4:7 (NKJV), "I have fought the good fight, I have finished the race, I have kept the faith."*

In this final letter to Timothy, Paul urges him to reject any temptation to be ashamed of the Gospel of Jesus, or of his association to Paul.

Paul had been at odds with the law of the day and imprisoned for his work of Gospel ministry, which led to some of his co-workers jumping ship. They didn't want Paul's negative reputation and record of imprisonment to taint their own reputations. Paul wanted Timothy to keep Jesus and his purpose the core focus in his life. Paul had personally been given his ministry by Jesus, and he was completely committed to follow through regardless of any opposition - even his own friends turning away from him. Perhaps what impresses us the most is Paul's response to these hardships.

He never allowed his heart to become bitter. He remained steadfast in his assignment; full of faith and confident expectation to see the Lord's deliverance from every evil attack; all the while giving glory to God (2 Timothy 2:16-17). If we follow his example to remain fixed on our purpose, and tender hearted towards others, allowing no bitterness or resentment to harden us - we too will it be able to say we have fought the good fight; finished our race; and kept the faith.

# Day 29

## Don't Settle for Less

***Acts 9:15 (NLT), "But the Lord said, 'Go, for Saul is my chosen instrument to take my message to the Gentiles and to kings, as well as to the people of Israel.'"***

As born-again believers, we are called to be God's chosen instruments here and now. However, many settle for an average Christian experience and never respond to the call of God.

Ephesians 2:10 says we were predestined to work in an inseparable partnership with Jesus, doing the good works He has already empowered us to do! The kingdom of God is within us and as we daily acknowledge His Presence in us, He empowers us to release His righteousness, peace, and joy into the earth - wherever we go!

The Bible says He seeks out those whose hearts are loyal to Him, and ready to live for Him. These are those He shows Himself strong to, on their behalf. How would the course of history be changed if Ananias didn't understand this truth and refused to lay hands upon Saul that day? It would have been natural for him to withdraw in fear and resentment towards Saul - but he obeyed the Lord, stepped out in faith, and released the power of God into a man who subsequently, significantly impacted this world with the gospel. God never overrides our freewill. We get to choose to either settle for an average Christian life, or to change this world for His Kingdom.

So, make your choice to not settle for less, knowing the Greater One dwells in you to work through you.

# Day 30

## Don't Lose Heart

*Luke 18:1 (AMPC), "Also [Jesus] told them a parable to the effect that they ought always to pray and not to-turn coward (faint, lose heart, and give up)."*

Our lives as God's covenant children must be centered around fellowshipping with God and spending time in His Word every day. There should always be a constant interaction between us and Him, through His indwelling Holy Spirit.

Romans 6:11 calls it being in **unbroken fellowship** with Him. This drawing near to Him, by acknowledging His Presence in us and turning our attention towards Him is as conversational as prayer. Not rambling on with complaints or demands but seeking His heart and having His word on a matter. The outcome will always produce faith. We cannot meet the Lord in prayer and not be strengthened in hope, peace, and joy. This is the doorway into the presence of God. It's the avenue through which needs are met, answers come, and strength is regained.

Remaining in unbroken fellowship with the Lord keeps us spiritually fruitful and in the center of His will for our lives. Fiercely treasure your inseparable connection with the Spirit of God today, take every advantage of acknowledging His Presence in you, and let His love, peace, and wisdom flow freely from His throne room into your life - ensuring you never lose heart or give up.

# Day 31

## Jesus, Our Good Shepherd

*John 10:14 (TPT), "I alone am the Good Shepherd, and I know those whose hearts are Mine, for they recognize Me and know Me"*

Jesus is our Good Shepherd who leads us in triumph and teaches us to remain in victory.

This should be the way of every child of God - we are either overcoming or learning how to overcome, but we are never failing. When Jesus truly has our hearts, it means we recognize His voice and obediently follow it. It means we are confident in His good nature and completely trust Him with our lives.

Jesus Christ is faithful. He has given us Himself, by giving us His Word. He has given us His Spirit to teach and lead us into all truth. His Spirit guides our steps, steers our thoughts, and empowers us to release His kingdom in the earth.

We can experience days of heaven on earth when we choose to follow our Good shepherded closely.

Today, choose to surrender to Him in every way. Yield to His voice and live from the victory He has already established for you as you walk closely in His ways.

# APRIL

# Day 01

## It is Well

**2 Kings 4:26 (NKJV), "Please run now to meet her, and say to her, 'Is it well with you? Is it well with your husband? Is it well with the child?' " And she answered, "It is well.".**

What a powerful declaration: "IT IS WELL!"! It is well with my family; it is well with my finances; it is well with my business; it is well with my health, in Jesus Name. Today, we can boldly make this our own confession because we serve an all-powerful, all-knowing, and always present God. We can boldly declare that there is nothing that life or the devil can do to us, that we cannot do something about because of our trust in God and our authority in Christ Jesus! This truth should fire up your spirit today. God sees your situation, but His intervention is determined by your faith in His trustworthy nature, and your refusal to be moved by circumstances.

The Shunamite woman, in 2 Kings 4, confessed that all was well, even after knowing her son was dead. She refused to let go of her confession of faith, even amid the trial she was in. She wasn't in denial, she simply knew that the God Who had worked a miracle by opening her womb to conceive the child, would not renegade on His Word (Hebrews 6:18). Now that miracle child was lying dead, but she refused to accept this was the will of God for her. She knew in her heart that God would not steal away the promise He had already fulfilled. As a result, the prophet raised her son back to life! Today, let God know that you trust Him by refusing to be moved by your circumstances.

Hold on to your confession of faith and get ready to see the intervention of heaven on your behalf! Decide to declare today, "IT IS WELL!".

# Day 02

## Only Advance

***Isaiah 60:3 (NKJV), "The Gentiles shall come to your light, And kings to the brightness of your rising."***

No matter how difficult our path ahead may seem in the natural because we belong to the kingdom of God, our only option is to move forward in victory! 2 Corinthians 2:14 says, *"Now thanks be to God who always leads us in triumph in Christ, and through us diffuses the fragrance of His knowledge in every place."* The reality of triumphant advancement is part of our inheritance through the glorious work of redemption. When we know and believe what the Word of God says about our new life in Christ Jesus, we begin to walk in victory even in the face of real adversity; real giants; real storms and real challenges. Remember, you are what God says you are, and not what you think you are. It's time to discard all those preconceived ideas of your worth and potential that keep you in a place of limitation. Believing the truth of who God says you are in Christ will change your way of life. That's because believing is power, and as you declare what you believe over your life, your present reality changes from what you are going through to what you believe and speak! Job 22:28 says, "*You will also declare a thing, and it will be established for you; so light will shine on your ways*." This is the mentality of the Kingdom, and as ambassadors of this Kingdom, we are required to possess it to be effective and impactful. In famine we're prospering like Isaac, in a pandemic were healthy like the early church; in persecution were prevailing like Daniel; in crisis we're flourishing like Goshen. This wonder of advancement is the life of the believer, step into it and begin to be a sign and wonder to all men, resulting in the lost coming to your light and kings to your rising!

# Day 03

## Hold Fast and Believe

*Ephesians 3:20 (NKJV), "Now to Him who is able to do exceedingly abundantly above all that we ask or think, according to the power that works in us,"*

Nothing is too difficult for God! The truth is many believers have confidence in the ability of God but lack the confidence in knowing His willingness to move on their behalf. They believe that He is all powerful and are fully persuaded of His greatness and majesty, but they're unsure of His willingness to keep His Word concerning them. In Hebrews 6 we are reminded of Abraham's journey of faith. The Bible explains how He was more persuaded in the integrity and faithful character of God to keep His promise, than his confidence in the promise itself. That's why he was prepared to kill his son, completely believing that God would raise him from the dead - because He would never renegade on His promises! God always watches over His word to perform it, and it is impossible for Him to lie or go back on what He has promised! (Hebrews 6:18, 10:23). We must have the same confidence in God's *integrity* to honor His word as we do in His *ability* to do so. The Word reveals the will of God concerning us, and His ability to fulfil His promises in our lives. The moment we believe what God has promised, without doubting, faith is produced inside us. Then, when we declare what we believe, our faith is released and becomes fully committed to see what we believe become our reality! (Mark 11:23). Just as Abraham held fast to his confession concerning the unchanging, faithfulness of God to come through on every promise, we must do the same. Remember the steadfast, never-failing character of God, He will do just as He has promised, as long as you hold fast and believe!

# Day 04

## The Clash of Two Kingdoms

*2 Corinthians 10:3-6 (NKJV), "For though we walk in the flesh, we do not war according to the flesh."*

It is very clear that every child of God engages in a spiritual battle in the journey of faith. The fight is on and it's a good fight according to 1 Timothy 6:12. There is a clash of two kingdoms. The kingdom of darkness that rules this natural world, and the kingdom of light. The latter has the power to overrule and subdue the work of darkness through us - God's own representatives. We are made in His image and likeness and have been given His authority to rule and reign in this life, by Christ Jesus. Satan, being the enemy of the Kingdom of God, is also our enemy. It's in his nature to steal, kill and destroy, but while we are hidden in Christ, we are always led into victory on every account. Our victory is secured in our position in God and our faith (1 John 5:4). This is our greatest weapon: Word of God that has become alive inside us and declared by us. The devil is defenseless against it. Our ignorance concerning the word is his greatest, most effective weapon against us. Make knowing and meditating on God's Word your primary goal. That way you will always have the upper hand, even before the battle arrives. God's Word is light, and nothing disarms darkness like light does. So let your light, which is the truth of God's Word alive in you, be the answer to every reproach, accusation, and onslaught of the enemy. When God's Word is released through your words, from the conviction of your heart - your victory is secured, and the battle is won.

# Day 05

## Call on Him

***Psalms 145:18 (AMC), "The Lord is near to all who call upon Him, to all who call upon Him sincerely and in truth."***

The Lord is near. As believers, we must remain aware of this truth. When we have revelation knowledge of our position in Christ Jesus, understanding that we have been made alive with Him, raised up together with Him, and are seated together with Him in heavenly places, we will have the confidence to call upon Him knowing He hears and answers us (Ephesians 2:4-10). Because of the finished work of the cross, we have been given the same access to the Father as Jesus has (Hebrews 4:16). We have the same position of victory to overcome as He has (1 John 5:4); and we have the same authority over the devil as He has (Luke 9:1, 10:19). Staying aware of **Who** we carry, and **Who** has taken possession of our inner man enables us to live intentionally and with purpose. Even when we don't feel that He is near, we choose to believe the truth of God's written word above our feelings. Deuteronomy 30:14 says, *"...the word is very near you, in your mouth and in your heart, that you may do it."*

Jesus is the Living Word, and by His Holy Spirit, He reveals the truth of who we are in Him, and what we have because of Him! He promises that whenever we call to Him, He will answer us and show us great and mighty things we can't possibly know with our natural intellect but will perceive with our spirits which are alive in Him (Jeremiah 33:3, 1 Corinthians 2:10-11). Calling upon Him in truth, means that we approach Him based on His Word. So, call upon Him today, fully expecting Him to answer you and show you truth that will make and keep you free and living in victory!

# Day 06

## No Dead Wood

*John 15:2 (NKJV), "Every branch in Me that does not bear fruit He takes away; and every branch that bears fruit He prunes, that it may bear more fruit."*

When we read this verse in context of the chapter, we see the analogy of the connection between the vine and its branches. The clear theme is that growth is expected. Jesus clearly emphasizes the necessity of having a personal, abiding relationship with Him to move from a place of barrenness to productivity, and then abundance. As we prioritize spending time with the Holy Spirit in the Word, learning to hear His voice and following His lead, He 'prunes' those things that hinder us from spiritual growth and fruitfulness. For instance, instead of being easily offended, He teaches us to let go of resentment and walk in the love He so freely pours into our hearts towards others. As we renew our minds to His way of doing things, we begin to see the transformation take place - every barren part is replaced by a bud promising fruitfulness. There is of course a serious warning in the analogy too. Those branches that are not connected to the vine are not able to receive its life and vitality and as a result will not produce fruit. They are dead and will be cut off and discarded. People who choose to simply associate with Christ in a casual, noncommittal manner, pretend to be connected to Him, but refuse to enter a meaningful relationship with Him will never produce evidence of His work in their lives. They will remain spiritually dead and be removed to make room for those who are truly connected to Jesus, to thrive in fruitfulness. This will not be your story! As you abide in Jesus, you will begin to overflow with evidence of His life in you!

# Day 07

## I Died with Christ

*Romans 6:6 (AMPC), "We know that our old (unrenewed) self was nailed to the cross with Him in order that [our] body [which is the instrument] of sin might be made ineffective and inactive for evil, that we might no longer be the slaves of sin."*

The death, burial and resurrection of Jesus was far more than just a physical, natural event. What took place in the spirit that day was not bound by the limitations of time or space. It transported our unrenewed, sinful natures directly to that cross with Jesus, the moment we surrendered to His Lordship. The Bible says we were placed in Him and He absorbed into Himself every part of our sin-stained natures (1 John 3:5). Not only did He remove our vial, sinful selves that were burdened with sin and cursed to eternal death; but He wiped away every memory of our oppression too (Isaiah 26:13-14). This means, the devil, our former master, has absolutely no legal accusation to make against us, we have been washed by the shed blood of Jesus! This is the exact time the greatest miracle and act of redemption took place! As Jesus absorbed our sinful nature into Himself, He exchanged it for His own righteous nature. He placed His own righteousness into us. 2 Corinthians 5:17 says that if any man be in Christ, he is a NEW CREATION, the old nature has passed away and EVERYTHING has been made new! Our spirit man was placed in Christ, it's old nature died with Him, and while we were in Him, He recreated our spirit-man and placed His Own sinless, perfect nature into us. What is essential for every born-again believer to grasp with full certainty, is that we, our re-born spirit man has never left this position of being in Christ! We remain hidden in Him, sinless and free of any hold of the devil! Hallelujah!!! Let this truth saturate your entire being as you celebrate the miracle that took place at that cross when you died with Christ!

# Day 08

## I was Raised Together with Christ

*Ephesians 2:6 (AMPC), "And He raised us up together with Him and made us sit down together [giving us joint seating with Him] in the heavenly sphere [by virtue of our being] in Christ Jesus (the Messiah, the Anointed One)."*

Our identification with the resurrected Christ is the center truth that has the power to transform and influence every area of our lives - so we can enjoy a reality of overcoming victory (2 Corinthians 2:14)! At the point of our salvation, we were placed in Christ and our old, unrenewed selves died with Him. Then, the Bible teaches that we were made alive together with Christ (Ephesians 2:4)! That very same mighty power that raised Jesus from the dead raised us up together with Him! 1 Corinthians 6:17 says that we have become one spirit with Him! In fact, we have no existence outside of Him! Acts 17:28 says, *"for in Him we live and move and have our being, ... 'For we are also His offspring.'"* Here's another beautiful truth for us to enjoy: Colossians 2:9-10 says, *"For in Him dwells all the fullness of the Godhead bodily; and you are complete in Him, Who is the head of all principality and power."* What does this mean? Since we have been made alive in Jesus and have been raised up with Him, being one spirit with Him - EVERYTHING that is in Jesus is in us too! His righteousness, life, joy, peace, love, compassion, power, wisdom, knowledge, authority, and victory flows from His Spirit into our spirits! Just as the resurrected Jesus is right now - we are too, in this world! Hallelujah! (1 John 4:17). It's time to see yourself as Jesus has made you to be - alive in Him and full of everything He is. You were raised together with Him, and made to be seated with Him, far above and victorious over every principality and power! Because of the finished work of the cross, this is your new identity in Christ Jesus!

# Day 09

## He Has Risen and I am Seated Together with Him

*Ephesians 1:19-20, "...and (know) what is the exceeding greatness of His power toward us who believe, according to the working of His mighty power which He worked in Christ when He raised Him from the dead and seated Him at His right hand in the heavenly places..."*

In Just 3 days, the Son of God was risen from the dead! He wears the victor's crown because He conquered death and hell for us! Now we know the privilege of enjoying every victory because we are hidden in Him! The Bible says that not only were we raised up together with Him, but we have been seated with Him in heavenly places too! We must understand what this means for us. Firstly, we have been given the same access to the Father as Jesus has. Ephesians 2:18 says, *"For through Him (Jesus) we both (saved Jews and Gentiles) have access by one Spirit to the Father."* Hebrews 4:16 says we can come boldly, fearlessly, and confidently into the throne room of God to receive mercy and grace to help in our time of need. Secondly, we have been given the position of overcoming victory, far above every principality and power (John 16:33, 1 Corinthians 15:57, 2 Corinthians 2:14, 1 John 4:4, 1 John 5:4). Thirdly, we have been given the Name of Jesus and the authority to use it over the devil and all his evil work! (Mark 16:17-18, Ephesians 1:21-23, James 4:7, Luke 10:19). Since we are seated with Christ, and all things are placed under His feet, they are placed under ours too. We don't face the challenges in this life from the perspective of victims. We face every troubling circumstance from a place of victory! Hallelujah! There is nothing too difficult or even impossible for us who are in Christ Jesus! Live your life from the perspective of who you are in Christ Jesus. He paid with His life to give you this position with Him, so do Him justice - step into your life of victory by renewing your mind to who He has made you to be in Him.

# Day 10

## Rich Evidence

*Psalm 1:3 (NKJV), "He shall be like a tree Planted by the rivers of water, that brings forth its fruit in its season, whose leaf also shall not wither; and whatever he does shall prosper."*

The Psalmist says that those who meditate on God's Word will bear fruit. Jesus confirms this truth by saying that unless His Word abides in us, we will have no evidence of our union with Him (John 15:3-5). So, we can easily conclude that without God's Word welcomed, received and acted upon in our lives, there will be no indication that we belong to Him. This first Psalm, as well of Joshua 1:8, give us a good idea of what this evidence or fruitfulness looks like. A life that is always vital, refreshed, prosperous and successful! Colossians 3:16 says that the Word of God should dwell in us richly! When it does, there's no looking back! David said he valued God's Word more than precious gold, and when he acted on it's wise ways, he succeeded in everything he put his hand to! Endeavour to treasure and value God's Word in your life, make it the final authority over all you do. You will be amazed at how it goes to work in your life, enriching you in every way!

# Day 11

## Powerful Praise

*Psalm 8:2 (NIV), "From the lips of children and infants You have ordained praise because of Your enemies, to silence the foe and the avenger."*

Praise has the power to silence the enemy! It was proclaimed by David and captured in the Word of God. In the same chapter David writes that the Lord made man ruler over the works of His (God's) hands and put everything under His feet. This means our praise has a powerful part to play in completing our God-given assignment. Many books have been written and sermons preached on this topic, but praise is more than just a personal fixer-upper or way to start a church service. Praise is more than white noise in the background while doing exercise or getting ready for the day. Praise is a conscious and deliberate action of wielding a powerful sword in the spiritual domain. We can start by expressing thankfulness and meditating on what His Name represents. When we praise, we literally declare God's Name over our lives and circumstances! This is so powerful because His power, His eternal plan and His character are encapsulated in His name. When we declare the Name of Jesus, we declare the Name above all other names, and open a vault of power, possibilities, and solutions! When we praise, we use the Word of God and release the working power of the Blood of Jesus. Singing in the Spirit, as a form of our praise, commissions ministering angels to fulfil their assignments. Praise doesn't account for isolated moments or scheduled events – it is boldly entering His presence where we are accepted and expected before the throne. So let praise be continually on your lips and rejoice as God's enemies (and yours) are scattered before you!

# Day 12

## God's Way - The Blessed Way

*Hebrews 8:5 (NKJV), "...For He said, 'See that you make all things according to the pattern shown you on the mountain.'"*

When God told Moses to build a tabernacle, He gave him a clear description of what it should look like and instructed him to build according to that description. In your walk with the Lord, as you work in His kingdom, don't just run off with every idea that comes to mind, just because you think it's good. Never choose what's best over what's blessed. Be sure you're following God's blueprint; the pattern and description He has given for you.

Ephesians 2:10 tells us God has good works, already planned for us to walk in. Which is why we must know His will for ourselves. In His Word, we find patterns and descriptions of how He wants us to live, the things He wants us to do, and how to do them. Most importantly, He instructs us to work together, as His body, in unity of faith and love. We are expected to be accountable to those in spiritual leadership over us, so that their wisdom provides safeguards and protection.

Today, thank God for the access of His Word into your spirit. Determine to be a diligent doer of the Word, not just a hearer. Keep playing your role by winning souls into the Kingdom and working alongside His body, contributing to His master plan. Together we will populate heaven and plunder hell - doing things the blessed way!

# Day 13

## Unshakable

***Psalm 16:8 (KJV), "I have set the LORD always before me: because He is at my right hand, I shall not be moved."***

When we fix our focus upon the Lord, we cannot be moved! While Peter was walking on the water, with his gaze set on Jesus, he prevailed against the natural forces of the gusting wind and breaking waves. For as long as Stephen's eyes remained on the vision of Jesus, the stones that blunt his body paled in comparison to the glory he was experiencing and the Divine presence that captivated him. Years later, Paul proclaimed: *"... We are troubled on every side, yet not distressed; we are perplexed, but not in despair; Persecuted, but not forsaken; cast down, but not destroyed; Always bearing about in the body the dying of the Lord Jesus, that the life also of Jesus might be made manifest in our body."* (2 Corinthians 4:7).

Fixing and settling our hearts upon Jesus causes us to not be moved – no matter what comes our way. We know, beyond a shadow of doubt, He truly is for us. That He sustains us and lifts us up. He quickens us and causes us to triumph! When we set the Lord before us, we place ourselves on the Rock – He is our fortress and our exceedingly great reward! As He becomes our focus of attention, and the object of our desire, His life and power are manifest in us and we become unshakable in our faith.

# Day 14

## Follow Him

*Psalm 23:4 (NKJV), "Yea, though I walk through the valley of the shadow of death, I will fear no evil; For You are with me; Your rod and Your staff, they comfort me."*

Psalms 23 paints a beautiful description of the Lord as our Good Shepherd. Have you ever taken time to contemplate a shepherd's duties? There are certain responsibilities he will never abdicate from fulfilling. He feeds, guides, and shields his flock. He always takes care of them, keeping them well-fed, groomed and sheltered. The shepherd constantly keeps his eyes alerted to anything that would harm his sheep, ensuring no threat comes near them before passing through him first (John 10:7-13). He always leads them out of where they are into a place of provision and safety, always going before them (John 10:3-4).

A good shepherd knows his sheep and they know him, recognizing His voice and following him because they trust him. It's a well-placed trust, because he is willing to lay down his life for them (John 10:14-15). Jesus is our Good Shepherd. He identifies Himself as having all these characteristics. He will always take care of our needs, physically, emotionally, financially, and spiritually. He will forever provide, protect, and promote those who choose to draw near to Him, learn from Him, and abide in Him. We will never be ashamed for placing our full trust in Jesus (Romans 10:11). Draw near to Him today, listen to His voice and follow Him wherever He leads you.

# Day 15

## Faith and Love

*Galatians 5:6 (NKJV), "For in Christ Jesus neither circumcision nor uncircumcision avails anything, but faith working through love."*

While it's impossible to please God without faith, if we "have not love" our faith will not "avail anything". That means our faith will not benefit us at all if the love of God is not ruling in our hearts as we release words of faith. Paul writes,"...and though I have all faith, so that I could remove mountains, but have not love, I am nothing" (1 Corinthians 13:2).

Under the old covenant, God's people had outward signs symbolizing they were His people. However, under the new covenant, loving others with God's love is evidence that we belong to Him and know Him personally (1 John 4:7-8). Without the love of God filling our own hearts, we will be susceptible to insecurities, wrong motives, doubts, and fear. This is the very atmosphere that makes faith inoperative. You see, God's love keeps us rooted and grounded in Him - where our eyes are fixed on Him, and our ears remain attentive to His voice. Without this, we can easily be moved and swayed with incorrect doctrine and step out of His perfect will for our lives. But when we open our hearts to the love of God, it drives out all fear and empowers us to endure all things without weakening (1 Corinthians 13:7-8). Since God's love never fails, decide to receive, and experience it daily. This way our faith will always work, and we will live in the reality of God's provision and promises.

# Day 16

## Perfect Peace

*Job 22:21 (AMPC), "Now yield and submit yourself to Him [agree with God and be conformed to His will] and be at peace; In this way [you will prosper and great] good will come to you."*

Peace. Something people are willing to fight for, pay money for, and even depend on medicine for. So where does peace come from? That would depend on your definition of peace. God's peace is supernatural and far more powerful than anything the world can offer. It's not a temporary relief from trouble, it's an ability to live in perfect rest amid trouble. The Bible says **Jesus is the Prince of Peace** (Isaiah 9:6). Yielding and submitting to Him means hooking into peace itself. Jesus is the Living Word, so becoming intimately acquainted with the Word of God, is to intimately connect ourselves to peace too; especially since God and His Word are one (John 1:1). When we appropriate God's Word as if our lives depend on it, we become acquainted with the lover of our souls. This is where deep trust in Him is formed and established. This is where we see His heart towards us, and we can experience peace in turmoil, because He is our peace. Here are some verses that lead us into that place of perfect peace: He knows me by name (Isaiah 43:1). He is a shield around me and answers me (Psalm 3: 3-4). The LORD is my light and my salvation – whom shall I fear? (Psalm 27:1). He is my hiding place (Psalm 32: 7). He is my refuge (Psalm 91:2). The righteous will flourish (Psalm 92:12). He put a new song in my mouth (Psalm 40:3). Spend time meditating on these scriptures as a good place to begin your journey of trusting Him and keeping you in perfect peace!

# Day 17

## Live Strong and with Purpose

**2 Timothy 4:7, "I have fought the good fight, I have finished the race, I have kept the faith."**

In this scripture, Paul looked back and gave three positive statements about his ministry. Firstly, he indicates that in all he endured, he didn't shrink back from his mission or call! He remained faithful and full of purpose - fighting the good fight of faith! Secondly, he declared that he had completed the call God had personally given him. When Paul encountered Jesus at his conversion, He showed him all he would do for the kingdom, including all he would endure in the journey (Acts 9:15). Then in 2 Corinthians 12:2, we read how he was later caught up to the third heaven and received revelation knowledge, again from Jesus Himself, unfolding the glorious mystery of the new-man and life we have in Christ Jesus! Paul was mandated to write all this down and teach it to the church. Praise God - he did it all, and he did it well! Thirdly, Paul says he kept **the faith**! He wasn't speaking about a casual, sub-standard faith either. He was talking about a faith completely fixed in the resurrected Christ. His faith was rooted in the truth that we were made alive in Him, raised together with Him, and seated together with Him in heavenly places (Ephesians 2:4-10). All three statements he made with the encouragement and intent for every one of us to walk in too. He expected us to imitate him as he imitated Christ. Paul demonstrated how through the work of the Holy Spirit in us, we are well able to fulfil the mandate God has given us and finish strong - declaring the same three statements: *"I have fought the good fight, I have finished the race, I have kept the faith."* Hallelujah!

# Day 18

## We Belong to Him

*Acts 17:28 (KJV), "'For in Him we live and move and have our being.' As some of your own poets have said, 'We are His offspring.'"*

God loves people. He created man for fellowship with Himself. He designed mankind in such a way that we would find Him to be all we need! He made a way for His Own, perfect love to be poured into our hearts by His Holy Spirit (Romans 5:5). He chose us to be the vessels that carry His Own presence (2 Corinthians 4:7). There is simply no disputing the truth - we belong to God. We are the people of His pasture and the sheep of His hand – He is our faithful Shepherd – how can we be in want? Our existence is wrapped up in Him. Our spirit-man, or inner-man is the part of us that is directly connected to the Spirit of God (1 Corinthians 6:17). This is significant to understand, because according to the word, we have a Father of spirits, who we can trust in and rely on to train us to live the life of the spirit, that always leads to life and peace (Romans 8:5-7). Hebrews 12:9 says, *"Furthermore, we have had human fathers who corrected us, and we paid them respect. Shall we not much more readily be in subjection to the Father of spirits and live?"* Just as the physical traits and human natures between fathers and sons, in the natural, hold strong resemblance - we resemble our Heavenly Father. The essence of our lives; the way we look, speak, and behave must cause an overwhelming awareness that we have a wonderful Father Who pours His love into us, and His attention upon us - because we belong to Him.

# Day 19

## Stronger than before

*Psalms 27:14 (NKJV), "Wait on the Lord; Be of good courage, And He shall strengthen your heart; Wait, I say, on the Lord!"*

There is a promise found in the Word of God when we are faced with situations that seem to diminish all the strength within us. God promises us renewed strength when we wait on Him. The Bible goes on to say that we will mount up on wings like an eagle, run and not grow weary, walk, and not faint (Isaiah 40:31). Learning to take time to block out all distractions and focus ourselves on His Presence that is within us, produces a flow of unstoppable grace directly from God's Own Spirit into ours. That grace is a supernatural empowerment to keep moving forward in faith!

An interesting fact about an eagle is its ability to soar at unusually high altitudes. At a particular time within its lifespan, an eagle goes into hiding, plucks out all its feathers, and breaks its beak for a new beak and feathers to grow out. This is done deliberately to increase the eagle's durability and lifespan. In our time of waiting on the Lord, it's as if we empty ourselves of ourselves to have Him fill us with a fresh surge of His Own wisdom, love, peace, joy and power. We are renewed with supernatural strength to carry on. Wait on the Lord, you'll move up further, faster and stronger than you were before.

# Day 20

## A Double Heritage

*Romans 5:17 (NKJ), "For if by the one man's offense death reigned through the one, much more those who receive abundance of grace and of the gift of righteousness will reign in life through the One, Jesus Christ."*

The entire human race originated from the Garden of Eden out of the first man, Adam. We could not have come into this earth any other way except through his lineage. Adam was the 'master' or 'prototype' for all mankind. He was created righteous and with direct, personal fellowship with God. Adam and Eve were blessed, happy, victorious, and prosperous; this is what they would pass on to their lineage. Adam was given the responsibility to guard the garden, take dominion, and keep the devil out. Due to his negligence and disobedience sin entered in and the 'master' or 'prototype' developed a defect. Sin, sickness, death, depression, confusion, and defeat marred the master. As a result, when Adam and Eve began to reproduce, that defect was carried over and produced in every person that was ever born. But thank God for Jesus! God, the creator, allowed His only Son to become a man, born of a woman, conceived by the Holy Spirit! A brand-new seed produced a brand-new humanity, a whole new creation! Jesus Christ became the new 'master' or 'prototype'! When we become 'born-again' we inherit a double heritage! Where our old nature carried the defect of guilt, our new nature carries the state of righteousness! Where our old nature carried the defect of being alienated from God, our new one is born of Him, we are His Own offspring! This new heritage gives us the freedom to reign in life in Christ Jesus!

# Day 21

## The Effective Word

*1 Thessalonians 2:13 (NKJV), "For this reason we also thank God without ceasing, because when you received the word of God which you heard from us, you welcomed it not as the word of men, but as it is in truth, the word of God, which also effectively works in you who believe."*

Paul taught that the good work God began in us, He will bring to completion (Philippians 1:6). The way God has chosen to do this, is through the Word we believe! Paul said, God's Word effectively works in those who believe. The Word of God is alive, and it is powerful (Hebrews 4:12). That's why the devil does his best to keep us from getting and keeping the word in our hearts (Luke 8:12). It's the Word of God that we believe that saves and brings life. The way we move from just agreeing with the word to believing it, is through meditating on it. This is where it abides in us and powerfully enriches our lives. Psalm 1:2-3 says how meditating on the word causes us to prosper in whatever we do. 1 Timothy 4:15 says, *"Meditate on these things; give yourself entirely to them, that your progress may be evident to all."*

Meditating on God's word causes it to take root and grow, producing everything it promises in our lives, making our progress evident to others! The stronger the root, the more difficult it is for our enemy, the devil, to steal it from us. For God's Word to work effectively in us, we must be vigilant concerning what we allow into our hearts through the things we see and hear. Make the word of God the loudest voice in your life, give it your full attention so that it rules over every other opinion. This way it will work effectively bringing the good work God has begun in you to completion.

# Day 22

## Lay Hold

*1 Samuel 17:51 (NKJV), "Therefore David ran and stood over the Philistine, took his sword and drew it out of its sheath and killed him, and cut off his head with it. And when the Philistines saw that their champion was dead, they fled."*

Goliath was brought down, and David triumphed over him. That is our position in Christ. We are seated together with Him far above all principalities, powers, and rulers of darkness, ruling and reigning victoriously over all the wiles of the devil. We have also been given the Name that is above every other name! That just at the mention of it, every knee must bow! Paul so aptly captures the victory of Christ in Colossians 2:15, *"He spoiled principalities and powers, and made a shew of them openly, triumphing over them in it."* Our victorious Jesus made a public display for everyone to see that the enemy of mankind has forever been defeated. So, our battle against him is fixed, we win in all things, always, through Christ.

Today, no matter what comes against you, understand God has already secured your victory. Stand in faith as you hold fast to your confession that God cannot lie! (Hebrews 6:18). He is faithful to always watch over His word to perform it in our lives (Hebrews 10:23).

So, having done all, stand and stay in the good fight of faith. As you are faithful to walk in His ways, lay hold of every promise in God's word, because it is yours through the death, burial and resurrection of Jesus Christ. Glory to God!

# Day 23

## Empowered for Success

*Acts 22:14 (KJV), "Then he said, 'The God of our fathers has appointed you to know His will, and to see the Righteous One, and to hear His voice."*

Paul was designated by God to do great exploits for His kingdom. When he was appointed to see and hear Jesus, the Righteous Son of God, he received all he needed to accomplish the work he was called to do. This is not exclusive to the Apostle Paul. Every believer has the privilege and opportunity to know, to see, and to hear the Lord! We are exhorted to grow in grace and the knowledge of Jesus (2 Peter 3:18). We do this by knowing Him, His ways, and His will by His Spirit, through the written word. The words Jesus spoke to Paul were His unuttered thoughts He took with Him when He left the earth. He couldn't release them while He was here because they were about our new life in Him, through His death, burial, and resurrection.

Now, those thoughts are recorded in Paul's letters to the church, for every believer to receive for themselves! This means we can personally walk in the same revelation knowledge Paul walked in. We are able to experience God's love and live according to His ways because we get to see and hear Jesus in His word, through His indwelling Holy Spirit. The Apostle Paul was supernaturally empowered to successfully fulfil all he was called to do because of his encounters with Jesus. I declare that as we encounter the Lord in His word, we will be as effective in the Kingdom of God, as Paul was, living a life hidden in Christ.

# Day 24

## The Glory Light

***2 Corinthians 4:6 (NKJV), "For it is the God who commanded light to shine out of darkness, who has shone in our hearts to give the light of the knowledge of the glory of God in the face of Jesus Christ."***

In Psalms 24:1, the Bible declares that the earth is the Lord's and the fullness thereof. That means everything created has been made from the glory of God, for the glory of God - including you and I. There is no such thing as a 'self-made man'. God is the one who formed us in our mothers' wombs (Jeremiah 1:5). Every day of our lives has been recorded in a book before Him (Psalm 139:16). He created us in His Son, for a purpose that He already prepared for us to walk in (Ephesians 2:10).

If we choose to daily receive and meditate on His Word, trusting the Holy Spirit to make it alive in us, that glory light will shine and reveal the truth of who God is to us. We will see Jesus in His word, and who we are in Him; and our lives will begin to reflect the glory from within.

The Bible says God has shone His glory light within our hearts. It says we have this hidden treasure in earthen vessels, showing that the excellency of that glory power is from God, and is not of ourselves (2 Corinthians 4:7). We remain in the light of His glory by fixing our eyes on Jesus, and continuously walking in the revelation truth of His Word. As we behold Him in His word, we become more like Him, shining His glory light to everyone, wherever we go.

# Day 25

## Boast in the Lord

*2 Corinthians 10:17-18 (NKJV), "...he who glories, let him glory in the Lord. For not he who commends himself is approved, but whom the Lord commends."*

We are not to boast in anyone or anything but the Lord. If anyone had reason to boast it was Paul. He was tutored by Gamaliel, one of the greatest Jewish leaders of his era. He was also a Pharisee, the strictest sect of the Jewish faith at the time. This gave him an excellent command of knowledge concerning all Jewish laws and customs. After His first supernatural encounter with Jesus, which led to his conversion, Paul lived out his purpose of spreading the Gospel and building the New Testament church with great zeal and astounding accomplishments! He goes down in history as one of the greatest champions for the Christian faith who endured all kinds of hardships and persecutions with grace and courage, adding writing two-thirds of the New Testament to his extensive list of achievements! Yet he referred to all his accolades as folly.

He counted everything as loss compared to the excellence of personally knowing Jesus Christ, and enjoying an inseparable, intimate relationship with Him. While others sought to glorify and commend themselves, Paul sought to boast in nothing but Christ. The truth of the matter is this: Once we have personally tasted and experienced what it is to walk with Jesus and know the reality of His personal, intimate touch on our lives, we find there is simply nothing in this world to compare with it. As we humbly seek knowing Him and His ways, treasuring our relationship with Him, through His precious Holy Spirit, He approves of us, and promotes us into all He has destined for us to walk in.

# Day 26

## If not You, then Who?

*Esther 4:14 (NKJV), "For if you remain completely silent at this time, relief and deliverance will arise for the Jews from another place, but you and your father's house will perish. Yet who knows whether you have come to the kingdom for such a time as this?"*

It's amazing to celebrate what God has done for us in Christ! We have received everything we need to live a life of victory and triumph. The question is, what are we personally doing to fulfil God's kingdom agenda for our lives? We must begin to use our God-given advantage to impact our world. With the Holy Spirit living in us, continuously working His mighty power inside us so He can work through us, we have more than what it takes to give out what we have freely been given!

In the fourth chapter of the book of Esther, Mordecai informed Esther of Haman's plot against their nation, and urged her to do something about it. He felt she had got so caught up in her position and privilege of being queen, that she had forgotten the reason she was placed in the kingdom to begin with. Many believers have forgotten that they were saved to do the good works of God. They have failed to remember that they have been placed in their positions to represent Jesus and glorify Him. God wants to use us now.

When we refuse to build ourselves up in faith and yield ourselves to the leading of the Holy Spirit, we will miss out on the wonderful purpose He has created us for! Allow the Holy Spirit to flood your heart with His love, and be purposeful to let Him use your gifts, talents, and abilities to invest into His kingdom for such a time as this.

# Day 27

## See God

***Matthew 5:8, "Blessed are the pure in heart, for they will see God."***

A generation that pursues the heart of God by seeking His face in daily communion, will be the generation that ushers in the glory of God collectively! Imagine revival fires in every city, every country, and every continent at once. We cannot continue to be satisfied with religion - it may look like Christianity, but it always leads to dissatisfaction and disappointment, because it has no power!

Those whose hearts are ablaze for God pursue Him. They enjoy times of refreshing in His Presence and thrive on deepening their relationship with Him as they spend time meditating on His Word. Their lives are marked by active obedience to the Holy Spirit, motivated by sincere love for Him and intense delight to please Him. The more we fall in love with Jesus, our spiritual eyes are enlightened, and our spiritual ears become attentive to His voice. There is an inclination to the Spirit of God and what He is doing.

More and more believers are becoming aware and are being moved to yielding to the Spirit of God, with a zeal and boldness likened to the early church believers. They were called, "The ones who turned the world upside down"! This could be said of you too! Be enlightened to the power that's at work within you. The earth is about to burst forth in manifestation of God's love and the demonstration of His power through those who know Him and move at His will!

# Day 28

## Set Your Heart on Him

*Jeremiah 29:13 (NKJV), "And you will seek Me and find Me, when you search for Me with all your heart."*

Many people avoid quiet moments alone to not face the dissatisfaction and loneliness in their hearts - something that can only be filled by God. The yearning in our spirits is for more of Him. Understanding this truth sets us free from searching to fill any void in our hearts with anything outside of Him!

In the Psalms, we see David pouring out his heart of thankful praise to the God who satisfies his soul (Psalm 42)! If you find yourself needing a fresh touch of His refreshing grace, and warm embrace, simply open your heart to Him and thank Him for His faithfulness and love. Philemon 1:6 says that as we acknowledge every good thing we have in knowing Christ, our faith is made effective! We become increasingly aware of His presence that wells up within us, causing us to overflow with His tender care and kindness towards us. In this, our hearts cry out to Him to fill us up with more of Himself!

This is where the Spirit of God within us helps us to express our grateful love to the Lord in return, and like the psalmist, we declare that our hearts will be devoted to Him, all the days of our lives! When we use those quiet moments doing this, we will never face moments of dissatisfied loneliness again!

# Day 29

## God's Treasure in You

*2 Corinthians 4:7 (NKJV), "But we have this treasure in earthen vessels, that the excellence of the power may be of God and not of us."*

God created us to carry His glory! It's easy to disqualify ourselves for God's service when we focus on our lack of qualifications or insufficiencies. Paul wrote to the believers in Corinth about this, telling them to rather place their attention on the fact that God called them to be His vessels of honor! Even if by the world's standards we seem to fall short of qualifications - God has qualified us by placing Himself inside us!

Paul reminds us that God uses the things that are seen as weak or even despised by the world to display His goodness and power! (1 Corinthians 1:26). He does this so that no flesh can take the glory for something His presence within us can and will do. When God's power is displayed in someone that is seen as weak in worldly standards, one can only conclude that the work was done by God. What a wonderful encouragement to others - seeing what God can do in and through us, regardless of our station in life, education qualifications and popularity!

One Bible translation says, *"We now have this light shining in our hearts, but we ourselves are like fragile clay jars containing this great treasure. This makes it clear that our great power is from God, not from ourselves."* God's power is made perfect in our weakness. Never doubt what God can do in and through you. All He requires is your heart of obedience and submission.

# Day 30

## Build Up!

***Proverbs 27:17 (NKJ), "As iron sharpens iron, so a man sharpens the countenance of his friend."***

When we have the right people around us, through their positive attitudes and sincere love, they will always contribute to our moving forward in life. There will be times we need a strong word, spoken in love, to redirect our perspective in the right direction. On the other hand, we could have people around us that constantly discourage us with their consistent negativity. They have a way of taking drive, purpose, and passion right out of us.

That's why one of the most important decisions we make is choosing our friendships. We need to ask ourselves what type of impact certain friendships have on our pursuit of what God has told us to do. In 1 Thessalonians 5:11, Paul gave some expert advice on how to treat our friends: *"Therefore encourage (admonish, exhort) one another and edify (strengthen and build up) one another, just as you are doing."*

If you are needing to see good, godly friends come into your life, you can take the first step to see the turnaround! Begin to be a positive influence on those around you. Pray for them, see the good qualities in them, and build them up with encouraging words, not shallow flattery. Before you know it, your sincere, positive attitude will begin to attract the right kind of people to you that will influence you to keep moving in the right direction in life.

# MAY

# Day 01

## Seek, Listen, Follow

*1 Chronicles 16:11 (ESV), "Seek the Lord and His strength; seek His presence continually!"*

As children of God, seeking the Lord is a trait that should be found strong in our lives, especially in the hour we're living in. It's not to be only reserved for certain seasons, or when it suits our schedules or moods. For the believer, seeking the Lord is a permanently, essential part of our daily lives. Spiritually speaking, hearing God's voice, and knowing His will is the very nourishment our lives need to survive and thrive in this world. In John 4:34, Jesus said, *"My meat is to do the will of Him that sent me, and to finish His work."*

While He walked the earth, Jesus was completely reliant on the strength, wisdom, and direction of His Heavenly Father, through the Holy Spirit. He received all He needed to be successful in everything He did, through personally hearing God's voice and then obeying His leading. If this was so vitally important for Jesus, how could we not treat it as our most valuable need and privilege too? Spending time to hear the voice of the Lord sets us up for success because His words to us are life and peace (John 6:63). Then, following up on those words by applying their timeless wisdom to our lives brings us to a place of everlasting victory!

This is the reward for those who seek the Lord, listen to His voice, and obey His leading.

# Day 02

## A Delight that Inherits.

*Proverbs 8:21, "That I may cause those who love Me to inherit [true] riches and that I may fill their treasuries."*

The Lord is searching for those who will prioritize knowing Him and His ways over and above the temporary things of this life. The wonderful truth is that God will always reward those who seek Him. It's impossible to seek God at a loss. And yet, it's not the rewards of His hands alone that motivate true worshippers, it's the privilege of seeking His heart and finding Him that motivates us.

God is not moved by temporary faithfulness and manipulative worship. He examines our motives before He acts. He is not interested in blessing something that resembles the Tower of Babel, that's built for our own name's sake. He will only move on and bless what is invested in His Kingdom interests and its advancement. Seek the heart of God steadfastly; seek to know Him more and you will love what He loves and hate what He hates.

As we delight in Him and His ways, we will secure His hand of provision with ease. Proverbs 3:4 says this will cause us to find favor and high esteem in the sight of God and man. His goodness and mercy will follow us all the days of our lives, and where His goodness flows, His provision is seen!

Let's decide to seek the Lord sincerely and consistently in all things, so that we will inherit His true riches and He will fill our treasuries with His abundant provision!

# Day 03

## Turn Your Affection Within

*__Psalm 150:6 (NLT) "Let everything that breathes sing praises to the Lord! Praise the Lord!"__*

Praise and worship are a direct and instant way to enter the presence of God. When we abandon every other thought and completely fix our attention on the Lord, gratefully considering His excellent nature, and His exceeding kindness towards us - our souls (intellect, will and emotions) are brought into the awareness of the reality our spirits enjoy.

1 Corinthians 6:17 -20 tells us about this reality. It says that because of our union with Christ, our spirits and God's Spirit are inseparably connected and that our bodies are the dwelling place of His Holy Spirit. A simple shift of our un-divided attention onto this reality, coupled with our personal words of praise and worship towards Him causes His Presence to overwhelm our senses with supernatural peace, love, and joy. When the Presence of Jesus invades a room, the entire atmosphere changes because of the power His presence carries. All darkness, doubt and fear are dispelled. Demons tremble and leave as bondages are broken off people's lives. As we learn to practice personally acknowledging God's Presence and releasing our heartfelt reverence and adoration to Him - we begin to recognize and experience how everything we need is in His presence. The fullness of joy, wisdom, healing, inner strength, and peace can only be found in Him. We are complete in Him and He couldn't have made our access to all that He has for us any easier.

Tap into the well of life that dwells, in fullness, inside of you, as you turn your affection towards His Presence within today.

# Day 04

## Marvelous Meetings

*Hebrews 10:25 (AMP), "...not forsaking our meeting together [as believers for worship and instruction], as is the habit of some, but encouraging one another; and all the more [faithfully] as you see the day [of Christ's return] approaching."*

People often think that they simply choose a church, whereas it seems that God places us with (or sends us to) a family of believers. It's a privilege and responsibility that should be prayerfully considered. However, this journey unfolds, one thing is illuminated from this scripture – we should not give up meeting together.

The New Testament church set a pattern for us to follow, where church resembles a place where the Word is preached uncompromisingly, where the heart of the Father is hunted, where everything is soaked in prayer. A place where we are encouraged, but also challenged with the Truth. Where we get to witness the presence of the Lord and see the Holy Spirit in operation. A place to practice our gifts (both spiritual and natural) and see the valuable contribution of other believers. We worship together. We surrender. We give of ourselves.

Something powerful and precious happens when a body of believers joins in unity. God speaks. Healings manifest. Lives are touched and changed by the power of God's love. There is protection in accountability with other believers, and we are empowered to go out and DO the great commission. Church is a place of marvelous meetings, so be sure to get connected to the one God has for you! Let's go to church!

# Day 05

## The Lord Delights in You

*2 Samuel 22:20 (NKJV), "He also brought me out into a broad place; He delivered me because He delighted in me."*

Have you ever considered just how much God loves His church? We are His workmanship, a royal priesthood, a holy nation, His Own chosen people, called out of darkness into His marvelous light. The Bible says He rejoices over us with singing (Zephaniah 3:17).

Undoubtably, the greatest demonstration of God's love for us was when He freely gave up His only Son, not only for our redemption, but that we could live a life of abundance in Him. Romans 8:32 says, *"He who did not withhold or spare [even] His own Son but gave Him up for us all, will He not also with Him freely and graciously give us all [other] things?"* Ephesians 1:22 says that after Jesus rose again from the dead - triumphant over it, God placed all things under His feet and gave Him to be the head over all things **to** the church! Then He said that we, the church is His body, the fullness of Him! Hallelujah!

God loves us so much that He not only sent His Son to die in our place, He made us alive in Him too, gave us His Name and authority and victory, and filled us with the fullness of Himself through His Holy Spirit indwelling us! This demonstration of His love and goodness and kindness towards us is incomparable to any other! God chose to pour Himself into us, to empower us to live a full and victorious life - demonstrating His goodness wherever we go. There can be no doubt in your heart of how much He delights in you!

# Day 06

## The Mystery of God's Kingdom

**Mark 4:11(TPT), "He said to them, 'The privilege of intimately knowing the mystery of God's kingdom realm has been granted to you...'"**

Jesus said that the mystery of God's kingdom has been given to us to know (NKJ)! That word *know* means more than just knowing about something. It means intimately experiencing the reality of it. This same mystery of God's kingdom is spoken about again in Ephesians 3:2 and Colossians 1:26, where it's described as a mystery that has been kept secret, hidden in God, since the world began, and is now made manifest! In Colossians 1:27, Paul reveals exactly what this mystery is: He said it is, *"...Christ in you, the hope of glory."* That word *hope* in the natural sense, doesn't hold much weight. It implies a wistful, wishful thinking. However, in spiritual terms, *hope* is far more! It is the promise of a sure, guaranteed reality!

The word *glory* holds significant value too. It literally means the full, weightiness of all that makes God - God. The mystery of God's kingdom that has been hidden in Him since the world began and has now been revealed for every believer to experience - is that since Christ lives in us - we have the sure guarantee that everything locked up in God, is locked up in us! We have access to the full measure of God's Presence and power (John 3:34, John 1:16). Today, meditate on the wonderful truth of this glorious mystery! The fullness of God dwells in Christ, and He dwells in us too - making us complete in Him, and full of Him! Everything we will ever need is found in Him. We lack for nothing because Christ in us is our guaranteed reality of the glory of God!

# Day 07

## First Love Restored

***Revelation 2:4 (ESV), "But I have this against you, that you have abandoned the love you had at first."***

No matter what we accomplish for the kingdom of God, it holds little value in the eyes of God if it's not initiated and motivated by His love! Hebrews 11:6 tells us that without faith, it's impossible to please God, but even faith has no value outside of love. The entire chapter of 1 Corinthians 13 explains how any spiritual gift or endeavor, that is not motivated by love, is regarded as superficial and valueless. The church of Ephesus could testify of their good works and patient endurance. They were intolerant of those who were wicked imposters of the faith, and they demonstrated resilience for the sake of the Lord. Yet, the Lord clearly warned them to *return* to their first love or lose their position in His kingdom. They were encouraged to repent and do what was first done.

Just the same, we too must live being conscious of the goodness and grace we first experienced when we encountered our Savior. Our commitment to Him was based on our overwhelming gratitude to be counted as His Own! We must take care to not grow cold in our regard of Who He is and all He has done in and for us. Don't allow life and work, regardless of how noble, to get in the way of remembering His love and goodness towards you. Do the things that please Him, with a heart overflowing with sincere, joyful love for Him. Come back to your first love.

# Day 08

## Prepared for the End

*Luke 21:36 (NIV), "Be always on the watch, and pray that you may be able to escape all that is about to happen, and that you may be able to stand before the Son of Man."*

God gives us His word and signs of the times we are living in to prepare us for what is ahead. As the time draws near for our Savior's return, more than ever we must remain steadfast in our faith and first love for the Lord. 1 Thessalonians 5:2 says that the day of the Lord's return will come as a thief in the night, so we must be prepared and unmoved by the increased trouble that is about to hit the earth.

1 John 2:24 gives us sound advice on how to do this: *"As for you, keep in your hearts what you have heard from the beginning. If what you heard from the first dwells and remains in you, then you will dwell in the Son and in the Father [always]." One translation describes what we have heard as the message of life.* In other words, the life we have in Christ Jesus must be what is constantly burning and alive in our hearts! The identity of the *new man*, hidden in Christ must remain the dominating truth inside us! It will keep us dwelling in the Son and in the Father - exactly where we must be found if we are going to overcome all we are to face, victoriously and unashamedly! Be diligent to meditate on the scriptures that secure your core identity in Christ and you will find yourself living the reality of 1 John 2:28, *"And now, little children, abide (live, remain permanently) in Him, so that when He is made visible, we may have and enjoy perfect confidence (boldness, assurance) and not be ashamed and shrink from Him at His coming."*

# Day 09

## Never Look Back

*Genesis 24:5-6 (NKJV), "And the servant said to him, 'Perhaps the woman will not be willing to follow me to this land. Must I take your son back to the land from which you came?' But Abraham said to him, 'Beware that you do not take my son back there.'"*

Isaac was to remain in the land of promise that God had given to him and his father. By leaving the land of Canaan, he would be positioned outside the promise of God! He was to avoid the past at all costs! When we decide to turn our back on wickedness and leave our old, sinful nature at the cross, we die to its existence and every bondage attached to it. The Bible says we became a brand-new creation, the old, previous moral and spiritual condition has literally passed away! Now a fresh, new life in Christ Jesus has begun! (2 Corinthians 5:17). Our journey of faith in God always looks ahead. It only focuses on the truth and hope we have in Him. The only time we are to look back is to celebrate past victories and all that the Lord has done in our lives. Colossians 3:1-3 says, *"If then you were raised with Christ, seek those things which are above, where Christ is, sitting at the right hand of God. Set your mind on things above, not on things on the earth. For you died, and your life is hidden with Christ in God.."* In the wilderness, the children of Israel complained, saying it was better in the land of Egypt. They bought the lie that the past was better. However, they forgot that when they were in Egypt they were slaves, living in bondage to a people who were strangers to the covenant keeping God. Just as Abraham refused to send his son back to the past, we must refuse to have any association with what we were saved out of! Our eyes are to remain fixed on Jesus, the author and finisher of our faith!

# Day 10

## Don't Keep Him Waiting

*Hosea 6:6 (NLT), "I want you to show love, not offer sacrifices. I want you to know Me more than I want burnt offerings."*

The most valuable possession under the sun is the wonderful gift of knowing the Lord. There is nothing else worth boasting about in this life. Knowing the Lord is what every man should glory in according to Jeremiah 9:24. What a glorious and wonderful reality we have been afforded through the precious work of redemption. The blood of Jesus afforded us access to dwell in the Son and the Father (1 John 2:24). Never allow yourself to become familiar with the gift we have been given to be intimate with the God of creation. Do you know the Lord desires for you to know Him? He would rather have your intimacy than an offering. He would rather have your love than your sacrifice. You mean so much to the Lord, but I want you to know today that intimacy will never happen by accident. We have a role to play!

The Bible tells us to draw near to God. It also says that His response is immediate - He will draw near to you. He responds to us when we pursue and seek to know Him. He is not hiding Himself from anybody, if you want to see Him, it will take all your heart to find Him. Friend, today I want to provoke something in you to seek and know the Lord. It's the most important thing you can have in this life. It's from a life of intimacy with the Lord that impact and influence will flow. He desires for you to know Him, how long are you going to make Him wait?

# Day 11

## Know the Word, Know God

*Psalms 9:10 (AMPC), "And they who know Your name [who have experience and acquaintance with Your mercy] will lean on and confidently put their trust in You, for You, Lord, have not forsaken those who seek (inquire of and for) You [on the authority of God's Word and the right of their necessity]."*

What we believe and know of God is through the revelation of His Holy Spirit, based on the authority of His Word. The sad reality is that many believers don't walk in true revelation knowledge of God because they have been led off course either by religion, passed down traditional views, skewed doctrinal beliefs or simply the devil lying to them! They may believe what is written in the Bible, but they don't necessarily believe its truth applies directly to them. As a result, they miss out on the wonderful blessings and life God has for them to enjoy now. The greatest ploy of the enemy is to overshadow the Word of God with doubt or deception - just like he did to Eve in the Garden of Eden. Faith is believing God at His Word, regardless of people's opinions, or the circumstances surrounding us. Abraham's faith was credited to him as righteousness because he was fully persuaded that God's character was completely trustworthy. He believed it was impossible for God to lie, and that He would always honor His Word concerning him. This is how he inherited the promises of God - through his faith and refusal to be moved concerning what he believed (Hebrews 6:12). We are instructed to imitate Abraham in this regard. Our guarantee of personally knowing the true nature of God and experiencing the fullness of His Presence in our lives is based on our faith to believe His Word. Pursue knowing God through the leading of the Holy Spirit as you give yourself to His Word. This way you will know the truth, and it will set and keep you free.

# Day 12

## Let's Go to God's House!

***Psalm 122:1 (NIV), "I rejoiced with those who said to me, 'Let us go to the house of the LORD.'"***

In the book of Hebrews, we are admonished, as some translations put it, to not forsake the gathering of the saints. This reprimand comes shortly after the verse which declares that we now have confidence to enter the Most Holy Place by the blood of Jesus. Can you see the beautiful golden thread from the Old to the New Testament?

Going to the Lord's house was important and treasured then. You can search for yourself what David so passionately wrote about it. Even though we have individually become the temple of the Holy Spirit, neglecting the coming together to worship the Lord and fellowship with other believers is most detrimental to our spiritual growth and well-being. As we serve together, we grow and become extremely effective for the kingdom of God. We can hide behind so many excuses as to why we have chosen to not connect and commit to a local church. However valid they may be, there is no denying the power, peace, and blessing released into our lives as we obey the Word.

As we joyfully obey the Lord and join in the corporate gathering of the saints, we will see how there is a crossover from the natural to the supernatural, from the physical to the spiritual, and from the mundane to the marvelous. What a joy to go to the house of the Lord together!

# Day 13

## Your Set Time!

**Psalm 102:13 (NKJV), "You will arise and have mercy on Zion; For the time to favour her, Yes, the set time, has come."**

For every prophetic declaration there is a set time of fulfilment. God works with time and seasons. According to Psalm 102:13, there is a set time for God's uncommon favor to manifest in our lives, and that time is now! John 1:16 says, *"For out of His fullness (abundance) we have all received [all had a share and we were all supplied with] one grace after another and spiritual blessing upon spiritual blessing and even favour upon favour and gift [heaped] upon gift."*

Because of the finished work of the cross, since we have been made alive in the resurrected Jesus, we have received and been supplied with grace, spiritual blessings, favor and gifts! The set time to enjoy all this is determined by when we choose to appropriate our faith to receive it!

Time is generally defined in the Greek as *"chronos"* and *"kairos"*. *"Chronos"* represents a chronological time; where *"kairos"* represents a God-appointed time. It's God's divine intervention in man's life to accelerate or bring to pass what has been promised. God's set time is now! So, release your faith through joyfully thanking and praising Him for His goodness and faithfulness towards you! He said He has given you all these marvelous things, now your appropriate response is to thank Him, knowing He always watches over His word to perform it in our lives! Hallelujah! Rejoice for your set time has come!

# Day 14

## Love's Proven Hope

*Romans 5:5 (ESV), "...and hope does not put us to shame, because God's love has been poured into our hearts through the Holy Spirit Who has been given to us."*

This hope spoken of here, is a developed hope in the Lord that cannot put us to shame. For some, hope may have started during some form of tribulation, that led us to the word to find an appropriate promise. Then it grew to produce patience, which is a stubborn refusal to be moved from the conviction of our hearts. This patience turned into experience, where we saw God's promise fulfilled, and so that hope finally became an established trust in the Lord that will never be shaken! We call this: hope that has been proven! In the realm of the spirit - hope is a joyful, confident expectation of the future! It is a secure foundation we can wrap our faith around and hold fast to - no matter the outward circumstances.

When we recognize how God's strength is made perfect in us when we can't rely on our own, we are so encouraged! Joy floods into us from our spirits and we're able to endure because we know He is empowering us to overcome! The Holy Spirit doesn't just release joy, like a fountain, into our hearts, He pours God's supernatural love into us too! This love that NEVER fails! It bears up under anything, giving us God's grace to perfectly respond every time! (1 Corinthians 13:7-8). Open your heart to the Holy Spirit today, trust Him to develop this hope inside you as He reveals more and more of God's love for you, and what that love can achieve.

# Day 15

## Trust in the Lord

*Psalms 121:1-2 (NIV), "I lift up my eyes to the mountains where does my help come from? My help comes from the Lord, the Maker of heaven and earth."*

When Adam sinned, he and all his descendants (humanity) were cursed, causing man to become self-dependent instead of remaining God-dependent. Men's hearts were turned away from the Lord and they became obsessed with a man-centered faith rather than a God-focused trust. Jeremiah 17:5 says, *"Cursed is the man who trusts in man and makes flesh his strength, whose heart departs from the LORD."* The new-man in Christ understands that his God-focused heart must never be replaced with a self-centered mindset that relies on his own fleshly abilities, instead of depending on the Lord's almighty provision. We place ourselves in a dangerous position when we formulate a dependency on a manmade system, or our own fleshly achievements, or negotiating skills.

In truth, these things become a point of idolatry and begin to heap up curses not blessings. There is nothing secure in a system that is outside of God. It's time to examine our hearts and consider where we have placed our trust and on whom we have anchored our hope. All our help comes from Him. Psalm 46:1 says He is an ever-present help. We are promised that He who keeps us will not slumber, nor sleep. He watches over us to help and preserve our very souls (our minds, wills, and emotions)! Today, choose to trust in the Lord your God with all our heart, and place your hope in His unfailing love and promised provision - He will never fail you!

# Day 16

## Fan the Flame

*Daniel 7:10 (NLT), "...and a river of fire was pouring out, flowing from His presence. Millions of angels ministered to Him; many millions stood to attend Him. Then the court began its session, and the books were opened."*

Daniel's end time vision revealed a river of fire pouring out from the presence of God. Hebrews 12:29 describes God as being a consuming fire! If a river of fire is constantly flowing from the throne of God, and we have been given access into this throne room through the blood of Jesus - what is preventing us from receiving a fresh touch of this fire flowing from His throne? In the book of Leviticus, it says the fire on the altar of our hearts should never go out!

We have a responsibility to keep it burning strong. Paul told Timothy to fan into flame the gift that was in him. We constantly must fan into flame the fire that is in us to keep our hearts burning for Him. We do this by remaining aware of His Presence in us. 1 John 2:24 says that as we allow the message of our new life that is hidden in Christ, and all that it entails to abide in us, we will actively abide in the Son and in the Father! Our hearts will continuously be alight with His fire that is streaming from His Presence inside us! This way we will not be found lukewarm in His returning, but red hot with the fire of passion burning for Him and His ways.

# Day 17

## Look to Him

***Psalm 34:5 (NKJV), "They looked to Him and were radiant, And their faces were not ashamed."***

In today's world it's almost impossible to not be drawn into the issues and challenges all around us. If we allow them to become our primary concern, we become prey to feelings of worry, anxiety, and depression. This doesn't mean we must choose to live in denial, it just means we must decide where to fix our attention on and use it as the filter for everything else. Scripture says the people whose eyes are fixed on Jesus will live in peace and joy amid the challenges that surround them. That's because every born-again believer has a hope which is anchored in God!

It is impossible for Him to lie or deceive us, so we have an unshakable, joyful, earnest expectation for the future because of His faithfulness towards us and His covenant promises! Our hope in God reaches from the visible into the invisible, from what is temporary into the permanent, and from what is in the present into the eternal! Hebrews 6:18-19 (TPT) says, *"...we can run into His heart to hide ourselves in His faithfulness. This is where we find His strength and comfort, for He empowers us to seize what has already been established ahead of time—an unshakeable hope!"*

# Day 18

## Remain in Him

***Hebrews 13:8 (NLT) "Jesus Christ is the same yesterday, today, and forever."***

There is great peace and security in knowing we belong to a God Who will never change His mind about us. His plans for us were already pre-determined. He saw us in Him before the foundation of the world! (Ephesians 1:4). Just as our God remains consistent in His excellent ways, we need to remain steadfast in our faith in Him. We must never allow our devotion and loyalty towards Him to be determined by what we see happening around us.

Our relationship with our Heavenly Father should only grow in love and appreciation for His perfect love and abounding goodness. The word says He is a rewarder of those who diligently seek Him! One great truth to hold fast to, is that while God will never change, we must! The more we learn about Him and who we are in Him, the more the Holy Spirit does a transforming work in us. We change one glorious degree after another into the very image of Jesus! Colossians 2:9-10 tells us that the fullness of the God-head dwells in Jesus, and since we are in Christ, the fullness of the God-head dwells in us too! Our spirits are not just inseparably connected to God's Spirit - we are also filled with His fullness! But only when we allow these wonderful truths to dominate our thinking will the transformation take place. Because as a man thinketh in his heart - so is he! Determine to consistently renew your mind to what God's word says you are in Him, and you will see while His faithfulness to you never changes - you will continuously move to new levels of victory and blessing in Him! He takes us from glory to glory and strength to strength!

# Day 19

## Complete in Him

*Colossians 2:10 (NKJV), "and you are complete in Him, who is the head of all principality and power."*

Our spiritual identity is found in who God's Word says we are. There are over 130 scriptures that help us see and understand who God has made us to be from the moment we surrendered our lives to the Lord Jesus. At our new birth, we were made completely new creatures in Christ! (2 Corinthian 5:17). That phrase **in Christ** is literally where we find ourselves as God's children. Just as He died on the cross, our old, sinful natures died with Him. And just as He was raised from the dead victorious, and seated at the right hand of the Father, in heavenly places - we were raised up together with Him! (Ephesians 2:5-6). The Bible says we have become joint heirs with Christ so everything the Bible says is ours in Him, is ours legally. That's because the Bible is a legal document, sealed by the Blood of Jesus. However, it's our believing it and confessing it that makes it a reality to us. God wants us to enjoy and know the reality of what He has provided for us! In Philippians 3:9, Paul made it clear that he preferred the man he was "in Christ" far more than the man he had been before he knew Him. Out of all his accomplishments for the kingdom of God, what he desired above all else, was to know and experience the Person of Jesus more - because he really *believed* he was complete in Him. Let the reality of your new-man in Christ become the truth that dominates you today - you will find yourself walking in glorious victory, peace, and joy because you know, beyond any doubt, that you *are* complete in Him.

# Day 20

## Love to Keep God's Word

**John 14:15 (ESV), "If you love Me, you will keep My commandments."**

The proof of our love for God is our obedience to His words. Having said that, the Word of God is not burdensome. It is alive with power and truth that leads us into a lifestyle of prosperity and fruitfulness (Psalm 1:2-3; Joshua 1:8). When we meditate on God's word, the Holy Spirit reveals its practical wisdom to us in a way that fills our hearts and minds with great peace and life-giving faith! (Romans 8:6; Romans 10:17). When we give ourselves to God's word by giving it the honor it deserves, which means loving it and welcoming its truth into our lives, and doing what it says - it not only deepens our love for God and strengthens our response of faith, but it also adds virtue to us! (Mark 4:24). That word virtue means excellence of soul. It's where our minds, our wills, and our emotions are kept in a place of prosperity! They become anchored to God Himself! (Hebrews 6:19-20). As a result, our physical bodies prosper too and remain in good health! (3 John:2). Colossians 3:16 tells us we can let the word of God dwell in us richly by maintaining an attitude of thankfulness towards it! If we really understood the priceless treasure we have in knowing and keeping God's word - we wouldn't think twice about making it our priority and the ultimate authority of our lives. Loving God's word keeps us loving Him and His ways, and it releases strength and joy into our lives! This is how Jesus felt about the scriptures when He lived as a man here on earth. Hebrews 1:9 records this about Him, *"You love righteousness and hate wickedness; therefore God, Your God, has anointed You with the oil of gladness more than Your companions."* Let these words be said of you - as you too love to keep God's Word!

# Day 21

## Live to Please Him

*Galatians 5:16 (NIV), "So I say, walk by the Spirit, and you will not gratify the desires of the flesh."*

In the beginning, was the Word as John 1:1 clearly states. It says The Word became flesh and dwelt among man. In other words, Jesus was The Word made flesh. The Bible says that when He came to earth, although He remained God, possessing all the attributes that make God; He emptied, or stripped Himself of the privileges and rights of being God (Philippians 2:5-7). This deliberate act of true humility caused Jesus to experience everything we do. He was not exempt from experiencing the full human nature, but He never allowed His flesh nature to override His spirit and defer Him from His assignment. Through everything He had to endure, He kept Himself dependent on the strength of the Holy Spirit and maintained an inseparable connection with His Father. He continuously sought His Father's will and only did what His Father told Him to do (John 5:19,30). This is the greatest example for us as believers. The Lord Jesus always subjected Himself to the obedience of His Father's voice! At the point of our salvation, the Spirit of Christ came to possess our own spirits and made us alive in Him. He empowers us to live the same way Jesus did when He was here as a man. We can hear His voice and always know the Father's will, in all things. When we make a moment-by-moment decision, like Jesus did, to ignore our flesh and yield to and obey God's voice instead, we live a life that is pleasing to God! This is something we don't do in our own strength - but through the indwelling power of the Holy Spirit! (Philippians 2:13). Living a life filled with faith that is well pleasing to God is fully obtainable when we choose to walk each day in the Spirit! You *can* live to please the Father in all things today!

# Day 22

## Determine to Hold on

***Deuteronomy 10:20 (ESV), "You shall fear the Lord your God; you shall serve Him, and to Him you shall hold fast, and take oaths in His name."***

Our goal, as children of God, is to be persistent in our walk with the Lord, refusing to let go of our faith in His trustworthy nature and His Word. Ephesians 2:12 tells us that true hopelessness is being without God in this world and being a stranger to His covenant promises. The Word tells us to hold fast to the Lord, to always cling to Him. We are not to lean on our own understanding, but to rather trust Him completely, and acknowledge Him in all things - putting us in a position to receive His clear instruction and guidance (Proverbs 3:5-6). Once we've received His instruction, we are to obey and never let go of our trust and confidence in Him to fulfil what He has promised.

When Jacob wrestled with the Lord, he refused to let go until he was blessed. As a result, He was given a new name and destiny. Instead of being known as Jacob (meaning "supplanter" or "deceiver"); He was given the name Israel (meaning "having power with God" or "God's fighter"). When Naomi told Ruth to depart from her, she refused to leave and clung to her mother-in-law. As a result, she was blessed with a husband and a son! When we determine to hold tight to trusting in the Lord and His Word of truth - we will see Him perform every promise He has made in our lives!

# Day 23

## Activate Your Faith

*Matthew 21:22 (NLT) "You can pray for anything, and if you have faith, you will receive it."*

The spiritual law of faith works when we have it dwell in two places: in our hearts and in our mouths. The Bible says when we pray, we must believe what we say, and we will have it! (Mark 11:23-24). Believing and speaking is the currency of heaven. When we believe what God's Word says we can have, faith is produced in our hearts, and it's transported on our words and released into the atmosphere where it produces exactly what we say (Isaiah 55:11). Through faith we access the things of Heaven and inherit God's promises (Hebrews 6:12). This is what pleases Him: To see His children access and enjoy every good thing He has made available for them! We will never receive what is promised if we don't believe it to be true, speak contrary to it, and never act upon it! Just thinking about something won't make it happen. God has instructed us to, *"speak to the mountain!"* When we speak, we act upon our faith and expect to see change come. This is how we activate what is already ours! We need to open our mouths and release words of faith to pull in what has been promised from the realm of the spirit into the natural one. When the world says, "No!", God says, "Yes!". When the world says, "It's impossible!", God says, "It's possible!"!

Activate your faith today and enjoy what God has promised you!

# Day 24

## Embrace the Holy Spirit

*John 16:7 (KJV), "Nevertheless I tell you the truth; It is expedient for you that I go away: for if I go not away, the Comforter will not come unto you; but if I depart, I will send Him unto you."*

The fact that you are connected to God means you are not ordinary. You have a life and power inside you that exceeds the natural. The way to access and draw from this life and power is by your daily, intimate communion with the Holy Spirit. He is our God-given advantage in this life. When Jesus said it was 'expedient' for Him to leave so that we would be able to receive the Presence of the Holy Spirit in our lives, He was implying our lives will become far greater with Him than without Him! In Greek, the word 'expedient' means 'to be at an advantage; profitable.' The Bible says the Holy Spirit will guide us into all truth and tells us things that will happen in the future. He will take what is on the heart and mind of the Father and declare it to us.

So, we will never be left in the dark, or hopeless concerning anything! (John 16:13-15). There is no such thing as victorious Christian living - without day-by-day dependence upon the Spirit of God. Don't fool around with your relationship with the Holy Spirit because He is your Helper. He will give you the edge over others who don't know Him and cause you to live in favor. He is available to tell you how to go about your business, your family, your finances, and your personal life. Thank God for the Holy Spirit and be careful to not neglect giving Him your attention throughout your day today - embrace the Holy Spirit.

# Day 25

## Keep His Presence

*1 Corinthians 3:16 (ESV), "Do you not know that you are God's temple and that God's Spirit dwells in you?"*

I don't think anyone in their right minds would allow someone to trash their house – to allow thieves to break in, steal and destroy what is meant for safety, peace, and rest. Yet, all too often, we allow sickness, sin, worry, unbelief, and lack of care to destroy God's temple – our bodies. When we understand that we are the house of God, that we carry His Presence within us, we will think twice about what we allow to influence our minds and bodies. From the time our spirits were made alive in Christ, we were set apart from living in a way that is common to those who don't know God. We have been given this treasure that deserves and desires our lives to be wholly consecrated and devoted to the One Who gave us this new life! God's Own Holy Spirit dwells within us.

His power and love can abound in us to heal and restore all that is broken, and then flow from us to touch others, allowing them to see His goodness and kindness through us. This happens when we constantly keep our minds stayed and hearts fixed on Him. This way no corruption or contamination can break through and violate what is sacred to us. When we spend time fellowshipping with the Lord and keep our hearts filled with the truth of His word, we remain aware and consciousness of His ever-present Presence in us and His readiness to help us. Protect the precious treasure that you carry, hate what is evil and carefully navigate this life to keep the overflow of His Presence diffusing through you.

# Day 26

## You are His Firstfruit

*James 1:19 (ESV), "Of His own will He brought us forth by the word of truth, that we might be a kind of first-fruits of His creatures."*

In the Old Testament the children of Israel were required to bring the first of their produce of the ground to the house of God. This was known as the firstfruits offering. It was holy and set apart for the Lord. The Lord also declared all the firstborn of the fruit of the womb to be holy and were to be set apart to live for Him. This was done as a reminder of His hand on His people when the angle of death passed over Egypt before Pharaoh finally set them free. In the same way, we, the firstfruits of God's new creation in Jesus, have been set apart and consecrated for Him. We have been set apart from the rest of the world. We are in this world, but we are not of this world (John 17:16). God has set us apart to carry His glory here on the earth. We are His bride and are expected to live in a way that our relationship with the Lord is our priority. The more we make time to sit at the feet of Jesus, to listen to His voice, through His indwelling Holy Spirit, and keep His written word alive in our hearts, our lives are transformed to resemble His nature. Ephesians 5:26-27 tells us that our souls (intellect, will and emotions) are sanctified by the washing of the water of the word, so that we are glorious before the Lord, without spot or wrinkle, and holy without blemish. In John 17:17 Jesus says that we are sanctified by the word of truth, so our relationship with God's word determines our readiness for His return. The more we give ourselves to the transforming work of the word, the more we resemble the bride Jesus will draw to Himself and carry away to the marriage feast. Let God's word sanctify you, so you are found ready, resembling His first-fruit.

# Day 27

## Set Your Mind on the Prize!

***Colossians 3:2 (NIV), "Set your minds on things above, not on earthly things."***

Life's true treasure is not found in earthly wealth or material possessions. Jesus is life's true treasure. Romans 8:32 says, *"He who did not spare His own Son, but delivered Him up for us all, how shall He not with Him also freely give us all things?"* When we live in Christ, we position ourselves in the place of God's continuous supply of provision. Everything we have flows from Him. As our hearts are fixed on Jesus and we prioritize spending time in His Word, and constantly acknowledge Him in all we do, loving Him and His ways - He becomes our treasure! When He truly has our heart and our affections - Jesus becomes our greatest reward! (Matthew 6:21). We soon discover there is absolutely nothing or no-one that compares with Him.

Even when God blesses us with earthly wealth or possessions, our hearts are never set on those things as they are on Him. Our hearts are so thankful for His blessings, but they are overwhelmed for the privilege of knowing Him. He enriches our lives. John 1:16 says the Lord gives us gifts heaped upon gifts - but the thrill of experiencing His tangible Presence any time we turn our attention towards Him is even greater! How wonderful to know we have a hidden treasure in our earthen vessels (2 Corinthians 4:7). The life of Christ in us is more valuable than silver or gold. Nothing will ever be able to take this prize away from us, and nothing will be able to separate us from His love that continuously pours into our hearts (Romans 8:38; 5:5). Determine to set your mind and heart on the higher things today, as you begin to acknowledge every good thing you have in Christ Jesus! (Philemon 1:6).

# Day 28

## Move on in Victory!

***2 Samuel 22:36 (NLT), "You have given me Your shield of victory; Your help has made me great."***

The David who stood before the ferocious Philistine army and brought down their hero-giant for all to see, attributed his unshakable confidence to the God he was in covenant with. Before David found himself facing Goliath, he had already seen and experienced the supernatural hand of God move on his behalf. While he tended his father's sheep, in deserted, lonely places, he was empowered to protect the flock from wild animals, including a lion and a bear, with his bare hands (1 Samuel 17:34-36). David didn't need to compare the size of Goliath against the size of the bear or the lion, he simply knew he was in covenant with a God who had proved Himself to be faithful. He had all the assurance he needed as he stood before the blaspheming rouge.

The moment after David cut the giants head off, he moved on in the victory God had given him. He continued to live his life devoted to the Lord, always remembering the victories He had allowed him to experience. God took this young Shepherd boy and promoted him into one of the greatest kings the nation of Israel would ever know. It's from his own lineage that the Son of God would come to this earth. God placed eternity in the heart of a young boy who had chosen to delight himself in his Creator and follow His heart. As we choose to delight ourselves in the Lord and follow His heart, we will see Him move supernaturally on our behalf, taking us from victory to victory, because like David, eternity has been placed in our hearts too.

# Day 29

## Prayers of Power

*1 Kings 18:38 (NKJV), "Then the fire of the Lord fell and consumed the burnt sacrifice, and the wood and the stones and the dust, and it licked up the water that was in the trench."*

The prevailing power of a prayer is not in the length of that prayer, as much as it's in the amount of time the person praying has personally spent in the Presence of God. While Jesus spent hours at a time in personal prayer with His Father - when it came to releasing and demonstrating His power for the miraculous - just a few, faith-filled words were required. Even the prayer that raised Lazarus from the dead after four days took less than two minutes. Before feeding thousands of hungry people with a small boy's lunch - a short word of thanks unleashed supernatural provision! When Elijah prayed down fire, he didn't break into a sweat from praying a long, sometimes energetic, sometimes tiresome prayer like the prophets of Baal. The prayer took less than two minutes and fire fell. Could this be, because just like Jesus, Elijah would often be found in a lonely place, for hours before the Lord in private prayer? A two-minute prayer that moves God to send down fire or raise the dead to life is not reserved for a set people. Anyone can see these powerful results, if they are willing to spend personal time in the Presence of God. When we wait on the Lord in private, allowing His Presence to flow strongly into our spirits - seeping into every thought, touching every emotion, and influencing every part of our wills - we become saturated by His love and the dynamic, demonstrative power that flows from it. Then, as the Lord directs us into circumstances that require that power to be shown - we simply open our mouths, speak His words, and watch Him move! Prayers of power come from the power of His Presence within.

# Day 30

## Ask, Listen, Receive

*Acts 10:19-20 (ESV), "And while Peter was pondering the vision, the Spirit said to him, 'Behold, three men are looking for you. Rise and go down and accompany them without hesitation, for I have sent them.'"*

The Spirit of God speaks all the time! He is always ready to reveal God's will to us, to enlighten our hearts to God's wisdom, or comfort us with His love and truth. The Bible says that while Peter was pondering the vision, the Holy Spirit spoke to him. We will always receive the Holy Spirit's input, while we are attentive to His voice. It's no good to ask the Lord to speak to us while our minds wander on everything else but on Him and His word. We all want to receive His wisdom concerning our current and future plans but spend very little time actually fellowshipping with Him to hear what He has to say. We have the un-divided attention of the Spirit of God who creates and knows all things, anytime we need it. But at times, we lack the discipline and desire to sit still and listen. God showed Peter a vision that left him complexed. But when he committed his thoughts and confusion to the Lord, he received the wisdom he needed to hear. When we find ourselves short of God's wisdom, our responsibility is to turn to Him, to ask and to listen – then He will speak!

# Day 31

## Mistrust Delays Destiny

*Exodus 13:17 (NLT), "When Pharaoh finally let the people go, God did not lead them along the main road that runs through Philistine territory, even though that was the shortest route to the Promised Land. God said, 'If the people are faced with a battle, they might change their minds and return to Egypt.'"*

As soon as the children of Israel came out of the land of Egypt, the Lord intentionally led them around the Philistine territory to avoid premature exposure to war. He knew they didn't have enough confidence in Him to take care of them. If they were exposed to war too soon, they would turn around and flee right back to bondage in Egypt. Since they were slow in trusting the Lord, the journey that could have easily taken days, ended up taking 40 years. Let's not be like those Israelites of old that refused to trust and obey the Lord. Their stubborn, rebellious hearts were set against being faithful to God because they would not let go of their past and place their total security in Him (Psalm 78:7-8). King David, on the other hand, had evil men plot against him, wanting to take him off his throne. Based on his personal trust in God, David resisted the urge to flee and instead, decided to place his confidence in the Lord, trusting Him to take care of his interests. (Psalm 11:1-7). His confidence was based on believing God was all knowing, all seeing, and all powerful - and that He was for him! David knew it was God who placed him on the throne, and that He had the power to keep him there. We should share that the same confidence in God too. He has planned every good work we are to do in Him, by Him, and through Him! All He needs is our trust and obedience to work with Him. Choose to lean on, rely on, and confidently put your trust in the Lord, so that you can, like David, obey His voice with joy and not be like the Israelites of old who delayed their destiny. He has prepared a way for you and empowered you to walk in it - with Him.

# JUNE

# Day 01

## Living the Good Life

*Ephesians 2:10 (AMPC), "For we are God's [own] handiwork (His workmanship), recreated in Christ Jesus, [born anew] that we may do those good works which God predestined (planned beforehand) for us [taking paths which He prepared ahead of time], that we should walk in them [living the good life which He prearranged and made ready for us to live]."*

The natural world has a warped view of success that is superficial and temporary. Success in the natural world is based on material wealth and gain, with no regard to spiritual wellbeing. So, the only way to sustain it, is through greed and selfish-ambition that is driven by the fear of losing it all. As believers, we live by a different set of rules! Since the unseen world of the spirit governs this seen, natural world, when we come into agreement with God's Word, His superior measure of success and prosperity becomes our reality.

Success for the believer, however, is prosperity without sorrow or fear! This prosperity comes as we surrender our wills to the will of God, who carries within Him all we will ever need for a life of abundant blessing! He empowers us to prosper and be successful in everything we put our hands to as we remain inseparably connected to Him. Pursue knowing God even more today, as you spend time with Him in His Word. Allow Him to influence your heart and mind so you can live the good life He has already planned for you to walk in.

# Day 02

## Established in Faith

***Isaiah 7:9 AMP** "If you will not believe [and trust in God and His message], be assured that you will not be established."*

God's purpose for us, as believers, is not only to stand firm, but to be established and rooted in His Word. That's because His Word is truth and becomes an anchor for our souls when trouble or confusion comes. No matter what we face in this world, circumstances don't determine our future outcome - not if we have chosen to come into agreement with God's Word.

As we remain rooted and established and refuse to back down, God will honor His Word concerning us. The Bible says it's through faith and patience that we receive the manifestation of every promise we have inherited through the finished work of the cross. That word *patience* means a steadfast endurance to never give up trusting God and His Word, until we see every promise become our reality. Remember, the power of His Word in us is greater than the troubles around us.

Remain rooted in God's Word and you will see your faith become strong and tenacious, establishing you in His promises as you gloriously overcome every obstacle that stands in the way of your victory.

# Day 03

## Learn to Overcome

*Jeremiah 12:5 (NKJV), "If you have run with the footmen, and they have wearied you, Then how can you contend with horses? And if in the land of peace, in which you trusted, they wearied you, then how will you do in the floodplain of the Jordan?"*

In the verses preceding this one, Jeremiah asked God why He would allow those who were persecuting him to be blessed and prosper. God's response directed Jeremiah to the truth that what he was facing now was only preparation for the challenges he would face in the future. He needed to learn how to trust God and draw from His strength in these meagre challenges to prepare him for the things to come.

We all have dreams we wish to achieve for God's kingdom. We want Him to use us more and to see His glory significantly impact this world. Yet many of us are unable or unwilling to overcome the small battles we are presently facing. We think that if God could spare us from them we would be able to move forward in life; not realizing our need to learn how to overcome before we can see Him move greatly in and through our lives. David, the young shepherd boy who faced and defeated Goliath, had to learn how to trust in the Lord to slay the lion and the bear before he had the confidence and courage to believe God to use him to slay the giant.

We will always need to fight the good fight of faith on this side of heaven. Until we learn to overcome the present battles, we will never be able to overcome the greater ones that lead us into greater victories.

# Day 04

## The Spirit of Faith

*Numbers 14:24 (NKJV), "But My servant Caleb, because he has a different spirit in him and has followed Me fully, I will bring into the land where he went, and his descendants shall inherit it."*

Unless we have a spirit of faith operating in our lives, we will not have the strength to survive the things we are going to face in this world. By redemption, every believer is granted the reality of a life filled with the promises of God - but it's going to take a spirit of faith to possess them!

For the Israelites to take possession of the promised land, they were going to have to overcome the giants that lived there first. Many children of God become discouraged at the first sign of trouble when they pursue what has been promised them. It's quite biblical for us to be challenged, however it's unbiblical for us to be defeated! Every challenge purifies and develops our faith in God, and makes us well able to conquer, through the spirit of faith. Because of his faith, Caleb and his descendants were allowed to enter and enjoy the Promised Land.

Let God's Word develop that overcoming spirit of faith in you, so every promise, despite any resistance, becomes your reality.

# Day 05

## Created to Flourish

*Psalms 92:12, "The [uncompromisingly] righteous shall flourish like the palm tree [be long-lived, stately, upright, useful, and fruitful]; they shall grow like a cedar in Lebanon [majestic, stable, durable, and incorruptible]."*

No matter what we face in this life, when we are rooted in Jesus, we will always flourish! Taking personal responsibility to nurture a quality relationship with the Lord must be our primary goal. Jeremiah 17:7-8 says that when we believe, trust in, and rely on the Lord, and make Him our hope and confidence, we will certainly flourish! That's because Jesus is the fountain of life, and His Holy Spirit is rivers of living water!

When we take the time to drink deeply of the Lord in His Presence and His Word - we become like a tree planted by the waters that spreads out its roots by the river. We won't be bothered or worried when the pressures of life come. Instead, our spirits will be full of strength, and our minds will be fixed on His faithfulness and goodness towards us. Psalms 92:15 says that if we are consistently faithful to abide in Jesus, we become living memorials to show that the Lord is upright and faithful to His promises! Our lives will demonstrate His goodness and faithfulness to us.

Invest in your personal relationship with the Lord today and see yourself flourish - just as you were created to do!

# Day 06

## Give Yourself to Prayer

*Mark 1:35 (TPT), "The next morning, Jesus got up long before daylight, left the house while it was dark, and made His way to a secluded place to give Himself to prayer."*

Jesus *gave* Himself to prayer! He fully understood the importance of meeting alone with God. Jesus knew His time of personal prayer was far more than just gleaming information and instruction from God, it was a time of being saturated with His life-giving Presence - to intuitively know Him and His heart, and to experience being known by Him.

In the secluded place, being alone with His Father, Jesus was filled with His Father's love and approval. The peace and joy that spontaneously flowed from this union fueled His confidence to obey every instruction as though it was done by the Father Himself - the One He was representing. Experiencing the Father's Presence like this, graces us with His glory, just as it did Jesus (John 17:23).

If we want to succeed the way Jesus did, we must understand the value of **abiding** as we give ourselves to **prayer**.

# Day 07

## Turn Your World Upside-down

*Acts 1:4-5 (NLT) "... He commanded them, 'Do not leave Jerusalem until the Father sends you the gift He promised, as I told you before. John baptized with water, but in just a few days you will be baptized with the Holy Spirit.'"*

The only way we will experience the fullness of the life and power Jesus secured for us on the cross, is to receive the baptism of the Holy Spirit. As recorded in Acts 2, the Holy Spirit descended on all who were present in the Upper Room. All were baptized in fire and filled with the Holy Spirit!

The evidence of what had happened to these men and women was so significant that it turned the whole world upside down for Jesus! According to Acts 9:31, with the power of the Holy Spirit working inside them, these believers were supernaturally built up, comforted, directed, and empowered, and they increased in every way! As we are filled with the Holy Spirit, and power, we can operate just as those early believers did! We are not here to bring a temporary change to people's lives; we are here to bring a supernatural change that will turn their lives around for the better.

Through the empowerment of the Holy Spirit, we have the boldness to take up our authority against the work of the devil and enforce his defeat over people's lives. The Holy Spirit in you will enable you to declare God's will and release the very atmosphere of heaven here on earth.

It's time to embrace His gift and turn your world upside down for Jesus!

# Day 08

## Discernment Trumps Intellectual Knowledge

*2 Corinthians 5:16a (NKJV), "Therefore, from now on, we regard no one according to the flesh."*

The natural, human way of development hinges very largely on the five senses; what we touch, taste, see, smell, and hear. As we grow, through training and education, our beliefs and abilities become more influenced by the knowledge we acquire over time.

However, as born-again children of God, we are called to a whole new way of growing. Discernment becomes more valuable than intellectual knowledge. Since we are new creations in Christ Jesus, our spirits become the primary receptors of information gleamed from the unseen world - that in truth - governs the seen world. The Holy Spirit, Who lives in our spirits, becomes our teacher and leads us into all truth. This is done when we rely on Him to reveal the truth of God's Word to us. Every principle in the Word is inspired by Him and is brought to life inside us when we receive its wisdom.

Through the power of the Holy Spirit, the Word washes over our minds, realigning our thoughts to God's truth and perspective. This becomes the essence of our vantage point! We see everything through His eyes and wisdom. So, what we know and believe is influenced by what God's Word says and confirmed by our inward witness of the Holy Spirit living inside us. Being continuously transformed to see and think like God gives us a far superior knowledge than that of our limited human understanding.

Cultivate your relationship with the Holy Spirit and grow in discernment above mere intellectual knowledge.

# Day 09

## Set Your Gaze

*Proverbs 4:25 (TPT), "Set your gaze on the path before you. With fixed purpose, looking straight ahead, ignore life's distractions."*

To walk out God's purpose and assignment for our lives, we will need to learn how to fix our focus on the things that will keep us moving forward, in the right direction. In the book of Psalms, David wrote that he always set the Lord before him. He confidently declared that walking in harmony with God secured him in a place where nothing would move him.

No matter the outward threat, while his gaze was fixed on the Lord, and His instructions, nothing would hinder the blessing, protection, and favor he would receive - in the presence of his enemies. Isaiah 26:3 says, *"You will guard him and keep him in perfect and constant peace whose mind [both its inclination and its character] is stayed on You, because he commits himself to You, leans on You, and hopes confidently in You."*

As you choose to keep your eyes fixed on the Lord, He will keep you steadfast and immovable in all our ways. Don't allow people or things to distract you from your walk of faith in Him. This way your life will be marked by victory and unprecedented favor, regardless of any outward circumstances! Set your gaze on Him and you will not fail!

# Day 10

## Obedience - Better Than Sacrifice

*Isaiah 1:11 (NKJV) "To what purpose is the multitude of your sacrifices to Me?" Says the LORD. "I have had enough of burnt offerings of rams and the fat of fed cattle. I do not delight in the blood of bulls, or of lambs or goats."*

In the first chapter of the book of Isaiah, the Lord rebuked the children of Israel for their disobedience. Despite the large sum of offerings and sacrifices they brought God was not pleased. He considered their offerings as hollow and superficial because their hearts were not in the least bit after Him. They thought they could use their offerings to manipulate His hand. They wanted to appease Him to hold back His punishment, without having any intention to change their ways.

The offerings themselves were not out of place, they simply served no purpose if the people's hearts were set to live independent of God, in disobedience. In 1 Samuel 15, King Saul made the same mistake. After attacking the Amalekites, for good reason, God instructed him to destroy everything. Saul disobeyed. He thought his decision to keep the best of the cattle for sacrifices was a better plan, and that the Lord would bless him for it. The prophet Samuel rebuked him and said, *"To obey is better than to sacrifice"*. If we want to please the Father, then we must understand it's our hearts He requires above all else. When we truly love Him, obeying Him becomes our pleasure because we trust His wisdom and know it always works towards our benefit and blessing.

A heart after God that trusts Him and is willing to obey His Word is far more appealing to Him than any offering. Give Him your heart, and He will give you everything in return.

# Day 11

## Your Supernatural Weapon!

*Jude 1:20 (NLT), "But you, dear friends, must build each other up in your most holy faith, pray in the power of the Holy Spirit,"*

There is a powerful, spiritual weapon every Christian who is baptized in the Holy Spirit has access to here and now. It's the weapon of praying in the Holy Ghost. The book of Jude tells us to build ourselves up in our most holy faith by praying in the power of the Holy Spirit. When we are feeling discouraged or battle-weary, praying in the Spirit is the quickest way to recharge our spiritual power levels!

The Holy Spirit, with all His power, lives inside our spirits. When we pray in tongues, God's Spirit prays His perfect will from our spirits. He by-passes our intellect, so we can't understand what we are praying, but we can sense the life and power that is energizing us from our spirit man. This power quickens our mortal bodies! It's the same resurrection power that raised Jesus from the dead hallelujah!

So, the more you take the time to do this, the more every weary, discouraged part of you will get revived and energized! It builds your most holy faith, preparing it to act! Don't allow the devil, or circumstances to steal your peace, joy, or strength! Pray in the Holy Ghost and the devil will regret ever messing with you!

# Day 12

## No Substitute for His Presence

*Exodus 33:16 (AMPC), "For by what shall it be known that I and Your people have found favor in Your sight? Is it not in Your going with us so that we are distinguished, I and Your people, from all the other people upon the face of the earth?"*

We serve a God that is alive. He is mighty to save, heal, and deliver us, and move us into everything He has promised us. But more than just seeing us blessed, He wants us to personally know Him and His ways - because this is the ultimate reward! In truth, there is nothing worth substituting the tangible Presence of God for. Moses knew this too well. God had promised to send an angel with them on their journey to the land flowing with milk and honey. He had promised to conquer every ferocious enemy that would oppose them.

Basically, He was guaranteeing them all that He had promised, however, they would not have Him in their midst anymore. This was something Moses refused to accept. He knew the only thing that distinguished him and his people from all others, was the tangible Presence of the Lord being with them. He was unwilling to settle for anything less. We would be wise to learn from Moses here, seeking God's benefits above a pursuit to know Him and His ways is pure foolishness. It sells us short of experiencing the only thing that can truly satisfy the longing and desire of our hearts.

Make your choice today - seek knowing God first, and every benefit and blessing will supernaturally follow suit.

# Day 13

## Jesus in You

**Mark 1:37 (TPT), "And when they finally tracked Him down, they told Him, 'Everyone is looking for You-they want You!'"**

Long before daylight Jesus went to a deserted place to spend time in prayer with His Heavenly Father. The One who knows all things, and is wisdom itself, found it necessary to spend time with His Father in prayer.

The Bible teaches us that between themselves, Jesus and His Father demonstrated a powerful and intimate connection. He confessed that He would do nothing without first seeing His Father doing it and would only say what He heard His Father say. This deep, constant connection between them fueled Jesus with the confidence to do the work of His Father. In so doing, He made the Father's good, generous nature known to us. Wherever He went people marveled at the authority by which He spoke, and at His overwhelming love and compassion that led Him to deliver the oppressed and heal the sick.

Everyone was looking for the kind man whose love healed them. The man who spoke and demons trembled, obeying His every command. When we delight ourselves in knowing the Father, just as Jesus demonstrated for us to do, His Presence within us will flow strong within our spirits, diffusing into every part of our lives, until we take on the very nature of Jesus Himself. The same expectation that was placed on Jesus to see the goodness and kindness of God powerfully in action, will be placed on us to display Him, who is living in us! Get ready to have Jesus live powerfully in and through you!

# Day 14

## Empowered to Do!

*Acts 2:3-4 (NLT), "Then, what looked like flames or tongues of fire appeared and settled on each of them. And everyone present was filled with the Holy Spirit and began speaking in other languages, as the Holy Spirit gave them this ability."*

We cannot expect to do the same works Jesus did with less than what He had! It was the empowerment of the Holy Spirit that enabled Him to do the works of His Father. After He was baptized in water, the Holy Spirit descended upon Jesus, like a dove. From that moment He was full of, and controlled by the Holy Spirit Who led Him into the wilderness for 40 days (Luke 4:1). Jesus spent this time fasting and praying. The Bible says that Jesus entered the wilderness full of and controlled by the Holy Spirit and then it says He left it, being full of power! (Luke 4:14).

His time of intense prayer energized the power that was within Him to not only stand up to and resist the devil's temptation, but to do the miraculous works of God! From this point we read about the many signs, wonders and miracles that took place through that power in Him. That same power filled those waiting in the upper room on the day of Pentecost. They were able to do the works of God with such power that the whole world was shaken by it! The same Spirit Who filled and empowered Jesus and the early Believers, has been given, as a gift from God to us today!

Open your heart to receive a fresh infilling of His power, by faith, right now. Be obedient to His leading and you will find yourself counted as those who do great exploits for His kingdom!

# Day 15

## The Valley of Decision

*Deuteronomy 28:11 (ESV), "And the Lord will make you abound in prosperity, in the fruit of your womb and in the fruit of your livestock and in the fruit of your ground, within the land that the Lord swore to your fathers to give you."*

In Deuteronomy 27, as the Israelites moved into the promised land, after crossing the river Jordan; they were to practically demonstrate their loyalty to the covenant God had made with them. There were two mountains of identical height and structure that stood opposite each other, forming a valley in-between. On top of the one mountain called Gerizim, six tribes were represented to pronounce the blessing of the Lord that would come on His people when they followed the covenant obligations. On the other mountain, called Ebal, the other six tribes were represented to declare the curses that would befall the people should they disobey God's law.

The rest of the nation along with Moses and the Levitical priests stood in the valley between the two mountains where they responded in agreement to each blessing and curse. In doing this they demonstrated their understanding the conditions of the covenant and the consequences of both keeping and violating it. Today, even under the New Covenant, we daily stand in the valley of decision. Yielding to the voice of the Holy Spirit within us and walking in His ways is a choice that will result in the covering of God's absolute blessing, favor, and grace over our lives. Refusing to do so will result in us walking right out from under that blessing and exposing ourselves to the curse that rests on a fallen world. Either way, we get to daily make the choice. Enjoy God's blessing and favor today as you choose to trust in, and yield to His Holy Spirit!

# Day 16

## His Mission is Our Mission

*Mark 1:38 (TPT), "Jesus replied, 'We have to go on to the surrounding villages so that I can give My message to the people there, for that is My mission.'"*

One of the main themes of the Old Testament is revealing the severity of sin and how it separates mankind from intimately knowing God, as a loving, generous Father. In the New Testament, Jesus comes as the express image of the Father - to demonstrate His true nature to us. Jesus understood the urgency of His mission. He carried His Father's heart of compassion for people and desired to see them set free from the bondage of sin and its consequences. Under the power of the Holy Spirit, He brought deliverance, healing, and wholeness, with sincere love, kindness, and joy.

Then, through the finished work of the cross He destroyed the work of the devil and triumphed over Him gloriously. He made a way for everyone to be raised to newness of life in Him! To stand redeemed and whole, and full of power and authority over our enemy the devil. This is the Gospel we must preach, with the same urgency Jesus did! That's because it is the power of God that snatches lives out of the kingdom of darkness and brings them into the kingdom of light! You and I are called as His ambassadors, with all of heaven backing us, to do the will of His Father!

Let His power and compassion well up inside you, as you enforce the devil's defeat over people's lives and see them delivered, healed, and made whole!

# Day 17

## Don't Change the Doctrine

*Matthew 11:4 (NKJV), "Jesus answered and said to them, 'Go and tell John the things which you hear and see:'"*

At that time, John the Baptist had been in prison for about a full year. He had very likely become disillusioned and struggling with doubt concerning Jesus. He had preached that Jesus was the coming Messiah - the One who would gather His people to Himself and judge their oppressors. He, like so many others, expected the Messiah to rule in a military fashion, much like King David did. But to that day, even though he had heard of the many supernatural works performed by Jesus, John had not seen Him take on their nation's oppressors.

So, he sent word to ask Jesus, *"...Are You the One Who was to come, or should we keep on expecting a different one?"*. To which Jesus responded, *"...tell John what you HEAR and SEE..."* The Supernatural demonstration that followed Jesus' ministry was verification that He had come to destroy the works of the real enemy - the devil; and to reveal and demonstrate the true loving nature of His Father to all people. Jesus told John to not become offended at Him because it would hinder him from seeing the full truth of Who He was.

We must always trust God's nature and His Word above all else, and never be tempted to change our doctrine to align circumstances we don't necessarily understand.

# Day 18

## Living From the Encounter

*Acts 4:14 (NLT), "But since they could see the man who had been healed standing right there among them, there was nothing the council could say."*

No one can deny the manifest power of God when they see it demonstrated in front of them. Once we have encountered the Person of Jesus and personally witnessed the demonstration of His miraculous power - we have no choice but to live expecting the supernatural.

Peter and John were men filled with the Spirit of God. When the council questioned and accused them of laying hands on a crippled man, releasing the power of God to heal him - they recognized these two men operated in the supernatural because of their association with Jesus.

When we spend quality time fellowshipping with the Lord, in prayer and in His Word - we begin to think like Him, talk like Him, and act like Him! Hallelujah! Jesus spent hours of quality time alone, in a secluded place with His Father. As a result, He lived from the reality of heaven towards the challenges of life. Even amid a terrifying, dangerous storm at sea - He slept soundly - unintimidated by natural, temporary circumstances. No matter what we will ever face in this life, if we have habitually practiced spending time in the Presence of Jesus, we will stop seeing things from the problem and begin to see things from our encounter with Him instead.

# Day 19

## The Glory of the Latter Temple

*Haggai 2:8-9 (NLT), "The silver is Mine, and the gold is Mine, says the Lord of Heaven's Armies. The future glory of this Temple will be greater than its past glory, says the Lord of Heaven's Armies. And in this place I will bring peace. I, the Lord of Heaven's Armies, have spoken!"*

A remnant of the Israelites had returned to Jerusalem following captivity. While there, Haggai spoke to them about prioritizing building the Lord's house before building their own. With repentant, obedient hearts, they heeded the call. However, their hopeful expectations were shattered when they realized the rebuilt temple was nothing compared to the glorious one King Solomon had originally built, generations before. Haggai encouraged the disappointed people, reminding them of God's promise. The future glory of the temple would be unmatched by any other before it. He was alluding to the prophecies of the Messiah. Jesus Christ, the light of the world would come as the expression of the glory of God. John 1:14 says, *"And the Word (Christ) became flesh (human, incarnate) and tabernacled (fixed His tent of flesh, lived awhile) among us; and we [actually] saw His glory (His honour, His majesty), such glory as an only begotten son receives from His Father, full of grace (favour, loving-kindness) and truth."*

And now we live in the reality of that prophecy - we have become the temple of the Holy Spirit Who lives in us! We are the temple not made of human hands, and we possess this precious treasure, the glory of His Presence, in our earthen vessels of flesh. Take time to become more aware of Who you carry within you today - as you turn your affection towards Him - you're guaranteed to experience the tangible Presence of His glory within you.

# Day 20

## Tested Faith

*James 1:2-3 (NKJV), "My brethren, count it all joy when you fall into various trials, knowing that the testing of your faith produces patience."*

Having your faith tested is scriptural. Being defeated is not. Sadly, many believers equate trials with defeat. They think the difficulties they're facing are a result of their lack of faith. The Word of God says differently. We are in fact, to be full of joy when trials come. That's because they are the perfect opportunity for us to have our faith tested and proven! In other words, when tough times come, the genuineness of our faith is tested. At the sight of trouble do we shrink back and quit? Do we panic and fear, allowing our emotions to carry us off into a downward spiral of despair? Or do we find that our first reaction is to thank God for the opportunity to see His Word go to work for us, as we trust in His faithfulness to equip us with everything we need to pull through victoriously?

The truth is the real testing doesn't just come at the face of the trial - it's the endurance we develop in the midst of it! Godly patience is a firm decision or resolve, to refuse to give up trusting God's Word on a matter, no matter how everything around us contradicts it. Remember, everything is subject to change, it's God's Word that remains forever. We just need to learn to get into that place of restful confidence, where we are convinced our faith in God's Word will outlast any trial! That's true faith, undergirded with the fruit of patient endurance!

# Day 21

## Develop Your Faith

*Romans 12:3b (NLT), "...Be honest in your evaluation of yourselves, measuring yourselves by the faith God has given us."*

We have all been given the measure of faith. Our responsibility is to grow that faith, by hearing the Word of God. As we expose ourselves to its truth, it becomes like a seed, attaching itself to the soil of our hearts. The more attention we pay that truth, the deeper its roots grow, and we don't just find ourselves agreeing with it, we actually believe it! At this point, that seed of truth has grown into a sapling of faith. That sapling grows in exponential strength and speed each time we expose ourselves to the truth of God's Word, no matter what scripture it is. Before long, we have a mighty oak of faith planted securely in the garden of our hearts!

At this point we've far surpassed just believing the truth and speaking in line with it - now it's become something we act on and live by! We begin to experience the fruit from that tree of faith in our hearts. Where others around us are in chaos and fear, we have a peace that transcends all understanding. We instinctively know what to do when others do not, and our hearts are always full of confident joy. Did you know, the only opportunity to please God in this manner, and develop a garden full of faith in our hearts - is on this side of eternity?

So, give yourself to the Word of God and develop your faith with all diligence!

# Day 22

## God's Word Prospers Us

*Matthew 8:8 (NKJV), "The centurion answered and said, 'Lord, I am not worthy that You should come under my roof. But only speak a word, and my servant will be healed.'"*

When we recognize God's Word to be His perfect will and wisdom for our lives - we begin to pay it the honor it truly deserves. This recognition stirs up a desire inside us to know the Word even more. When we discover that loving and obeying its wise instructions results in the favor and blessing of God - we hunger after it all the more!

In Mark 4:24 it says the amount of attention we pay to the truth (Word) we study and hear, will be the measure of virtue and knowledge that is produced in us. That word *virtue* means excellence of moral quality, or excellence of soul. In other words, the Word of God we give ourselves to, will cause our souls to prosper! Now, according to 3 John 1:2, when our souls prosper we prosper in every way and will experience good health!

The Centurion in Matthew 8:8 recognized that Jesus was under the authority of His Heavenly Father. He knew the words Jesus spoke were in absolute agreement with His Father's will and would prosper and produce whatever He said.

As we honor God's Word and yield ourselves to it, it will cause our souls to prosper and everything else in our lives will follow suit!

# Day 23

## Healing is God's Sovereign Will

*Psalms 103:3 (AMPC), "Who forgives [every one of] all your iniquities, Who heals [each one of] all your diseases,..."*

God is sovereign. One of the definitions of sovereign is a supreme ruler who acts independent of outside interference. John 10:10 declares that we have an enemy, the devil, who comes to steal, kill, and destroy everything good in our lives; however, Jesus has come to give us abundant life. This is His sovereign rule - to give abundant life, regardless of the enemy's interference. Through the finished work of the cross, Jesus literally destroyed the power of sin and death. His resurrection power destroyed every work of the devil and then came to live in us, giving us the authority to enforce that defeat.

All sickness and disease are from the pit of hell; and Jesus paid the price for us to walk in Divine health - in our souls and physical bodies. This was an intentional, sovereign act of God. He broke the curse of sin so whoever believes in and surrenders to the Lordship of Jesus can be healed and live whole. To say God is glorified in our sickness is to undermine His sovereignty and belittle the finished work of the cross. It is **always** the sovereign will of God to see us healed from all sickness and disease. When we experience anything that contradicts this, we cannot allow ourselves to resort to even the suggestion that God has somehow changed His mind or made an exception.

By His stripes we **were healed** - He shed His blood to seal this forever. (1 Peter 2:24; Isaiah 53:5).

# Day 24

## Obedient Faith

***Genesis 25:5 (NKJV), "And Abraham gave all that he had to Isaac."***

Abraham goes down in biblical history as "The Father of Our Faith". He entered a mighty covenant with God and the result was a lifetime of outrageous blessing and wealth. As a good father leaves an inheritance for his children (Proverbs 13:22), Abraham passed on all he had to Isaac when he died. Isaac could have lived in plenty without lifting a hand, but he knew the real prize was to live in the same covenant of faith his father prospered in. So when a time of great famine came upon the land, instead of relocating his entire family, Isaac obeyed the instruction of the Lord, and by faith, dug up the dry, parched ground and planted seed. In the natural this act was pure foolishness.

But Isaac was in covenant with God and knew this covenant operated by obedient faith. As a result, he reaped a hundred-fold harvest from that seed, in the same year! The bible says he began to prosper and continued to prosper until he became very prosperous! God has given us all things that pertain to life and godliness which results in great blessing! It's that blessing of the Lord that makes us rich and adds no sorrow with it. (Proverbs 10:22).

A life of abundant blessing is not our ambition, it's the inheritance of those who choose to live by obedient faith in God! Hallelujah!

# Day 25

## Worship - God's Circumcision of Our Hearts

*Psalm 89:15 (NLT), "Happy are those who hear the joyful call to worship, for they will walk in the light of Your presence, Lord."*

True worship begins in our hearts, when we are alone with the Lord and reverentially adore Him. This is a most intimate *experience* where our true, deep affections are turned towards the Lord. At this moment, His Spirit within us causes His tangible Presence to be unmistakably *felt* by us. Whenever our hearts are exposed and surrendered to the manifest presence of God like this, He begins to cut away any incorrect mindsets or unholy things that have attached themselves to our souls. This is what Paul called the true circumcision of our hearts, that takes place when we worship God in spirit (our own spirits) *and by His Spirit* (who lives within us). (Philippians 3:3).

As a result, our lives become transformed from the inside out. The change begins with the work of the Holy Spirit (from our spirits) to our souls (our intellect, emotions and will). Our physical bodies will follow whatever our souls dictate, so they are ultimately going to be included in this transformation process too! According to Psalm 89:15, this circumcision or sanctification process causes us to walk in the light of God's presence.

Today, allow the very truth and wisdom of God to become clearly seen and known to you in all you do by making the decision to worship Him in spirit and truth.

# Day 26

## Praise God for Your Increase!

*Psalm 67:5-6 (NKJV), "Let the peoples praise You, O God; let all the peoples praise You. Then the earth shall yield her increase; God, our own God, shall bless us."*

According to 1 Corinthians 3:6-7, increase comes from God! Yet it is our responsibility to give Him something to work with. Our PRAISE tills and cultivates our hearts to believe God's Word which produces the powerful, spiritual force of faith inside us! Faith is the substance that brings the promises of God from the spirit realm into our natural realm (Hebrews 11:1).

So, giving or sowing financial seed with a heart full of active faith will certainly produce increase in our lives. However, praise does more than just cultivate our hearts for faith! It also cultivates the ground into which we sow our seeds. Psalm 67:6 says the ground we sow into will respond to our praise and yield an increase! When you have prayed in faith, and sowed in faith, yet it seems as though the breakthrough is slow in coming, it's not the time to relax courage, it's time to **praise**! When you do, the ground you put your seed into will yield an increase! This is more than enough reason to cultivate a lifestyle of **praise**!

This way, always and in all seasons, we are prepared and ready for increase! Today, PRAISE God for your increase!

# Day 27

## Prosperity from the Inside Out!

*Joshua 1:8 (NLT), "Study this Book of Instruction continually. Meditate on it day and night so you will be sure to obey everything written in it. Only then will you prosper and succeed in all you do."*

When God passed the baton from Moses to Joshua, He gave Joshua the key to success. The key was to keep God's Word before him, and to never deviate from any of its instructions. True prosperity comes when we keep God's word as the final authority of our lives and make meditating on its truth a daily priority. When we do this, according to Romans 10:17, the truth of God's Word we hear roots itself into our minds and hearts and produces the spiritual force of faith.

Faith is a raw spiritual power, a substance that moves us from being a victim in this life, to an over-comer. Instead of just accepting circumstances that are contrary to the promises of God for our lives, when we have faith, we can confidently stand on the truth of God's word and with His authority, speak His Word into those circumstances - and watch them change. Now, while believing and declaring God's Word are essential for us to prosper; we must never neglect the instruction to obey the Word of God and live by it's principles. Without a life yielded to the work of the Holy Spirit, where we choose the will of God over our own - in all things; our faith will not produce the results we long to see. True prosperity has everything to do with hearing and obeying God's Word, allowing it to transform us from the inside - and then declaring its truth to see circumstances change on the outside!

# Day 28

## No Compromise

*Daniel 6:10 (NLT), "But when Daniel learned that the law had been signed, he went home and knelt down as usual in his upstairs room, with its windows open toward Jerusalem. He prayed three times a day, just as he had always done, giving thanks to his God."*

Each day we are presented with opportunities to compromise our testimony of faith. The devil doesn't really need to get us to backslide if he can get us to compromise. A compromised Christian is an ineffective Christian. Compromise makes us 'fence sitters', we are neither fully committed nor are we completely uncommitted. Another word for this state of indecision is lukewarm, and according to Revelations 3:16, it does not sit well with God! The fact is, we are living in times where we will need to make a deliberate decision to either live according to the world's standard of compromise, or fully commit to the standard of the kingdom of God. The Bible calls it being those who are in this world, but not of this world. Our stand either way will have enormous consequences, both for on earth, and for eternity.

Choosing compromise may make you more acceptable to society at large while you are here, but it will cost you your salvation. However, choosing to live on purpose for the kingdom and all its ways will certainly cause the world to despise and persecute you, while your eternal reward remains secure. It's the Daniels who will rise in the face of opposition and refuse to compromise. They will remain unmoved and unshaken in their faith until they meet Jesus, face to face. Remember, in the end, standing for Jesus will result in Him standing for you (Matthew 10:33).

# Day 29

## Know the Person Who Is the Word

*Galatians 1:24 (ASV), "...and they glorified God in me."*

Prior to his encounter with Jesus, Paul had quite literally made himself an enemy of God. Though he believed, at the time, he was justified in his acts – it took a drastic visitation from the Lord Himself to intervene and show Paul the truth. He had been so consumed with the written law (without revelation) and the observance thereof, that he found himself in direct disobedience to God. The truth of God's character and His perfect will is most certainly found in His Word, however without a personal relationship with Christ, through His Holy Spirit, the word does not produce life - it simply remains a letter of the law. 2 Corinthians 3:6 says the letter kills, but the Spirit gives life! Only through reading, receiving into our hearts, and obeying the Word of God through the work of the Holy Spirit, will bring the reality of God's kingdom into our lives!

Paul soon found that only through personally knowing the God of the Bible was he able to live in righteousness, peace, and the joy of the Holy Ghost! Be very careful to approach the Word of God through your relationship with the One Who inspired it. He will teach and lead you into its truth and cause it to produce life inside of you. As a result, it will cause others to see Him at work in you! Without Him, however, the word will only produce dead religion and disappointment. None of which glorifies Him.

# Day 30

## Know the Person Who Is the Word

*Psalm 18:34 (TPT), "You've trained me with the weapons of warfare-worship; now I'll descend into battle with power to chase and conquer my foes."*

In Psalm 18:33, it speaks of the Lord setting us securely upon high places. The Passion translations calls these high places, heavenly places, where we are strong and secure in God. According to Ephesians 1:20, this is quite an accurate position we have as believers. Psalms 18 proceeds to say it's from this position of victory and freedom that we are in fact trained to powerfully overcome every opposing force, that would seek to contradict, steal, kill, or destroy God's perfect will for our lives.

The yoke-breaking anointing and courage we need to conquer any obstacle that dares to come our way is found in personally knowing Christ and His victory He has already won for us. 1 John 4:4 tells us that we are *of God* – and have overcome every opposing force that would try to dissuade us from God's truth, will and purpose. In Him we are strengthened, courageous, swift, and sure-footed. In His strength even the hardest, most stubborn resistance and obstacle can not only be pushed back but will be destroyed.

As you spend time in the Presence of the Lord, allow Him and His Word to train and equip you for victory today!

# JULY

# Day 01

## Showcase His Good Character

*1 Thessalonians 2:10 (NKJV), "You are witnesses, and God also, how devoutly and justly and blamelessly we behaved ourselves among you who believe;"*

Paul told the church at Corinth that they were, *"known and read by all men"* (2 Corinthians 3:2). Our lives are a living testimony of the influence the Spirit of God has inside us. The extent to which we allow the Word of God to renew our minds is very evident to others. Our consistent conduct, the same way we act over time - clearly tells if we have made the Presence of God our habitation or not. When our lifestyle contradicts what we profess, it weakens the authenticity of our testimony.

In Romans 2:24, it says the name of God is blasphemed among the Gentiles because of our sinful conduct. Living contrary to a life filled with and under the control of the Holy Spirit, drives people away from wanting to know the Lord. Hypocrisy repels, but living in the reality of an intimate relationship with the Presence of Jesus and His Word attracts the unsaved to know Him, and those who are saved - to know Him more!

Let your life be marked by your good works as you showcase the good character of God (Matthew 5:16).

# Day 02

## Honor - the Key to Blessing!

*1 Corinthians 10:10 (NKJV), "... nor complain, as some of them also complained, and were destroyed by the destroyer."*

God showed Himself to be a faithful protector and provider for the Israelites in the wilderness, as they journeyed out of slavery towards the Promised Land. In 1 Corinthians 10:3-4, we are told they were not just nourished physically, but God supplied them with spiritual food and drink from Himself too. And yet, most of the people insisted on seeking after the lifestyles and gods of other nations. They grew cold in their hearts towards the Lord and dishonored Him, not only in their actions, but in their consistent murmuring and complaining.

Dishonor opened the door for calamity and destruction in their lives. Paul warns us to not follow their example, but to cultivate and maintain a constant attitude of thankfulness and gratitude towards the Lord! When we keep our minds and hearts focused on His good and faithful nature, and the truth of His Word, we honor Him. We stop complaining and begin praising and thanking Him instead! A lifestyle of honoring the Lord through our thankful attitudes opens the door for supernatural favor and blessing over our lives. The Word is full of promises for those who choose to honor the Lord instead of giving in to the temptation to complain. It teaches us that a lifestyle of honor has a magnetic quality to pull God's goodness and favor into our lives and produce an income stream that not even money can supply!

# Day 03

## Effective Prayer

*Mark 11:24 (NKJV), "Therefore I say to you, whatever things you ask when you pray, believe that you receive them, and you will have them."*

There are some important keys to praying effective prayers. The first is to *ask*! Of course, the Lord knows what is on our hearts, and what we need, but like any loving parent, He delights in us coming to Him in confidence and communicating our needs and desires to Him. Secondly, effective prayer is always going to agree with God's Word. When we have His Word on a matter, we have His will! So, there's no guess work involved, hallelujah!

For instance, if His Word says He is our healer and He paid the price on the cross for us to be healed of all sickness and disease - then there's no question about **- it is His will for us to be healed**! Which brings us to the next key - faith! We must believe and not doubt when we pray. The book of James says that doubt will cause us to not receive anything from the Lord.

So, when do we receive what we've asked for? The Bible says the moment we prayed and believed - is the moment we received! Let me explain - faith is a supernatural power that reaches into the unseen realm of the spirit, takes a hold of the promises of God, and brings them into our reality. The moment we pray, believing - our faith grabs a hold of what we asked for and brings it into our reality! What do we do until we see the promise manifest? We thank the Lord for it - every day until it's right in front of us! Hallelujah! This is the prayer of faith, and it's the most effective way to pray!

# Day 04

## Represent Him Well

*Psalm 89:16 (NLT), "They rejoice all day long in Your wonderful reputation. They exult in Your righteousness."*

Throughout the Bible we read of the wonderful nature and character of our God. The God we serve has a reputation like no other. He is entirely faithful, marvelous in all His ways, forever good and His love and mercy continuously abounds! Perhaps the most glorious and mysterious quality of God, is His desire to dwell inside us, and transform us into His image and likeness. The more we yield to the working of His Word and Holy Spirit within us - the greater the transformation! The greater the transformation, the more accurately we represent Him to others. As much as this process may seem mechanical, it's entirely relational.

Spending time in intimate fellowship with the Lord and His Word results in our falling completely in love with Him. Yielding to His Spirit and the instructions of His Word become an absolute pleasure and delight. Our lives literally overflow with His love, peace, and joy as we live keeping an awareness of our inseparable connection with Him. No matter what turmoil or trouble brews around us - our hearts and minds are kept sound and secure in Him, and we remain steadfast and established, lacking nothing! This is how we represent Him well and His good reputation is made evident - through our lives surrendered to, and saturated with His Presence from within!

Let the Lord be revealed through your life today, and every day!

# Day 05

## Marked by Distinction

*Malachi 3:16-17 (NLT): "'They will be My people,' says the Lord of Heaven's Armies. 'On the day when I act in judgment, they will be My own special treasure. I will spare them as a father spares an obedient child.'"*

Amid grave concerns, tremendous social decay, and troubling daily news we are constantly bombarded with, we have a strategy that will always keep us in a place of hope and victory! That strategy is to keep speaking and declaring the truth concerning God's character - based on His Word and our personal testimony! This is how we stir each other up in faith and keep the fire of God burning in our hearts. We will have (possess as our reality) what we speak, whether it's life or death – this is a timeless truth and principle straight from His Word.

The confession of our faith will bring us distinction! In this passage of Malachi, we see the value of keeping our hearts (which influence our mouths) in alignment with God. The Lord says, in Malachi 3:18, concerning those who profess their faith and busy themselves with honoring His name: *"Then you will again see the difference between the righteous and the wicked, between those who serve God and those who do not."*

Because this is from the mouth of God, you can be sure it will come to pass! Your life will be marked by distinction as you choose to remember God and His promises and remind and encourage others of them too.

# Day 06

## Let Your Cup Overflow

*Psalm 23:5 (NLT), "...You honour me by anointing my head with oil. My cup overflows with blessings."*

When we receive a fresh infilling of the Holy Spirit, we become a magnet for the blessing and favor of God. That's because His Presence deals with all the doubt, disappointments, and sinful habits that had attached themselves to our minds through our experiences in life. 1 Thessalonians 5:23 calls them profane things, and they repel the blessing of God, and block the flow of God's life in us. But if we continually yield ourselves to the infilling of the Spirit of God, He will cause rivers of living water to gush into our lives, from His Spirit in us. That living water will push out every hinderance to the blessing of God in our lives and cause us to overflow with His grace, love, peace, and joy! We will experience a great hunger for more of His Presence and His Word!

God's Word is essential for renewing our minds, it causes the truth to replace incorrect mindsets that hold us in a place of defeat. It also produces faith inside us - a supernatural force that keeps us triumphing over every challenge! According to the Word of God, the only acceptable way for a believer to live, is by being consistently filled with and controlled by the Spirit of God.

So, keep your heart in a place of perpetual hunger for and surrender to a fresh infilling of the Holy Spirit's life and power, so your life overflows with the blessing and favor of the Lord!

# Day 07

## Become Unstoppable!

*Romans 8:31 (NLT), "What shall we say about such wonderful things as these? If God is for us, who can ever be against us?"*

One of the greatest miracles and mysteries of the kingdom of God, is that the creator of all of heaven and earth has chosen to make His dwelling place in the heart of man. God, by His Holy Spirit lives within us, and has promised to never leave us! Confess that out loud today and as you do, you will feel something wonderful rising up in your heart. Not only is your God in you, but He is also with you and for you too! The reality of God being in us, with us, and for us is what enables us to be **unstoppable** for His kingdom! No plan of the enemy can stop God, and because He is in you - it can't stop you either! There is no obstacle great enough, no situation strong enough, and no circumstance hard enough to stop God's perfect will for your life - except for you. Jesus said that while we choose to abide in Him, and have His Word remain alive in our hearts - there is nothing He will not do for us (John 14).

However, growing cold in our hearts towards Him, and losing our hunger for His Presence and Word will cause the things of this world to take preference over Him. Romans 8 teaches that we either live controlled by the spirit or we live controlled by the flesh. Living dominated by our flesh makes us victims to our circumstances and gives the devil the upper hand in our lives. However, living full of and controlled by the Holy Spirit, will keep us in a place of victory and make us unstoppable for the kingdom of God! Make your choice to be unstoppable today!

# Day 08

## Your Chief Cornerstone

*1 Peter 2:6 (AMPC), "...Behold, I am laying in Zion a chosen, precious chief Cornerstone, and he who believes in Him [who adheres to, trusts in, and relies on Him] shall never be disappointed or put to shame."*

When Jesus walked this earth, despite all the good He did, He was still despised and rejected by many people. Jesus was the chief cornerstone that many rejected. He is the One upon which every life must be built. He is a sure foundation that will never crumble or fail. To have our lives securely rooted in Jesus, means we live by the truth of His Word, and draw our strength, peace, and joy for life from our relationship with Him, through His indwelling Holy Spirit.

The decision to place Him and His Word first place in our lives not only results in His absolute provision and blessing, but a promise that we will never be disappointed or ashamed of putting our entire trust in Him! Absolute belief in Jesus Christ causes our spirit man to dominate our thoughts, our emotions, and our free will! Every decision is made influenced by His wisdom and perspective, and every motive is influenced by His love in and for us.

There is no greater, or more rewarding way to live - build yourself up in the Lord Jesus Christ!

# Day 09

## God in You

*Deuteronomy 1:21 (NKJV), "Look, the Lord your God has set the land before you; go up and possess it, as the Lord God of your fathers has spoken to you; do not fear or be discouraged."*

Throughout their journey, the Lord spoke to Israel with a strong message, *"Do not fear or be discouraged"*. Before they entered the promised land, the Lord always went ahead of them and fought for them. Once they lived in the promised land, they were required to dress and arm themselves for battle. The manna from heaven also ceased the moment they ate from the produce of the land. They had entered a new maturity in their covenant with the Lord - which was signified when the men were all circumcised days before crossing the Jordan and entering the land. In their own land they would learn to work and live in partnership with God as He established them.

Since the finished work of the cross, believers have entered an even better covenant with God. Before, His Presence was with His people, training them in battle and teaching them how to grow food to nourish themselves. Now, we have His Spirit within us! He teaches us the Word and leads us into truth, so our spirits are nourished and minds renewed. He trains us to stand strong in faith and use our authority to defeat our enemy, the devil. Embrace this awesome partnership you have with the Lord as together with Him - you step into every promise He has for you. You can move forward with boldness and confidence without fear - because the Lord is in you!

# Day 10

## Trained to be Led by Him

*John 16:13 (NKJV), "However, when He, the Spirit of truth, has come, He will guide you into all truth; for He will not speak on His own authority, but whatever He hears He will speak; and He will tell you things to come."*

The Holy Spirit is the ultimate partner for life. We can train our spiritual senses to immediately recognize and respond to His leading. Ephesians 3:19 says we are filled with the fullness of God, having the richest measure of the divine Presence in us, so we have become a body wholly filled and flooded with God Himself! Then in 2 Peter 1:4 it says we can experience a partnership with the divine nature of God, which causes us to escape the corrupt desires that are in the world. This means, the Holy Spirit within us is as willing as He is powerful to perform His mighty work in us to train us to continually stay free from incorrect mindsets, and things that would hinder us from moving forward in a life of victory and freedom!

As we remain conscious of His Presence abiding in us, we are more inclined to practice listening to His voice and yielding to His leading in all things. We literally become trained by Him to be led by Him. This is the unbroken fellowship with God we can enjoy that Romans 6:11 speaks about. What's more, it leads to us reigning in life in Jesus (Romans 5:17). Pursue being trained by the Holy Spirit by being sensitive to be led by Him today - it's the only way to reign in this life, in Him!

# Day 11

## Ready for Jesus

Hebrews 12:14 (NKJV), *"Pursue peace with all people, and the holiness without which no one will see the Lord."*

The Bible makes it clear that without holiness we will not see God. In Matthew 5:8, Jesus says, *"Blessed are the pure in heart for they shall see God"*. So, purity of heart and holiness are essential for our walk of intimacy with the Lord. Psalm 24:4 tells us that only those with clean hands and pure hearts will stand in the holy Presence of the Lord. Now, in Titus 1:16, it says there are those who profess to know God, but in their actions they deny Him. It says their actions are abominable, disobedient, and disqualified for every good work. That's a serious rebuke. We know that when Jesus returns, He will not come for a bride that is filthy or stained with elements of this world, but one that is without spot or blemish. It's true our spirits, that are connected to the Spirit of God, are perfect, however, it's our souls (intellect, emotions, and free will), that are constantly being exposed to the unholy things of the world and are in constant danger of being pulled in and influenced by it. So how do we keep our souls in a position of being holy and blameless before the Lord?

1 Thessalonians 5:23,24 tells us that God's Presence within us can do this - provided we continuously abide in Jesus and welcome the grace (supernatural power) of the Holy Spirit to do His sanctifying work in us. This is how we remain holy and blameless in our spirit, soul, and body. It's also how we stay in love with Jesus, ready to meet Him when He comes for His bride.

# Day 12

## Supernatural Strength

***Psalm 89:17 (NLT), "You are their glorious strength. It pleases You to make us strong."***

Our faith pleases God! Anything outside of faith, is not pleasing to Him! This way, when we face challenging circumstances that contradict God's will for our lives, we can draw from the strength of His Spirit within us to contend for His promises and overcome! How does this practically work in our lives? Well, faith comes from the Word of God we hear (Romans 10:17), which means we must always be in a position of hearing it. God's written word is alive with His power, but this power is a latent power, which means it exists in it, but is not yet manifest. Proverbs 2:4 and 7 reveal God's power is hidden or concealed within His written word.

When we read that word, agree with it, meditate on it, and receive it into our hearts, the Holy Spirit gets all over it and causes it to come alive within us. When the Holy Spirit speaks that word directly into our spirits it instantly infuses our minds with peace and life. This is what we call the spontaneous, freshly *spoken* word of God, or His rhema word. As it's **spoken** into our spirits God's power is released. That power holds within it the supernatural strength we need to fully trust, stand our ground, and see that word become our reality.

# Day 13

## Faithful Provider

*Genesis 22:14 (AMPC), "So Abraham called the name of that place, 'The Lord Will Provide'. And it is said to this day, 'On the mount of the Lord it will be provided.'"*

For most, just the possibility of Abraham having to sacrifice his son, stirs up feelings of horror. For Abraham, this was the ultimate test of his trust in the love and faithfulness of his God. The journey he and Sarah took just to conceive Isaac was enough to become overprotective in their care of him. Isaac was the son of promise. From him would come the fulfilment of the covenant that promised descendants as numerous as the stars of the sky. God's instruction to Abraham concerning laying Isaac on the alter would seem unthinkable in the natural, and yet Abraham knew and trusted the nature of God to the extent that he was completely convinced that He would keep His promise, even if it meant raising his son up from the dead (Hebrews 11:17-19).

While faith in God and His promises is essential, unless it's grounded in an absolute confidence of His good, loving, and trustworthy nature - it really has no value (1 Corinthians 13:2). Our personal revelation of God's love for us is the basis on which our faith operates and produces in our lives. Abraham obeyed because He was fully persuaded in God's faithfulness and had absolute confidence in God's ability and *willingness* to do exactly what He had promised. When our obedience to the Lord is based on the same confident trust, there will never be a time we won't experience His faithful provision.

# Day 14

## Supernatural Strength

*Daniel 11:32 (NKJV) "Those who do wickedly against the covenant He shall corrupt with flattery; but the people who know their God shall be strong and carry out great exploits."*

We cannot afford to be a people that only know about God, and don't know Him personally! Jesus set the standard for our intimacy with Him and the Father. He said we are to be deeply aquatinted with Him, to lean on, confidently trust in, and completely rely on Him. The reality is we are the only ones who determine the depth of relationship we have with the Lord. When we abide in Him, and continually allow His Word to transform us, through our relationship with the Holy Spirit - we will know Him!

In Philippians 3:10, Paul explains that truly knowing God means knowing His resurrection power! This is what courses from our spirits like a mighty force, infusing us with supernatural strength to do the works of God! The truth is, knowing God doesn't happen by accident. It's a result of intentionally engaging in a relationship with Him and His Word, through the Person of the Holy Spirit.

Increase your commitment to studying the Word and understanding the relationship you were created to enjoy with the Holy Spirit. He will lead you into all truth and reveal the exact nature and will of Jesus and the Father to you. He will show you how to work in partnership with Himself, as He equips and empowers you to accomplish supernatural feats in this natural world.

# Day 15

## Walking with God

*2 Peter 3:18 (AMPC), "But grow in grace and recognition and knowledge and understanding of our Lord and Saviour Jesus Christ..."*

Walking with God is what gives value to working for God. The closer our walk with Him, the greater the impact we will have for His kingdom. When we take the time to draw near to Him, and get His heart on a matter, we align ourselves with Him and His grace (supernatural power). This is where understanding begins to flow to us from His Spirit. 2 Peter 3:18 tells us to grow in grace and the knowledge of Jesus Christ. God's practical wisdom to carry out His will, empowered by His anointing - makes what we do for Him effective and efficient. We develop this closer walk with the Lord by dwelling in His Word and spending time with Him in prayer. His Word reveals the character and knowledge of God and His ways, and our time fellowshipping with Him is where we can speak to Him and hear from Him to receive the personal guidance we need. This time of walking with the Lord grants us access to the secrets of His heart that gives purpose and value to everything we do for Him. Instead of just working for Him, we carry His grace to reflect Him too, causing what we do to be impactful and extremely satisfying.

# Day 16

## Strong and Sweet

*Judges 14:6 (NLT): "At that moment the Spirit of the Lord came powerfully upon him, and he ripped the lion's jaws apart with his bare hands..."*

Samson was on a mission to find a wife. Along his journey, he was suddenly attacked by a young lion. Through the strength of God, when the Spirit of the Lord came powerfully upon him, he easily killed the attacking lion, and moved on swiftly. At a later stage, when he went past his battle ground to look at his conquest, he found some honey in the lion's carcass. In Psalm 81:16, honey is described as something God personally provided for His people to satisfy them. In Exodus 3:7-8 it's used to describe abundance, and in Psalm 119:103, and Proverbs 24:13-14, it is used to describe the sweetness of God's life-giving Word that brings wisdom and enduring hope. Like honey, God's Word personally fed to our souls by His Holy Spirit - brings a steady flow of His nourishing, satisfying goodness that is full of hope and unfailing expectation. The Spirit of God came upon Samson that day and caused him to supernaturally conquer and overcome a dangerous enemy.

Out of something strong, came something sweet and satisfying. No matter what battle we encounter in this life, when the Spirit of God makes His Word come alive inside us, it will not only give us the strength to overcome but will fill our lives with a satisfying hope and expectation to see His abundance and victory every time we face a challenge in the future.

# Day 17

## Resurrection Power

*Matthew 27:52-53 (AMPC), "The tombs were opened and many bodies of the saints who had fallen asleep in death were raised [to life]; and coming out of the tombs after His resurrection, they went into the holy city and appeared to many people."*

The resurrection power of God that flowed strong inside of Jesus as it raised Him from the dead caused many other people to be raised with Him that day! This resurrection power is stronger than any power that exists, and according to Romans 8:11 - it dwells in every child of God! What's more, this power that resides in us is there for a purpose! It will restore our bodies to life! You may be feeling like there are areas of your life that have been shut down, or laid to die, due to circumstances or disappointments. You may even feel that the hope you once had for a destiny that was full of promise has been buried and forgotten. Even changes in your physical health may seem to have nailed the door closed on the promises you were believing to walk in.

Well, today, understand that within you is the resurrection power of God! There is nothing that can oppose its power to bring life to all those dead-end areas of your life! Let the faith of God rise strong inside you today as you draw from the flow of that power and declare it quicken, and bring to life what Jesus said you can live in! From today see yourself moving forward from defeat into victory, enjoying the reality of God's abundant life and promises!

# Day 18

## Let Your Spirit Take the Lead!

*2 Peter 1:3 (AMPC), "For His divine power has bestowed upon us all things that [are requisite and suited] to life and godliness, through the [full, personal] knowledge of Him Who called us by and to His own glory and excellence (virtue)."*

As believers, we have everything we need to live a life of victory! The Bible teaches that man, like God, is made of three distinct parts: the spirit-man (directly connected to God when we are born-again; the soul (mind, will, and emotions); and the physical body (our earth suit that houses the spirit and soul). With regards to 2 Peter 1:3, some argue that this verse only covers the provision we need as far as our spiritual wellbeing is concerned, and not our mental, physical, or financial health.

The truth is, the Bible is full of promises concerning the prosperity of our minds and emotions, our physical health, and our financial provision. However, to believe God for those promises to become our natural reality, we must be in a position where our spirit-man begins to take the lead and becomes dominant enough to influence our souls and physical bodies. When we trust the Holy Spirit to make the Word of God come alive in our hearts as we meditate on its truth, we get to know more of Who God is, what His will is for us, and what He has already done for us to live in victory and abundance. As this knowledge becomes a revelation to us, God's power is set to work inside us, causing our faith to grow, so we can receive every promise that exists in the realm of the spirit, and believe it into our natural realm! It's time to let your spirit-man, by the power and partnership of the Holy Spirit, lead you into the life of victory you have been promised!

# Day 19

## Develop Patience

*Hebrews 10:36 (AMPC), "For you have need of steadfast patience and endurance, so that you may perform and fully accomplish the will of God, and thus receive and carry away [and enjoy to the full] what is promised. For ye have need of patience, that, after ye have done the will of God, ye might receive the promise."*

In our journey of learning to walk and live by faith, we will face some challenges that when we don't see the results we are believing for as quickly as we desire, we could become discouraged. Unless dealt with, discouragement can quickly lead to bitter disappointment. Very soon we will begin to question and doubt everything we believe about walking in faith and make the mistake of measuring what we believe by the circumstances we are experiencing. Our impatience can cause us to literally back out of a position of faith. In Hebrews 10:38-39 says the person who draws back from their walk of faith positions themselves in a state of perdition, which means eternal misery. That's why we cannot become people who quit when things get tough because we have impatient, short-lived faith. We must give faith time to work! If God has spoken to you, His written word will confirm it. Which means there is no other option than to stand fast and refuse to waver until you see the manifestation of that promise. Patience and endurance are power twins! Patience is a spiritual quality that undergirds our faith - refusing to be moved by anything that contradicts what the Word of God has promised. Develop patience by refusing to let go of God's promises and you will have them!

# Day 20

## Greater Determination

*Nehemiah 6:9 (NLT): "They were just trying to intimidate us, imagining that they could discourage us and stop the work. So I continued the work with even greater determination."*

Nehemiah was a man on assignment. He was focused on his mission and determined to see it through. Even when an enemy, Sanballat, tried to distract him with lies and threats to make him pause from his assignment, he continued with the work, *with even greater determination* than before. The day you committed to serving the Lord by pursuing Him and fulfilling His call on your life, the enemy felt the threat to his kingdom. He made it his business to deter you from completing your assignment. But praise God, because of Jesus and the finished work of the cross - the devil is a defeated foe! Anything he tries to use to hinder and dissuade you from confidently taking possession of what God has already provided for the success of your assignment, will fail - if you refuse to give in.

Here's what the word says to do: 1) Refuse to be intimidated and fearful. 2) Press even harder into spending time with the Lord in prayer and the Word and praying in the Holy Spirit. When you do this, faith will arise strong inside of you and the grace of God will increase - infusing you with supernatural strength, energizing you and empowering you to keep moving forward in the task God has given you. Great success and overwhelming victory are at hand as you move forward in an even greater determination than before!

# Day 21

## Godly Authority

*1 John 3:8 (NKJV), "...For this reason the Son of God was manifested, that He might destroy the works of the devil."*

When Jesus left heaven and lived with us on the earth, He demonstrated how we can walk in our God-given authority and undo the evil work of the devil, through the power of the Holy Spirit living within us. The Holy Spirit has not changed, He is operating in the same power He did in the book of Acts. We should expect to live this way. Walking in God's power is essential to see us accomplish the assignment He has for our lives. The power already exists in every believer who has been baptized in the Holy Spirit. To increase the potency and effectiveness of that power, we must learn how to draw, and practice drawing from the source of that power. Habitually acknowledging the presence of the Holy Spirit being within us and spending time listening to His heart and walking in obedience to His voice will keep His love, life, and power flowing from His Spirit into ours.

The confidence of knowing God is in you and with you, will give you a boldness to stand up to the devil, resist him and drive him out of the way. Then, with that same authority, you can declare the will of God directly over circumstance and see things turned around for the good. Submit yourself to the Lord today, stand in the authority He has given you, and enforce the devils defeat everywhere you go.

# Day 22

## Your Glorious Life in Christ

*1 Peter 2:9 (AMPC), "But you are a chosen race, a royal priesthood, a dedicated nation, [God's] own purchased, special people, that you may set forth the wonderful deeds and display the virtues and perfections of Him Who called you out of darkness into His marvelous light."*

This scripture is speaking about those who have surrendered their lives to Jesus, and are born-again, by His Spirit living inside of them. If that is you, then the Word of God says you are chosen by God for a specific purpose. That purpose is to live in a way that demonstrates the wonderful deeds, virtues, and perfections of Jesus. We do this by acknowledging every good thing that is in us because of Him being in us! Here are just a few of the many things we have because of Him: We have brand new spirits that are one with His Spirit and carry His nature, His supernatural gifts, and His power. We are redeemed, healed, and have been made righteous. We have a sound mind and a life personally planned out by Him that is loaded with good works, prosperity, and success in every area! Hallelujah!

1 Peter 2:9 says we are His royal priesthood. The word priesthood speaks to the power and authority that God has given us to act in all things necessary for our salvation and victory. Any time the devil tries to kill, steal, or destroy any of the benefits we have in Christ, we have the authority to resist him and send him fleeing. Use the power and authority you have been given to demonstrate the glorious life you have in Christ Jesus, today!

# Day 23

## Secret Things

**Deuteronomy 29:29 (AMPC), "The secret things belong to the LORD our God, but the things that are revealed belong to us and to our children forever, that we may do all the words of this law.**

God holds the knowledge to everything because He is the Creator. All wisdom, insight and understanding belong to Him. Colossians 1:17 says the Lord is before all things, and in Him all things consist. That's why there isn't one problem that will not have its solution found in the Lord. There is absolutely nothing He cannot fathom or solve, and if we just seek His face and ask - He will not hold the answers we need back from us! (Psalms 84:11). When we are in Him, we can receive a continuous flow of His revelation knowledge to know His perfect will in every situation (Colossians 1:9). Jesus said that the secrets of the Kingdom of heaven were given to us to know (Matthew 13:11) and all who receive God's Word as little children, in simple faith – to them shall these mysteries be revealed (Matthew 11:25). Hallelujah!

As children of God, we are privy to knowledge and wisdom that many will never attain. Remember, since we have the Spirit of God who searches the deep things of God within us (1 Corinthians 2:10), we have the mind of Christ (1 Corinthians 2:16)! How does this become our reality? Proverbs 25:2 says it is the glory of God to conceal a thing, and the honor of kings to search out a matter. All that we would ever need to know is found on the other side of seeking. When we seek, *we shall find*. Whatever answer you are looking for – find it in our Glorious Father, the All-knowing One!

# Day 24

## Power of the Gospel!

*1 Thessalonians 1:5 (NKJV), "For our gospel did not come to you in word only, but also in power, and in the Holy Spirit..."*

When Paul preached the Gospel to the Thessalonians, the word he spoke was accompanied by the power of the Holy Spirit. Similarly, Paul says to the church at Corinth that the kingdom is not in word but in power (1 Corinthians 4:20). So, the words we speak must be accompanied by the power of God, if not, we haven't preached the Gospel, we've preached religion. Mere words and eloquent speech don't change the lives of people. Only the Word of God, undergirded by the power of the Holy Ghost can bring about change.

When people are bound by the power of the devil, whether it's a destructive addiction, a spirit of heaviness and depression, a generational curse of poverty or divorce - only the truth of the Gospel accompanied with power is going to break off that yoke of bondage and set those people free! Religion is powerless, it doesn't set people free, it keeps them in bondage and adds disappointment and disillusionment to their broken state.

When you open your heart to the Holy Spirit and the Word of God comes alive inside you, let that revelation power flow so strong in you, that when you share it with others, that power is carried on the words you believe! You will see the Holy Spirit use those power-filled words to bring change, deliverance, freedom, life, peace, and joy to yourself and those who listen to you! That is the power of the Gospel!

# Day 25

## One Thing Needed

*Luke 10:42, "But one thing is needed, and Mary has chosen that good part, which will not be taken away from her."*

Instead of being consumed and focused on what was going on around her that day, Mary chose to give her full attention to Jesus. She didn't even sit or stand in a distant corner of the room, where she could become easily distracted by Martha's busyness. Instead, she found her spot at His feet, listening intently to His words. Mary had made a deliberate decision to position herself in a place where she was able to be more consumed with what He was saying than anything else! We can make the very same choice, every day of our lives. If necessary, we can make the decision to get up earlier, find a secluded place where we can be alone with the Lord and His Word, and learn from Him. Of course, we all have responsibilities that need to be taken care of, but if we make spending time alone with God our priority, He will order the rest of the day in a way that not one thing will be neglected. Make time to seek the Lord each day and you will not only succeed, but everything else will also fall into place and bring Him glory too!

# Day 26

## Refuse to Waver

*1 Peter 2:24 (AMPC), "He personally bore our sins in His [own] body on the tree [as on an altar and offered Himself on it], that we might die (cease to exist) to sin and live to righteousness. By His wounds you have been healed."*

Do you know that the glorious God you serve, Who lives in you - is the Healer. He gave Himself to ensure your divine health and He has declared His Own wounds *have* healed you. In the Old Testament, God commanded His people to diligently hearken to His voice and be obedient to Him (Exodus 15:26). He told them that if they would simply keep His ways, they would enjoy freedom from all disease, because He was their Healer!

Now that was under an inferior covenant, since the finished work of the cross, even though the curse still exists in the world around us, we have a far superior covenant (Hebrews 7:22)! Jesus became the sacrifice that took on the full impact of the curse, with every sickness and disease so that we wouldn't have to suffer under it anymore! Today, if we choose to personally reject Jesus and the finished work of the cross, even by wavering in our belief by thinking it may not be God's perfect will for us to be healed - we will not receive what Jesus has paid for us to have. Why? Because according to the Word of God, anything outside of faith is sin. James 1:6-8 tells us that any wavering concerning walking in the fullness of what God has promised us will cause us to not receive *anything* from Him.

Today let the truth of God's Word so saturate your thoughts that you begin to fully believe what is yours through Jesus. Refuse to waver in your faith and expect to receive every promise now in Jesus Name!

# Day 27

## Refuse Suffering

*Philippians 3:10 (NKJV), "...that I may know Him and the power of His resurrection, and the fellowship of His sufferings, being conformed to His death"*

Jesus said we must become vitally united to Him (John 15:7)! Since God is our source, our primary pursuit should be to truly know Him, because it's from knowing Him that everything else begins to flow. Intimately knowing God leads us to knowing and experiencing the power of His resurrection in our lives too. The last part of this scripture says we should know the fellowship of His sufferings, being conformed to His death. That word *sufferings* in this scripture in the Greek speaks to hardships and pains undergone by someone. When we become aware of the sufferings Jesus bore at the cross - we become well aware of all He took on Himself, on our behalf, so that we don't have to bear them! Hallelujah! He suffered everything for our sake! And when He died carrying those things - our old sinful nature died with Him! That's why He wants us to be fully aware of what He suffered so that we, with full boldness and confidence, will refuse to allow the devil to put those things on us! To do anything less would be to insult Jesus and all He endured on the cross for us. Today, make it your business to know what Jesus suffered for you, so that you can honor Him and refuse it in your own life.

# Day 28

## Supernatural Wealth

*Deuteronomy 8:18 (NKJV), "And you shall remember the Lord your God, for it is He who gives you power to get wealth, that He may establish His covenant which He swore to your fathers, as it is this day."*

Abundance is part of our redemption. For us to experience supernatural wealth we must remember where it comes from! Heaven's wealth is an entrustment not an achievement. In our covenant relationship with God - He gives us power to get wealth. His Word, which is His perfect will for our lives, is full of kingdom, financial principles. Tithing and sowing and reaping are extremely powerful spiritual laws that were established far before the law given to Moses for the people of Israel. They are and will always be essential tools that, when mixed with faith, will release supernatural power to bring wealth into our lives. God's responsibility is to honor His Word, our responsibility is to give Him something to work with by obeying His instructions and implementing His principles. It's our willing, faith-filled obedience that activates the power to get wealth! In summary, we could say that giving is a covenant obligation that empowers believers to access the realm of supernatural wealth. Regardless of the economic climate in the world around us, believers can operate in a supernatural economy, with supernatural principles that unlock and activate supernatural wealth. Decide to become familiar with these principles, apply them to your life with faith - and you will see the benefits of your kingdom covenant pour into your life!

# Day 29

## Trained for Good Success

**Hebrews 5:14 (NLT), "Solid food is for those who are mature, who through training have the skill to recognize the difference between right and wrong."**

God created Adam and Eve and blessed them. That blessing was an empowerment for them to increase, prosper, and have dominion over the earth. They were expected to use their God-given authority to continually increase and prosper (Genesis 1:28). The starting point of humanity shows God's original intent for us. We are meant to consistently progress in life. To move from faith to more faith, from glory to glory, and from strength to strength! Proverbs 4:18 says, *"But the path of the uncompromisingly righteous is like the shining sun, that shines more and more brighter and clearer unto the perfect day".*

This is the mark of a true believer, where despite challenges and opposition, there is always growth and increase. As we continually advance in faith and the strength of the Lord, we see the outflow of increase in every other area of our lives. As we consistently renew our minds to God's Word, pursue His Presence, and walk in His ways - our souls prosper; and the extent to which our souls prosper - we prosper! (3 John 1:2). Hebrews 5:14 shows how growth comes through consistent training and enhances the skill to recognize what is right and wrong. This discernment is *trained* through exposure to God's Word by His Holy Spirit. From this day, determine to take the path that leads to increase as you yield to the Holy Spirit and allow the Word to train you for good success.

# Day 30

## A Holy Life of Power

*2 Peter 1:3 (AMP), "For His divine power has bestowed on us [absolutely] everything necessary for [a dynamic spiritual] life and godliness, through true and personal knowledge of Him who called us by His Own glory and excellence."*

After Jesus ascended to Heaven, He didn't leave us abandoned, incomplete or hopeless. Instead, He gave us the greatest gift of all, the gift of the Holy Spirit! Through the finished work of the cross, God gave us personal access to Himself! He made a way for His Own Spirit to come and live inside of us. Now we can have true and personal knowledge of Himself. This is how we have everything we need to live a dynamic spiritual life! We are well able to live holy before the Lord because He is holy and lives in us! It's His Presence in us that makes us holy and empowers us to live holy! Why is this so important? Because a life made holy by God's presence is a life that is led by the Spirit and empowered to operate just like Jesus did when He walked the earth! We operate in mighty power and authority over the devil when we have nothing in common with him! Every demon spirit sense and knows the power of a true believer who walks holy before the Lord, and wastes no time getting right out of that believer's way. Decide to know God more by spending time in His Word. Let it teach you how you can be just like Jesus as you walk being led, controlled, and empowered by the Holy Spirit who lives in you.

# Day 31

## Love Righteousness!

*2 Corinthians 7:1 (NKJV), "Therefore, having these promises, beloved, let us cleanse ourselves from all filthiness of the flesh and spirit, perfecting holiness in the fear of God."*

Paul instructed the believers at Corinth to cleanse themselves from all filthiness of the flesh. As believers, we are required to live holy and to keep our garments of righteousness clean. The way we achieve this is through fearing the Lord. That's because to fear the Lord means to hate what is evil. Paul instructed the church at Rome to regard with disgust and hatred what is evil and to cling to what is good. The Bible says the fear of man brings a snare, but the fear of the Lord produces holiness and obedience. Religion will take this truth and make it seem as though we are sacrificing or missing out on enjoying life for a legalistic way of life. But the truth is, living for the Lord is the most joyful, rewarding life there is!

Ask anyone who knows what it is to be saved out of a life that was bound by the bondage of sin and its destructive consequences, and into the glorious life of love and freedom in Jesus! Righteousness, peace, and the joy of the Holy Ghost is the hallmark of the believer who fears the Lord! Psalms 45:7 was written to describe the life of Jesus - the most joyful person who ever walked the earth: *"You love righteousness, uprightness, and right standing with God and hate wickedness; therefore God, Your God, has anointed You with the oil of gladness above Your fellows."* It's time to love righteousness and hate wickedness so you can live in the fullness of God's joy every day of your life!

# AUGUST

# Day 01

## Your Path of Victory

*Philippians 4:4 (NKJV), "Rejoice in the Lord always. Again I will say, rejoice!"*

What kind of life would you desire for someone you love and truly care for? Would you be delighted to see them walking in purpose and full of the joy and life God has made available for them? Is there any lid of limitation you would put on their wellbeing and success? Now take a moment to consider this: God, the author of life itself, so loved you that He gave Jesus, so you are able to live in and with Him, enjoying the fullness and abundance of a life well worth living! How do we get to experience this kind of life that seems too good to be true, especially when the circumstances we find ourselves in contradict it? Well, the Word of God is powerful enough to change your circumstances.

All you need to do is *choose* to believe what it says, meditate on it and speak in agreement with it - even before you see the change take place! When we delight in the Lord and choose to rejoice in Him and in His Word - we set the course of our lives in the right direction! Understand, your Heavenly Father loves you so intensely, and desires to see you walk in an even richer, fuller life than you could ever dream or imagine! So, work with Him - choose to delight in Him. Make an unwavering decision to rejoice in Him letting His Word influence your thoughts, words, and actions; paving the path of victory He has always intended for you to walk in.

# Day 02

## A Carrier of Your Encounter

*Exodus 3:2 (NKJV), "And the Angel of the Lord appeared to him in a flame of fire from the midst of a bush. So he looked, and behold, the bush was burning with fire, but the bush was not consumed."*

This encounter Moses had with the Living God changed his life forever. The Moses who returned to deliver Egypt was not the Moses who had previously fled Egypt in fear. He met with God and became a carrier of that divine encounter! Today, know that you were created for a purpose. It doesn't matter how you got here, all that really matters is that you're here now. You were created to personally encounter the Living God, have Him so impact your life, that you carry what He has placed on you to change the world around you. You are destined to carry the One you encounter because He is the Divine solution to every problem the world has right now.

So, take a good look at yourself today, through the eyes of the Word. See that the One who is the Divine solution, dwells in you! Impact doesn't flow by accident. It flows because of an encounter with the Lord. He desires to encounter you in a wonderful and powerful way, but He waits on you to get hungry to seek Him! It's when we seek Him with all our hearts that He promises to manifest Himself to us. As you encounter Him, know He makes you whole, empowers, and deploys you into your destiny! God will not disappoint you, cry out to Him today for a fresh encounter and begin to carry Him to a world that desperately needs to know Him too.

# Day 03

## Saved, Redeemed, Delivered

*Galatians 1:4, "...(Jesus) gave Himself for our sins to deliver us from the present evil age, according to the will of our God and Father,..."*

The moment we became born-again, God recreated our spirit-man, and placed His Own spirit inside our spirits. We became inseparably connected to Him. The previous life of sin we once led has died and is buried with Christ. Now, the same Spirit that raised Jesus from the dead, lives inside us, and has raised our spirits, that were once dead in sin, to a brand-new life in Him! We have been saved, redeemed, and delivered from the curse of sin and its wicked control over our lives. When this becomes a revelation to us, we never have to live under the weight of condemnation from the past, nor do we ever feel the pull back into a life of sin. Before meeting Jesus, the Apostle Paul had persecuted thousands of believers in his attempt to snuff out the Christian faith. The guilt and condemnation must have been a terrible weight for him bear.

However, Paul experienced the depths of God's love, compassion, and forgiveness when he realized the truth. He received a solid revelation that Jesus Christ paid a hefty price for his salvation, redemption, and deliverance from sin. Don't give despair over the past the luxury of hanging around you. Look full into the joy and freedom you have in the Lord. You have been saved, forgiven, and empowered by God's Spirit, to live free and full of purpose in Christ Jesus.

# Day 04

## Victory From the Inside Out

*Numbers 10:35 (NLT) "And whenever the Ark set out, Moses would shout, "Arise, O Lord, and let Your enemies be scattered! Let them flee before You!"*

In the Old Testament, whenever the Israelites moved, the Ark of the Covenant would go first. It carried the presence of God before the people. When they stopped to camp, the Ark would be placed in a tent in the center, and the people would camp around it. It was the heart and the life of the people. How wonderful it must have been to live, knowing the presence of God was right there, tangibly with and amongst them. But praise God - through the finished work of the cross, the presence of God, in the form of His Holy Spirit is no longer confined to a wooden box. Now His presence inhabits every born-again child of God! He is not just with or amongst us - He is in us! Hallelujah! And not just in a tiny measure - the Bible says we have the fullness of God, the richest measure of His Presence within us! (Ephesians 3:19).

Jesus taught that while we are in this world, we will experience trials, tribulations, and challenges, but we will never face them alone. We will always face and overcome each one from a position of victory, from the presence of God, looking toward the trouble. Today, have a revelation of who Jesus is, what He has done for you, and how He has empowered you, through His Own Spirit living in you. While you live recognizing this truth - your enemy, the devil - will flee before you as his plans concerning you fail every day, in every way!

# Day 05

## Prove Your Faith

*James 2:26 (NKJV), "For as the body without the spirit is dead, so faith without works is dead also."*

Faith without a corresponding action is dead! If we truly believe in the faithful, trustworthy character of God and every promise and principle in His Word concerning us, we wouldn't think twice to act on what it says. It's simply impossible to demonstrate faith without action. The day Abraham offered his son Isaac on the altar, the validity of his faith was proven! He trusted God enough to be fully convinced that no matter what, He would keep His promise. He knew that even if Isaac died by his hand that day, the Lord would raise him again from the dead because He promised that Isaac would carry on his linage. Isaac's descendants would form the nation of Israel. In the same way our faith in God is made perfect by our obedience to Him. We cannot profess to believe in God and not wholeheartedly apply His principles to our lives. Let the validity of your faith be proven as you decide to act on the Word of God, being fully persuaded that the Lord will honor His Word concerning you.

# Day 06

## A Powerful Impact

*Psalm 45:7 (AMPC), "You love righteousness, uprightness, and right standing with God and hate wickedness; therefore God, Your God, has anointed You with the oil of gladness above Your fellows."*

We were saved by the grace of God and redeemed by His precious blood to make a powerful impact for the kingdom of God in this world! As we surrender to His transforming power we become more and more like Him! We begin to think like Him, speak in line with His Words, and act just like He does! The glorious, victorious image of the resurrected Jesus is the image we are changed into! No matter how troublesome and hopeless the world around us seems - Jesus said that as He is **now** - so are we **in this world**!

If you want to know how you are going to make an earth-shaking impact in this world - look at **Who** is inside you! Read everything the Word of God says our victorious Jesus is, and then realize this is the very image He is transforming you into! God's presence in you is full of glory, and the fullness of joy! It has a voice that only speaks faith, thanksgiving, and praise! This is what marked Jesus when He walked this life, and it's what will mark us too! Let God live strong in and through you to mark this world for generations to come!

# Day 07

## Imprinted in Your Mind

*Joel 3:10 (AMPC), "Beat your plowshares into swords, and your pruning hooks into spears; let the weak say, I am strong [a warrior]!"*

The third chapter of the book of Joel is prophetic and speaks to God's final judgement and rule. A people who was oppressed, scattered, and subjected to severe cruelty under the hands of their enemies are called to rise up from their position of weakness, and become strong in the Lord. The Word teaches that under the New Covenant, we have authority and a sure victory over our enemy the devil. While we walk with God, keep ourselves filled with His power, and consistently renew our minds to the truth of His Word - victory will be our experience.

The key to living in this place of perpetual victory, is to meditate on the truth of God's Word. That's because meditating involves imagination. Just like Abraham did, we must take God's promises and instructions and imagine them being a part of our lives. The prophet Joel used descriptive analogies that made it easy for God's people to imagine becoming strong in the Lord to defeat their enemies. This stirred up hope, faith, and extreme courage inside them. They believed themselves to be what they imagined in their minds, based on the truth of God's Word. Let God's truth become your reality as you meditate on it today.

# Day 08

## The Self-Surrender that Overcomes the Enemy

*Revelation 12:11 (KJV)  "And they overcame him by the blood of the Lamb, and by the word of their testimony; and they loved not their lives unto the death."*

The call of Christ upon every believer is a call to complete commitment. He doesn't lay claim to only certain aspects of our lives, He owns all of us! The Bible tells us Jesus came to give us a new life, marked by redemption and love. When He lives full in us, we reflect the abundance of His goodness, mercy, and kindness. The more we surrender all to Him, the more we walk in the fullness of what He paid for us to enjoy. He has given us the freedom and privilege to draw near to His throne of grace, and to be seated with Him in heavenly places as a lifestyle. And it's from this place, in His Presence, where there is no fear or intimidation, only pure faith and absolute confidence in Him. Here we receive grace (His supernatural power) to declare His Word over our lives, our families, and our circumstances. This is where we bind and loose as we operate in the authority He has given us, as His Own representatives.

When we abide in His Presence, we understand our lives are not our own. We gladly die to our own ambitions, and the desire to make our own names great. Instead, we live wholeheartedly for Christ and the glory of His Name. This is how we overcome! Today, lay your life down for Him. He will do more with your surrender than you can do with your control.

# Day 09

## Become a Living Proof

*John 5:36 (NLT), "But I have a greater witness than John—My teachings and My miracles. The Father gave Me these works to accomplish, and they prove that He sent Me."*

While Jesus was on earth, many people were desperate to receive a touch from Him, and yet there were those who were deeply offended by Him and the works He did. The religious leaders thought He went too far or was too bold. The freedom He offered people was inspiring them to too much free-thinking. The more they were around Him, the more they could think of and expect the impossible. Jesus came to show them a different kingdom to the one they had been living under. Every work He did broke the boundaries of what they were accustomed to. In comparison to what they had received from their religious teachers, Jesus was shockingly excessive! He was too generous, too kind, too compassionate, and acted in too much authority, and always seemed to be having too much fun doing it.

We know that everything Jesus did was intentional and became living proof that His Father had sent Him. We have been sent by God too. But, unless we continuously renew our minds to how He thinks and operates, we will never carry that same freedom or have the same impact on lives as Jesus did. Trust the Holy Spirit to reveal the real Jesus to you and let Him make your life a living proof of the Father's goodness, as He lives through you!

# Day 10

## Hold Fast to Hope

*Hebrews 10:23 (NKJV), "Let us hold fast the confession of our hope without wavering, for He Who promised is faithful."*

It's easy to believe and have hope when things are going well. However, when circumstances look opposite to what we are praying for, we need to let our spirits take the lead. Ephesians 1:18 says that the eyes of our hearts can be flooded with light, so that we can know and understand the hope we have in Christ. That hope is His rich and glorious inheritance for us! What is that inheritance? It's a guarantee that we can experience and enjoy the fulfilment of every promise in His Word - here and now! But it's only obtained through faith.

Faith sees God's promises fulfilled when our natural eyes can't. The Word instructs us to hold fast to this hope, until what has been promised becomes our natural reality! Keep your eyes fixed on the Lord, Who is the author and finisher of your faith. Only let your words mirror what God's Word has promised you. Then you will see the faithfulness of God come through - without fail!

# Day 11

## The Lord is My Banner

*Exodus 17:15 (AMPC), "And Moses built an altar and called the name of it, 'The Lord is my Banner'".*

A banner is a sign that informs and declares a certain truth. In the Old Testament, the Israelite army defeated their enemies because God was with them. In Exodus 17 we read that Amalek, a descendant of Esau, led his army against the Israelites. His hand was always set against God and this day, the Lord would prove to the nations that while His Name was lifted high - His people would always experience victory. Moses was to stand overlooking the battle, with the staff of the Lord raised high in his uplifted hands. It represented God's authority and a banner declaring He was with His people. As soon as Moses' arms grew tired and began to lower, the Israelites would experience defeat, but when those standing with Moses raised his arms up, the staff was seen by all, and victory came to the Israelites.

No matter how battle weary we become, when we stand in unity, under the truth of God's Word, we will be supernaturally strengthened and see every opposition to His rule be overturned! As the church of the Lord Jesus Christ, we must never be ashamed of upholding His truth and righteousness, no matter how fierce the battle, or ferocious the threat against us. While we carry His Name as a banner over us - He will deliver the enemy into our hands and secure our victory.

# Day 12

## Be Kind

*1 Peter 4:9 (CSB), "Be hospitable to one another without complaining."*

Part of the 'code of conduct' we're called to live by, especially when daily choosing to follow Christ, is to be sober-minded, prayerful, walking in love, and being *hospitable* without complaining. There is absolutely no way of fulfilling any of these instructions apart from the empowerment of the Spirit of God. Only His love at work within us enables us to do all of this without complaining. God's grace is a supernatural empowerment that gives us both the desire and strength to carry out His will.

Philippians 2:13 says, *"[Not in your own strength] for it is God Who is all the while effectually at work in you [energising and creating in you the power and desire], both to will and to work for His good pleasure and satisfaction and delight."* In the very next verse it says we are to do all things, *"...without grumbling and faultfinding and complaining [against God] and questioning and doubting [among yourselves]."*

Today, choose to yield to God's love inside you, and be hospitable to others. This is possibly one of the most powerful ways to displays His genuine love for them. Understand, your kindness will not go unnoticed by God as you represent Him well and impact others' lives with His love.

# Day 13

## Believe and Speak

***John 1:1 (NKJV), "In the beginning was the Word, and the Word was with God, and the Word was God."***

Since God's Word is inspired by the Holy Spirit, it holds within it the power to create and transform. However, this power is only activated when faith is applied. Hebrews 11:3 says, *"By faith we understand that the worlds were framed (fashioned, put in order, and equipped for their intended purpose) by the word of God, so that what we see was not made out of things which are visible."* When God created the world, everything He spoke came into existence, as He spoke from what He envisioned in His heart. Isaiah 55:11 says, *"So shall My word be that goes forth from My mouth; It shall not return to Me void, But it shall accomplish what I please, And it shall prosper in the thing for which I sent it."* God had already purposed what He wanted to see in His heart and mind before He spoke it into existence. Then, He told us to do the same thing.

In Mark 11:23-24, He says, *"Truly I tell you, whoever says to this mountain, 'Be lifted up and thrown into the sea!' and does not doubt at all in his heart but believes that what he says will take place, it will be done for him. For this reason I am telling you, whatever you ask for in prayer, believe (trust and be confident) that it is granted to you, and you will [get it]."*

Learn from God today, believe what He has promised you, speak it from the conviction of your heart - and you will walk in the reality of that promise!

# Day 14

## Strength in Words of Faith

*2 Chronicles 32:7-8 (NKJV), "'Be strong and courageous; do not be afraid nor dismayed... for there are more with us than with him. With him is an arm of flesh; but with us is the Lord our God, to help us and to fight our battles.' And the people were strengthened by the words of Hezekiah king of Judah."*

As a child of God, the words that flow from your mouth each day should build and encourage those who hear them! Understand, your words reveal the state of your heart. King Hezekiah was known for his trust in the Lord, and he had a track record to prove God's faithfulness. That's why, in the face of the most ferocious enemy that was sure to destroy them, his people were encouraged and strengthened when Hezekiah spoke. The Assyrian army were known for their barbaric, inhumane war tactics, and they held Jerusalem under siege. But God told Hezekiah that because he obeyed Him, and refused to bow to the foreign king, He would fight for them. That very night, God sent a single angel to kill 185,000 Assyrian warriors in their tents and gave Hezekiah and his people a glorious victory!

When we make a stand for righteousness, no matter the threat of those opposing us, God will take it personally as an attack on Himself, and single-handedly destroy the threat, and hand us the victory! Today, speak words of faith that reveal your trust in God. It will strengthen and encourage those who stand with you for His righteousness, and together you will watch Him take you from victory to victory.

# Day 15

## Your Path of Blessing

*1 Samuel 17: 38 – 39 (NLT), "Then Saul gave David his own armor—a bronze helmet and a coat of mail. David put it on, strapped the sword over it, and took a step or two to see what it was like, for he had never worn such things before. 'I can't go in these,' he protested to Saul. 'I'm not used to them.' So David took them off again."*

Hear this today; God desires for you to thrive in your calling! What He has placed inside you, and the path He has set out for you to walk in, has been designed and purposed to cause you to thrive and flourish! However, something that will quickly hinder your calling is comparison. Comparison breeds doubt, frustration, and the feeling of inadequacy. God has set before us a wonderful plan that is unique and specific to each of us. When David got ready to defeat Goliath, he was offered the armor of King Saul. He soon realized it didn't fit and would only weigh and slow him down. He wouldn't be able to defeat Goliath wearing someone else's armor. Instead, he took it off and placed his full confidence in Who he personally knew the Lord to be. David faced the giant wearing what God had already given Him, the anointing and strategy he was already familiar with to bring this enemy down.

If you live a life comparing your calling to the way others do ministry, you will never have the confidence and ability to overcome the challenges along the way. As you draw near to the Lord, and learn directly from Him, you will be fully equipped to stand confidently against any enemy you face. Only do what God has called you to do. He will give you the boldness and power to fulfil your call with great success and a maturity to confidently know your identity in Him as He leads you on the path of goodness, purpose, and blessing.

# Day 16

## Make Your Stand

*Daniel 3:25 (NKJV), "'Look!' he answered, 'I see four men loose, walking in the midst of the fire; and they are not hurt, and the form of the fourth is like the Son of God.'"*

The beauty of unapologetically taking a stand for God, in our rightful authority, is knowing that He is a very present help in time of trouble. He will never leave nor forsake us, and whenever we stand for Him, we can be sure, He stands for and if need be, vindicates His children. Shadrach, Meshach, and Abednego stood strong in their conviction. They refused to bow and worship the king. They were fully prepared to die for their stand, because they loved and feared God more than the authorities. They knew that the God they served was the God of the supernatural and that He was well- able to deliver them from the fiery furnace, should He choose.

Today, as you remain in intimate communion with the Lord, know you are commissioned to minister the Good News of the Gospel to this generation, with boldness and authority in the face of opposition. Regardless of whether you are well received or not, your God will be with you, and strengthen you as you make a righteous stand for Him.

# Day 17

## No Claim on Us!

*John 14:30 (AMPC), "I will not talk with you much more, for the prince (evil genius, ruler) of the world is coming. And he has no claim on Me. [He has nothing in common with Me; there is nothing in Me that belongs to him, and he has no power over Me.]"*

Jesus was preparing His disciples for what was about to take place – Judas, influenced by Satan, was about to give Him up to the authorities. Jesus willingly laid His life down for us. He was completely in agreement with, and fully committed to God's plan of redemption. He was innocent in every way, and yet He placed Himself between us, and the full onslaught of the fury of hell. He was the perfect sacrifice, taking our place on that cross. Scripture tells us He endured all He did for the joy of seeing us reconciled to the Father. John 14:31 tells us that it was His love for His Heavenly Father that compelled Him to obey the commandment to lay His life down. That love caused Him to agree to become sin, so that we could become righteous.

Now, we can declare boldly, that Satan has no claim on us! Now we can show the world the wonder of lives driven by love and obedience to a Heavenly Father Who gave up His only Son for our freedom. This is a beacon of hope to them - promising a life where Satan no longer has a hold over them.

# Day 18

## Secure and Without Fear!

*Proverbs 1:33 (NKJV): "But whoever listens to Me will dwell safely, and will be secure, without fear of evil."*

God's covenant promise to all His children, who choose to trust and obey Him, is a secure life - void of fear! The Bible calls this place of confident security - the Rest of God. This place of rest is not a place of being idle though. Instead, it's where we are constantly moving forward, taking territory and increasing in God's kingdom, with a mindset and perspective that is guarded by the peace of God! Where we are completely convinced that He is with us - continuously strengthening us with His supernatural might; and that He is fulfilling every promise while we remain full of His love and faith! When we live from this place of rest - no matter what circumstances surrounded us, we will always have an overflow of His joy, peace, and love.

Do you realize that this is *your* portion? If you are willing to take interest in His Word, root yourself in His love, and obey His voice - you can enjoy living in paths that overflow with His goodness. Even amid turmoil, trouble, distress and evil – you have no need to fear loss, lack, or any evil thing! Decide to devote yourself to delighting in the Lord and His ways today and watch how He will securely establish and settle your heart and mind in peace!

# Day 19

## I AM

*Exodus 3:14,15b (AMPC), "And God said to Moses, 'I AM WHO I AM and WHAT I AM, and I WILL BE WHAT I WILL BE;' and He said, 'You shall say this to the Israelites: I AM has sent me to you! This is My name forever, and by this name I am to be remembered to all generations.'"*

Throughout scripture, the Names of God are declared, each revealing a powerful truth of His character, His attributes, and His true identity. Knowing the truth of Who God is, by what He calls Himself, enriches and deepens the way we relate to Him, and builds our faith in His faithfulness towards us. Moses felt completely inadequate for the task he was given, and he knew the people would insist on knowing Who was sending him. So God told Moses to say, *"I AM has sent me"*. God was saying that He was exactly what His people would need when they needed it. He was their God, their protector, their deliverer, and their provider. They could trust Him to be everything they would ever need. This promise rings true for every born-again believer today! God has declared to be exactly who we need Him to be, in every season, and every circumstance of our lives! He wants us to trust Him with all things, always. His Word says He cares deeply for you, and that His hand is never too short to save and to bless you. Open your heart to receive a fresh revelation of Who your God says He is to you - today!

# Day 20

## Jesus in the Word

*John 5:39 (NLT) "You search the Scriptures because you think they give you eternal life. But the Scriptures point to me!"*

Jewish religious leaders were harassing Jesus after He healed a lame man. His response cut to the truth of what their hearts were full of. They insisted on judging everything He did according to the law. They were so intent on discrediting Jesus on technicalities, that they completely missed the truth being fulfilled in front of their eyes! The requirements of the law were being fulfilled by Jesus Himself. If their hearts were truly full of the scriptures, they would have recognized Who Jesus really was, and not been offended by Him, and everything He did. The doorway to eternal life and relationship with God was standing before them!

All scriptures point to Jesus, you can never separate Him from the Word. This was God's awesome plan all along. How wonderful to know that as we read the Word of God, we read Jesus Himself, and open our hearts to encounter Him through His truth. Just as the Word can never be separate from the person of Jesus, we can never be separate from Him when His Word is laid up in our hearts! Welcome the Word into your heart and expect to encounter the true nature of Jesus in its truth.

# Day 21

## Enriched by the Word

*Colossians 3:16 (NKJV), "Let the word of Christ dwell in you richly in all wisdom, teaching and admonishing one another in psalms and hymns and spiritual songs, singing with grace in your hearts to the Lord."*

Allowing God's Word to dwell in you richly is an intentional decision. The book of James tells us that we are to humbly accept the implanted Word, which is able to save our souls (James 1:21). The soul of man consists of his intellect, emotions, and free will. It's a place we make decisions from. Everything we experience in life is collected and kept in the recesses of our souls. Attached to those experiences are thoughts and emotions. Depending on each experience, the memory and information implanted in our souls can be both positive and negative. Each memory triggers a positive, healthy emotion, or a negative, destructive one. What we can be sure of is whatever our soul is full of, or influenced the most by, is what will chart the path and direction of our lives (Proverbs 23:7).

While we don't always have the power to control our circumstances and experiences, we do possess the power to influence the condition of our souls - and so direct the course of our lives into peace and prosperity. 3 John 1:2 says, *"Beloved, I pray that you may prosper in every way and [that your body] may keep well, even as [I know] your soul keeps well and prospers."* We must intentionally, and consistently renew our minds to the truth of God's Word. It's life and power will heal and redirect every thought, bringing it into agreement with His truth. It's time to live free and enriched by God's Word today!

# Day 22

## Change Your Perspective

*Deuteronomy 6:8-9, "You shall bind them as a sign on your hand, and they shall be as frontlets between your eyes. You shall write them on the doorposts of your house and on your gates".*

God told the children of Israel to always keep His Word before them. Why? Because God wanted to demonstrate His greatness, kindness, and generosity through them as a people to the nations. It was impossible to do this while they had the wrong mindset. Even though God had freed them from 400 years of Egyptian captivity, they still carried a slave mentality. The Bible says they had no faith, and consistently doubted Him and complained against Him. They simply didn't see themselves from His perspective. That's why they needed to constantly be reminded of His truth - He was their God and had set out ways for them to live so that it would go well with them and their descendants! This principle carries through for us today!

Under the New Covenant, we need to constantly renew our minds to the perspective of Who God sees us to be, so that we can live free and flourish! 1 Peter 2:9 says, *"But you are a chosen race, a royal priesthood, a dedicated nation, [God's] own purchased, special people, that you may set forth the wonderful deeds and display the virtues and perfections of Him Who called you out of darkness into His marvellous light."* As you meditate on God's Word, the Holy Spirit reveals truth to you that will bring supernatural change! You will see yourself as He does and live in the fullness of life He has saved you into!

# Day 23

## Well Able Through Grace!

*Ephesians 2:10, "For **we are His workmanship, created in Christ Jesus for good works, which God prepared beforehand that we should walk in them.**"*

Grace is God's supernatural empowerment to strengthen and equip us for a life of victory! Because of His grace, we don't just desire to do His will, we are well able to do it too! Philippians 2:13 says, *"[Not in your own strength] for it is God Who is all the while effectually at work in you [energising and creating in you the power and desire], both to will and to work for His good pleasure and satisfaction and delight."* In short, we cannot live victoriously for Him, without Him.

God never intended for us to live life where He is not the vital necessity. The only way to live the new life we have in Him is through faith, by grace! His grace empowers us to live above any and every circumstance, and it is a free gift we are to enjoy! This life that God has for us isn't difficult to attain, because it's God's original design for us! We are meant to be His workmanship, His masterpiece. At salvation, our spirits are recreated into this original design where we become one with Christ Jesus! Every good work has already been prepared for us to walk in, with Him, and by His grace. All we need to do is respond to His grace, step out in faith, and obey Him! His grace has made us well able to do it.

# Day 24

## Seasoned with Salt

***Proverbs 27:6 (NLT): "Wounds from a sincere friend are better than many kisses from an enemy."***

Have you ever had to engage in an uncomfortable yet essential conversation with a good friend? These are the kind of conversations where the discomfort makes them dreaded, but you just *know* they are necessary and will require growth from all parties. The Wisdom found in Proverbs teaches us that when we set our hearts on sincerity, love, and growth, it is far better than flattery or being left to destructive devices. While confrontation may be difficult, there is such a joy, gratitude and closeness that comes from being loved enough to be corrected.

If you know you need to bring correction to a good friend, be sensitive to the Holy Spirit with regards to the timing and speak the truth in love. If you are the friend who's received the correction from a sincere friend, take it before the Lord with an open heart and allow the Holy Spirit to illuminate what needs to be done to bring the change. Either way, be encouraged and grateful to have these difficult conversations, because they can save a soul from potential destruction.

Remember this effective way of speaking to others: *"Let your speech always be gracious, seasoned with salt, so that you may know how you should answer each person."* (Colossians 4:6 CSB)

# Day 25

## Far Above

*Ephesians 2:6 (AMPC), "And He raised us up together with Him and made us sit down together [giving us joint seating with Him] in the heavenly sphere [by virtue of our being] in Christ Jesus (the Messiah, the Anointed One)."*

According to the Word of God, every born-again believer has been given a position of right standing with Him (2 Corinthians 5:21). Have you noticed however that when some Christian's feel defeated, they often quote, "I'm just a sinner, saved by grace.". The truth is, we **were** all sinners before we came to know Christ Jesus! Sin **had** power over us, but now we have a brand-new nature that hates sin and loves righteousness! We also have the grace of God, that is His supernatural power inside our re-born spirits, to empower us to make the right choices in life. We are well able to walk away from the temptation of sin and choose to live holy lives, that are pleasing to the Lord! Hallelujah!

It's simply not in our re-born nature to sin! The more time we spend in the Word and fellowship with the Lord, the more His Spirit and Word washes over our minds and renews the way we see ourselves. We are not weak-minded people, struggling to try live right before the Lord. He has already made us right in our spirits and has given us the place of victory in Him!

Recognize that whatever is true of Jesus is true of you too. You are no longer subject to sin; you have been given the power and authority to **function in life from far above all evil influences** in Jesus Name.

# Day 26

## Fully Committed

*Galatians 1:10 (NLT), "Obviously, I'm not trying to win the approval of people, but of God. If pleasing people were my goal, I would not be Christ's servant."*

The Apostle Paul was writing to the Church, expressing the importance of preaching the good news of Jesus, and not altering doctrine to suit their audience. Our focus must always remain on being obedient to God and His Word. A well-known preacher said, "The anointing doesn't flow when you obey man, the anointing only flows when you obey God."

The Apostle Paul highlights the truth that if our goal is to please and win the approval of man, we might as well not follow Jesus! It certainly takes great conviction of faith to swim against the stream of popular opinion doesn't it. The truth is anything done outside of faith brings no pleasure to God (Hebrews 11:6). Since faith comes from and is exclusive to the principles of God's Word - anything that contradicts it is not pleasing to Him. In today's society moral corruption has become the norm to the extent that even those who call themselves Christians are confused about what they really believe. Be extremely cautious of the opinions you choose to side with.

If you know the truth, by the standards of God's Word alone, it will bring absolute clarity to you concerning the choices to make and stand by. Today, make the choice to remain fully committed and devoted to pleasing God. When this becomes your ultimate pursuit, you will never fall short of His approval, favor and blessing!

# Day 27

## Answered Prayer

*1 John 3:22 (AMPC), "And we receive from Him whatever we ask, because we [watchfully] obey His orders [observe His suggestions and injunctions, follow His plan for us] and [habitually] practice what is pleasing to Him."*

Obeying God's Word is the key to having our prayers answered. This probably doesn't sit well with believer's who don't believe there is consequence to an ungodly lifestyle. So let's look at this verse another way: *"And whatever we ask we will not receive from Him, because we do not keep His commandments and do not do those things that are pleasing in His sight."* Jesus made this same principle perfectly clear when He said, *"If you live in Me [abide vitally united to Me] and My words remain in you and continue to live in your hearts, ask whatever you will, and it shall be done for you."* (John 15:7).

According to these two scriptures, answered prayer is directly linked to the priority we place on our personal relationship with the Lord, and the measure of His Word we choose to keep alive in our hearts and allow to influence our daily lives. The book of Proverbs confirms that the Lord takes no pleasure in, in fact, He is insulted by the prayers of His children who have deliberately rejected His instructions and chosen to grow cold in their walk with Him. *"One who turns away his ear from hearing the law, even his prayer is an abomination"* (Proverbs 28:9). A heart that is truly pursuing God and the intimacy found in His Presence is a heart that deeply loves His Word and lives by its wisdom. His prayers are a delight to the Lord and will always be answered!

# Day 28

## Let Peace Rule

***Judges 6:24 (AMPC), "Then Gideon built an altar there to the Lord and called it, The Lord is Peace".***

We know that peace is not the absence of war, or the removal of challenging circumstances from our lives. True peace is being in a place of intimately knowing God, and not being a stranger to His covenant promises. It's something we are designed to experience amid turmoil and distressing circumstances. In John 14:27, Jesus assures us that this peace is found in Him, and that He gives it to us freely, so we don't let our hearts become troubled, or afraid. It stops us from being agitated and disturbed; and enables us to refuse fear to intimidate and unsettle us.

Isaiah 26:3, shows us how to enter this place of peace, and keep our hearts and minds there! *"You will guard him and keep him in perfect and constant peace whose mind [both its inclination and its character] is stayed on You, because he commits himself to You, leans on You, and hopes confidently in You."*

By training ourselves to constantly keep the Word of God running in our thoughts, we will experience perpetual peace that will never relent to outward circumstances. When we do this, the peace of God that surpasses all understanding will guard our hearts and minds. It's time to focus on God's truth and have His peace rule in your life!

# Day 29

## Wisdom's Benefits

*Proverbs 2:21 (NLT), "For only the godly will live in the land, and those with integrity will remain in it."*

Proverbs 2 details for us the profound benefits of acquiring wisdom. These benefits begin when we listen to and treasure God's commands; and lead to us inheriting His promises *and* remaining in them. What this means for us when we fully receive and engage in God's Word is this: not only will we be rewarded with God's promises, but we will get to see God's Word proven true again and again. We get to experience God's goodness in the land of the living. When we establish ourselves on the truth of God's Word, we will never feel shame for trusting in its truth and obeying Him! Hallelujah!

We never have to be concerned of being displaced from our blessed state. Because **the Lord** is our blessing, and our reward; and from Him comes every good and perfect gift. Whatever doubt has ever tried to convince you contrary to this truth, it disappears now as you decide to take God at His Word without exception. Living in His promises and benefits is His reward to you for following Him. You can set your hopeful expectation, confession, and testimony on the goodness of God – God's promises are there for *you* to inherit and enjoy.

# Day 30

## God's Precious Gift

*John 15:26 (NKJV), "But when the Helper comes, whom I shall send to you from the Father, the Spirit of truth who proceeds from the Father, He will testify of Me."*

We are extremely blessed to have the precious Holy Spirit dwelling on the inside of us. The very same Spirit that raised Jesus from the dead now dwells in us and quickens our mortal bodies. Every child of God *must* recognize this! Jesus didn't leave us high and dry when He ascended to heaven. He didn't leave us on our own to navigate life by our own power and our own sense of direction. He sent us the same wonderful Helper, the Holy Spirit, Who empowered and guided Him when He was on the earth. The ministry of the Holy Spirit is to guide, empower, and reveal the Person of Jesus to us.

Many believers fall from the faith because they refuse to embrace the gift we have been given, in having a relationship with the Person of the Holy Spirit. He makes fellowship with God possible. Jesus paved the way for reconciliation to the Father by His blood, now the Holy Spirit reveals the character, nature, and mysteries of God to us, and enables us to experience His manifest presence wherever we are. Decide to prioritize getting to know the Person of the Holy Spirit. Honor Him as the priceless gift He is to the body of Christ. He will reveal the Person and will of Jesus to you, and the deep things of God. However, He doesn't reveal these truths to casual enquirers, he looks for diligent seekers. Open your heart to Him today and see how He reveals the wonderful things of Jesus to you.

# Day 31

## Trust and Obey into Victory

*Deuteronomy 20:4 (ESV) "For the Lord your God is He who goes with you to fight for you against your enemies, to give you the victory."*

The God Who parted the sea for the Israelites to walk through on dry ground; and rained down manna from Heaven, and gushed water from a rock in the desert, is the same God we serve today. Hallelujah! When Moses led the Israelites out of Egypt into the promised land, they were only meant to spend a few days travelling, yet their stubborn disobedience and unbelief caused them to spend 40 years wandering in the wilderness. God's original plan and purpose for those who follow Him is always victory, but the length of the journey to it often depends on our willingness to enter a place of rest in Him - where we willingly and confidently trust and obey Him.

In Deuteronomy 28, we read of the blessings of God that overtake His people when we trust and obey Him. The word *blessing* means *God's favour and protection*. God blesses His children, and His attention is turned towards those who obey His Word! Understand today that His plan for your life and future is, and always has been for your good! It includes His abundant blessing and prosperity. Our only responsibility is to love Him and His ways, and walk in them, by the help of His Holy Spirit. The God we serve is fully able to lead us into all victory in this life, and because of Jesus, we already stand positioned for it! Choose to get on board with His plan as you trust and obey the One Who goes before you and leads you into victory!

# SEPTEMBER

# Day 01

## Take It Captive

*2 Corinthians 10:4-5, "For the weapons of our warfare are not carnal but mighty in God for pulling down strongholds, casting down arguments and every high thing that exalts itself against the knowledge of God, bringing every thought into captivity to the obedience of Christ."*

Every thought contrary to the truth of God's Word is in direct violation of His perfect will for our lives. Even though a thought may seem harmless, it is a seed that has the full potential to produce either life or death inside us. That's why we must be extremely intentional in recognizing and discerning the source of our thoughts, and whether they are inspired by the truth of God's Word, or by the lies of the enemy. The Bible says to take every thought that opposes what the Word says captive. That means to stop it in its tracks before it can cause us damage. Once we've recognized that it's not in line with God's Word, we refuse it and immediately replace it with what God says on the matter. Decide to take time to know what God's Words says so you can train your mind to quickly identify which thoughts are good and which thoughts are harmful. This way you will stop the enemy's plan to trip you up before it has an opportunity to prosper.

# Day 02

## A Lifestyle of Praise

*Psalm 113:3 (NKJV), "From the rising of the sun to its going down The Lord's Name is to be praised."*

When we praise the Lord, things begin to happen in the unseen realm that directly affect our natural one. In the Old Testament, the people of God didn't have the Name of Jesus as a weapon, but they did have praise. As New Covenant believer's we have both! As we declare the Name of Jesus in triumphant praise we align our affections and thoughts with the truth of Who God is, and the victory He has already won for us in this life. As a result, our faith in God and His promises is strengthened and emboldened! Which is extremely powerful since faith is the supernatural force that causes every promise of God to become our manifest reality! It literally grabs a firm hold of what exists in the unseen world of the spirit and pulls it into our natural world. It has the power to change every circumstance and cause all things to submit to and align with God's Word. Learn to praise God as a lifestyle, it will build your faith and release it to bring God's promises into your reality!

# Day 03

## Modern-day Religion

*John 2:14 (NLT), "In the Temple area He saw merchants selling cattle, sheep, and doves for sacrifices; He also saw dealers at tables exchanging foreign money."*

Knowing the importance of Passover for all Jews and how crucial it was to have the right, clean animal suitable for sacrifice; money-hungry merchants set up shop to bargain with and cheat God's people - distracting them from their true worship. Today we don't have to make animal sacrifices to the Lord but are called to give Him ourselves as **living sacrifices**. So, we go to church to worship Him and receive His Word that has the power to transform us. The modern-day merchants that come to distract us from this, come in the form of messages that are void of power and faith. They place more emphases on personal comfort and gratification than building us in the truth of God's Word and how to live full of and controlled by His Holy Spirit.

Instead of stirring up faith to make a stand for righteousness in this world, they soften and weaken our resolve and persuade us to conform rather than push against evil agendas. Don't get caught up in modern-day religion that distracts from the power and passion of the Gospel of Jesus Christ. Nothing can substitute the power of being transformed by the truth of His Word, and the joy of being filled and flooded by His Holy Spirit!

# Day 04

## We Shall Not Lack

*Psalm 23:1 (AMPC), "The Lord is my Shepherd [to feed, guide, and shield me], I shall not lack."*

God is our good Shepherd; to feed us, to guide us and to shield us. When we have a personal revelation that He is our source and only has our very best interests at heart, we will wholeheartedly devote our lives to know Him and His ways so that we can walk in them and never lack! Abraham, Moses, Joshua, David, Joseph, and the Apostle Paul all understood this and centered their lives around it. They were convinced that God's ways were the only one's worth following, and that positioning themselves in and under His personal care ensured that no evil thing could rise against them and win. We position ourselves under God's personal care by embracing His Word and not rejecting it. His Word produces faith and life inside us and aligns us with His perfect will for our lives. It empowers us to resist the lies of the enemy and remain focused on the life of victory we have in Christ Jesus. Keeping God's Word alive in our hearts will cause us to be well fed, furnished and fruitful in every aspect of life.

# Day 05

## The Power of God's Word

*Hebrews 4:12 (NKJV), "For the word of God is living and powerful, and sharper than any two-edged sword, piercing even to the division of soul and spirit, and of joints and marrow, and is a discerner of the thoughts and intents of the heart."*

The Word of God is not just some historical book that carries no relevance to our life here and now. In fact, it is very much alive and will always remain relevant for every generation. God's Word carries dynamic power that enables all who believe it to experience triumph, turnaround, and testimonies on a regular basis (Psalm 1:1-3). The devil is not afraid of the written Word however, he is terrified of the believer who has the Word dwelling in him and lives by its truth.

God's Word alive in us produces faith for victory and transforms us into the very image of Jesus - Who defeated the devil and took away his power to harm us. That's why the Bible says the devil comes to steal the Word from us. He is afraid of the Word of God mixed with the faith of the believer! The position the Word holds in your life determines the position God holds in you. He will always honor His Word concerning you. Never underestimate the power of the Word that is alive in you each time you believe it and act upon its truth.

# Day 06

## Equipped to Overcome

*Matthew 4:4 (NLT), "But Jesus told him, 'No! The Scriptures say, 'People do not live by bread alone, but by every word that comes from the mouth of God.'"*

Did you know that what is true of Jesus is true of you? When He walked the earth, Jesus was the perfect example for us and modelled the way we are well able to live in this world. Through the infilling of the Holy Spirit, we are empowered to live just as Jesus did. We were never meant to live out God's purpose for our lives alone! We have been given everything we will ever need to be perfectly equipped to handle every challenge victoriously. After Jesus was baptized in the Holy Spirit, He was led into the wilderness and faced a head-to-head confrontation with the devil. Each time Satan tempted Jesus, the response was the same. The Holy Spirit gave Him an inspired (rhema) Word to combat every deceptive ploy meant to steer Jesus off course from His purpose. Jesus knew He was not going to succeed in what He was destined to do by what the devil or world could offer Him. He had direct access to the very thoughts, guidance, wisdom, and power of God! The truth of God's Word carries it all! We too have been given the indwelling Holy Spirit and the privilege to experience ongoing in-fillings of His Presence and power. Just as He did for Jesus, He does for us. He will highlight the exact truth from God's Word we need to empower us to overcome whatever we face in this life, ensuring we stay on course and directly in line with God's perfect will. Trust the Holy Spirit to make God's Word alive in you and lead you in its truth today.

# Day 07

## Move Forward and Occupy!

*Deuteronomy 2:24-26 (NLT), "Moses continued, "Then the Lord said, 'Now get moving! Cross the Arnon Gorge. Look, I will hand over to you Sihon the Amorite, king of Heshbon, and I will give you his land. Attack him and begin to occupy the land."*

There could be no mistake in interpreting the instruction God gave to Moses through these two phrases: **"Now get moving!"** and **"...occupy the land."** Both are the result and reward of a mindset that is convinced that victory already belongs to us. According to the promises of God's Word, we are not fighting for victory in this life - Jesus has already obtained it for us (John 16:33). Our responsibility is to fill our hearts and minds with the truth of what God has already accomplished for us, and then full of faith, we are to steward that authority one instruction at a time. We occupy our inheritance through absolute faith and obedience, proving we are faithful and can be entrusted with the power to see God's agenda established in every area of our lives. Understand, to occupy there will be opposition. That's where our faith is proven to be true. Instead of drawing back in fear - we push forward in absolute faith and trust, knowing we are being obedient to the One Who has already made the way for us. God's love conquers all and when our hearts are continuously being filled with it - all fear will be driven out and replaced with the favor of God! It's time for you to occupy your spiritual inheritance, so move forward in confidence, knowing your absolute obedience with a heart full of faith and love will see every promise become your joyful possession!

# Day 08

## Divine Instruction

*2 Timothy 3:16-17(NLT), "All Scripture is inspired by God and is useful to teach us what is true and to make us realize what is wrong in our lives. It corrects us when we are wrong and teaches us to do what is right. God uses it to prepare and equip His people to do every good work."*

We serve a very intentional God Who has given us His Word to equip and guide us in His perfect will for our lives. There is no confusion concerning what is right and wrong in the Word. It clearly teaches us what is true so that we can see what deception is. It corrects incorrect mindsets and teaches us to do what is right and pleasing to God. It also trains and equips us to do every good work God has already planned and purposed for us to do (Ephesians 2:10). Hallelujah! How awesome it is to serve a God who gives us step for step wisdom and instruction to live a good, meaningful life; as well as the strength and ability to carry it out! Let's be clear on one thing - the world's definition of right is most often contrary to God's.

If we follow after any opinion that's outside of the truth of God's Word, it will certainly lead to corruption and destruction. So learn to remain attentive to the voice of the Holy Spirit as He leads you in truth, through the instructions of the Word. Rest assured, every instruction in God's Word is inspired by His Own Holy Spirit. He has lovingly given them to us to follow, because they are faultless and filled with divine truth for our good and His pleasure!

# Day 09

## Promise for the Faithful

*Ezra 1:4 (NLT), "Wherever this Jewish remnant is found, let their neighbours contribute toward their expenses by giving them silver and gold, supplies for the journey, and livestock, as well as a voluntary offering for the Temple of God in Jerusalem."*

This day marked the fulfilment of a prophecy God gave through Jeremiah. It stated that the exiles would return to Jerusalem. Just as the Jewish remnant saw the fulfilment of what God had promised – so will you and me. But they didn't just walk out of exile empty-handed, those around them gave them silver and gold, supplies for the journey, livestock, *and* a voluntary offering for God. This promise was for the remnant. The dictionary definition for remnant is a minority of people who have remained faithful to God. If we are faithful to the Lord, we are His remnant, and every promise He has made us, we can be assured we are going to see fulfilled! Not only will we possess it with joy, but we will also see His hand of provision accompany it!

Rejoice today knowing that not only is God going to bless you by delivering on His promises, but you will never walk empty-handed as you go to possess them. What a wonderful, generous God we serve! Psalms 37:25 says, *"I have been young and now am old, yet have I not seen the [uncompromisingly] righteous forsaken or their seed begging bread."* Enjoy His careful attention towards you as you walk faithfully before Him.

Day 10

One in Death and Resurrection

Romans 6:5, *"For if we have been united with Him like this in His death, we will certainly also be united with Him in His resurrection."*

Jesus Christ not only died for us, but we also died with Him! Our old, sinful nature died the moment we accepted the resurrected Jesus as Lord over our lives! The Bible says we became completely new! His Own Spirit recreated our spirit-man, and then He took occupation of it! Hallelujah! When we believe this reality - we begin to comprehend that we cannot live substandard lives. We now live as Christ because it's His Spirit that lives within us!

This means everything we experience in life must be seen through the filter of the victory He won for us on the cross. Nothing that contradicts God's goodness has the power to affect us! Sin, sickness, lack, and misfortune have no right to reside with us. Everything that Satan sends our way, is an illusion in the light of God's Word. Just the same, everything within us that contradicts God's Word must surrender to the Lordship of Jesus. Every thought must constantly be brought into obedience with His Word, as must our conversations and actions. This is what it means to be one with Christ in His death and resurrection.

The more we acknowledge the Person of the Holy Spirit living within us, the more sensitive we become to His leading and His resurrection power within us to release everywhere we go. This was Paul, the Apostle's prayer too - that he may know Christ and the power of His resurrection (Philippians 3:10). This is the key to abundant life - a daily pursuit to know the God that we died with, so He can live victoriously through us!

# Day 11

## Looking unto Jesus

*Hebrews 12:2 (NKJV), "Looking unto Jesus, the author and finisher of our faith, Who for the joy that was set before Him endured the cross, despising the shame, and has sat down at the right hand of the throne of God."*

Jesus endured the full impact of the cross fully focused on the result of reigning in life together with us! His ability to not become distracted by the pure evil, hate, and rejection that was thrust upon Him, kept Him moving forward in His ultimate purpose for our sakes! Hebrews 12:3 urges us to have the same fixed focus on Jesus as we push forward to fulfil the purpose we were set free to obtain! It says, *"Just think of Him Who endured from sinners such grievous opposition and bitter hostility against Himself [reckon up and consider it all in comparison with your trials], so that you may not grow weary or exhausted, losing heart and relaxing and fainting in your minds."* Living out God's purpose for our lives is never going to be without some serious opposition. In truth, there will be a testing of our faith that will require every ounce of steadfast endurance and faith we can muster.

No matter how tough it gets, we will always have a rock-solid hope to fix our eyes on. That hope is Jesus, He is the very reason we keep moving forward in faith! The more we focus on Him, the more we become just like Him, and can have Him live in and through us! Living full in Him is our reward. Destroying the work of the devil and releasing the love and power of God to others is our great prize. Decide today to keep your eyes fixed on the Author and Finisher of your Faith. He is the standard for our Christian living here and now.

# Day 12

## All Things Work to the Good!

Romans 8:28 (NKJV), *"And we know that all things work together for good to those who love God, to those who are the called according to His purpose."*

The Bible says that when God is a partner in what we do, all things will work together for our good. Not some things. All things. Often, the devil attempts to trick believers into thinking that their past will negatively affect the plan and purposes of God for them. However, God can turn around every mistake you've made and incorporate it into His divine plan and purpose, for your good. Take the life of David for example. There was a time when he neglected his relationship and faithfulness to God and fell into sin that had grave consequences for him and his bloodline. He committed adultery with a woman named Bathsheba, and to cover up his sin, he murdered her husband.

On repenting and turning wholeheartedly back to God, despite his serious errors, God raised up a king from the woman David committed adultery with – King Solomon! When David turned back to God, even though he suffered loss because of his sin, God restored him and caused all things to work together for David's well. We may have made regrettable mistakes in our past and wonder if they will handicap our future purpose in God. Understand, when we repent and chose to partner with God in all things, He restores us and causes them to work together for our good, just as He did with David. While we remain submitted and committed to Him, we will walk out His perfect will for our lives.

# Day 13

## Love Openly Displayed

*Mark 14:3-4 (AMPC), "Andwhile He was in Bethany, [a guest] in the house of Simon the leper, as He was reclining [at table], a woman came with an alabaster jar of ointment (perfume) of pure nard, very costly and precious; and she broke the jar and poured [the perfume] over His head. But there were some who were moved with indignation and said to themselves, To what purpose was the ointment (perfume) thus wasted?"*

Mary's display of pure love and devotion to Jesus caused others to become annoyed with her, especially those who didn't share the same devotion she did. This didn't dissuade her at all. She cared only about pouring her love and gratitude onto Jesus. Mary understood the power of sitting at His feet and receiving from Him (Luke 10:39). She experienced the miraculous resurrection power of God when Jesus raised her beloved brother, Lazarus, from the dead (John 11:43-44). Jesus and all He had personally done for her produced a heart of pure love, sincere devotion, and generosity inside her. She was merely acting out what her heart was overflowing with. This kind of sincere, genuine worship is obvious to everyone who witnesses it. That's why it cuts against the grain of those who don't feel the same way. Unless you have personally experienced the redeeming love of Jesus, you will never understand this display of passionate devotion. Those who do not love God wholeheartedly, because they have not recognized or opened their hearts to receive the full extent of His love for them, generally become offended at those who do! Our devotion to Jesus must expose the lack of devotion in others – not for shame, but for change. Jesus Himself endorsed Mary – declaring that her act will be remembered along with the spreading of the Gospel! That's because this kind of response to His undeserving love is the heartbeat of our salvation.

# Day 14

## God's Word - Alive in Us

*John 17:17 (ESV),* *"Sanctify them in the truth; Your Word is truth."*

God's Word is Truth. It's not the opinions or philosophies of man, or a record of hypocritical religious beliefs. It is God's Own thoughts, opinions and will. What's more, it is alive with His power to transform whoever believes in Him and accepts His truth as their own. When we believe that God's Word is the ultimate authority for our lives and choose to walk in its ways through the power of the Holy Spirit - we will inherit every promise it contains! 2 Corinthians 1:20 says *"For all the promises of God in Him are Yes, and in Him Amen, to the glory of God through us."*

The real evidence of our faith in God and His Word, is when we align the way we think, speak, and act with what the Word teaches. The result will be exactly what it promises us (Isaiah 55:11). If it declares peace, prosperity, healing, and life for those who believe it and do what it says - that's exactly what it will produce. In a day and age where many voices compete for our attention and affection, let God's Word be the truth we treasure most. It will set us apart to fulfil what we were born to do - invade this world with the atmosphere of heaven. God's Word, alive in us, will cause us to become living signposts of His blessing on the lives of His own.

# Day 15

## Wise Up and Stand!

*Luke 10:19 (NKJV), "Behold, I give you the authority to trample on serpents and scorpions, and over all the power of the enemy, and nothing shall by any means hurt you."*

When we understand the power of the finished work of the cross, we will acknowledge the truth that we are not to live under the circumstances of life anymore. We will understand that the tables have turned on the devil - he no longer holds the position of authority over us. Jesus took that power from him and transferred it to us (Matthew 28:18, Romans 5:17, Colossians 2:10). This means it's not biblical for us to live harassed and afflicted by the devil. We have been given divine dominion over all things under Christ. We have been delegated the authority to enforce the defeat of the devil on this earth by the power of the Name of Jesus (Mark 16:17). We have been authorized to drive out all darkness by the marvelous light we carry inside us - that light is Christ in us, the hope of glory! This is the reality of every child of God. It's what Christ purchased for us through our redemption. This is the freedom and power God offers us, but many don't operate in it, why? It's only the truth that we know that can set us free! Today, know what was won for you through the death and resurrection of Jesus Christ. Know you are His ambassador, backed by the armies of heaven! His Word in your mouth will cause demons to tremble and mountains to move. What is impossible in the natural becomes possible when you operate in the supernatural force of faith - that only comes as you grow in the knowledge of the Word. So wise up in the Word and stand your ground - In Jesus Name.

# Day 16

## The Anchor of Your Soul

*1 Corinthians 3:11 (NKJV), "For no other foundation can anyone lay than that which is laid, which is Jesus Christ."*

Jesus is the only foundation we are to build our thoughts, attitudes, conversations, and actions on. He is the truth that will hold through every season and storm for eternity. His truth is His Word (John 1:1-3; John 1:14). If the Word is not our firm foundation, we will always be unstable in all we do. Any construction worker knows that if the foundation is weak or poorly laid, it will affect the entire structure. In the same way, if we have not made God's Word the firm foundation of our lives, the moment trouble comes, the weaknesses in what we have built our beliefs on will be revealed. Whatever beliefs we've built that is contrary to the will of God will fall.

Jesus said that if anyone hears His words and does them, they will be like the man who built his house upon the rock (Matthew 7:24-25). That rock speaks of Jesus, and His truth is firm and immovable. Even though we live in a world driven by constant, contradicting change; the one thing that must remain constant in our lives is the unchanging Word of God. When everything around us is tossed about in confusion and fear, let God's Word become the anchor of our souls - keeping us safe and prosperous in all our ways.

# Day 17

## Personal Endorsement

*Acts 2:22 (NLT), "People of Israel, listen! God publicly endorsed Jesus the Nazarene by doing powerful miracles, wonders, and signs through Him, as you well know."*

As the issues of life become more demanding and the pressure to meet goals and accomplish responsibilities increases - prioritizing becomes invaluable. God has given us the capacity and ability to do all these things, provided we keep our time with Him our chief priority. His wisdom teaches us to follow the things of the Spirit before the things of the flesh. When our focus is first and foremost on the things of God, everything else falls into place, more efficiently than if we gave them a higher place of importance, above our time with the Lord. When we follow the life of Jesus, He never neglected the priority of meeting with His Father long before the responsibilities of the day began. Because He made His relationship with the Lord His essential necessity, above all else - God publicly endorsed Him and set His approval on Him by performing powerful signs, wonders, and miracles through Him.

The world will recognize the supernatural working of God in and through us when we choose to give Him the place of honor - the first place, above and before all else. Just like He did for Jesus, He will use this time to infuse us with His ability, strength, and wisdom to accomplish all things efficiently and with excellence. Just as we were created to never live apart from God, we were created to never fulfil our purpose independent of His power and Personal endorsement.

# Day 18

## Faith - Our Spiritual Currency

*Hebrews 11:1 (NKJV), "Now faith is the substance of things hoped for, the evidence of things not seen."*

Faith is the tangible substance of the Word of God we choose to believe before we see it in the natural. That's why God is so impressed by our faith - it's really the best way we can prove to Him that we believe and trust His Word on a matter, before we physically see it. The life of the spirit is based on the currency of faith. Just as we believed the Word for our eternal salvation, we believe what it says about our identity in Christ. None of these foundational truths become our reality without faith. Romans 10:9 teaches us that faith is in the heart and is expressed through our words. Scripture also teaches us that the source of faith is the Word of God (Romans 10:17). If our hearts are filled with things that are not in line with the truth of God's Word - faith will not grow in us, and it will certainly not be carried out in our conversations either. That's because it's from the abundance of the heart that the mouth speaks (Luke 6:45). If we are not speaking the Word of God that we believe in our hearts, we are not speaking faith. As a result, we will never walk in the reality of the promises the Word says we can have as children of God. Choose to fill your heart with the truth of God's Word so faith can grow and be carried on your words - making every unseen promise your physical reality!

# Day 19

## Surrender to the Word

***Revelation 19:13 (NLT) "He wore a robe dipped in blood, and His title was the Word of God."***

Whenever we hear the phrase, "Word of God", the first name that should come to my mind is Jesus! This is such a beautiful revelation. John 1:14 says Jesus was the Word made flesh and walked on this earth, representing His Father. Just as He came to reveal and represent the Father to the world, the Holy Spirit, Who lives in us, reveals Jesus to us as we spend time in the written Word. The Holy Spirit makes the written Word come alive in our hearts when we receive it with faith, believing what it says. It becomes powerful and active in our lives and can change the circumstances in our lives!

Revelation 19:13 says Jesus holds the title: 'The Word of God!' So as we surrender ourselves to the Word and accept it's truth as the ultimate authority for our lives, we are in fact, surrendering our lives to Jesus, giving Him the ultimate authority over us. Now, we can confidently know that as we hold on to His truth, God will perform everything He says in His Word concerning us! Release His Word over any impossible circumstance today, and see it go to work, in Jesus Name!

# Day 20

## Completely Yielded

*Ezekiel 2:2 (NLT), "The Spirit came into me as He spoke, and He set me on my feet. I listened carefully to His words."*

When Ezekiel had his encounter with the Lord, he was called and commissioned for a specific purpose that was set out for him before the creation of the world. His awe at the glory of God made him fall, face down, on the ground and he heard a voice speaking to him. Even when the voice told him to stand up, he could not on his own. It took the Spirit of God empowering him to stand and enable him to fully take in what God was saying, so he could obey it. When we recognize that we are not only called and commissioned by God for a specific purpose that was set out before the foundation of the world, but we also pay attention to every Word He speaks to our hearts and we read in His written Word. We also understand we are completely dependent on and empowered by God's Own Spirit to do what God requires. It will take our daily surrender to the power of the Holy Spirit to sustain and continue to empower us to walk in faith and obey - doing mighty exploits for His kingdom. Yield to the Spirit of God today. Let this same disposition that was in Ezekiel be in you as you say, *"I will obey God all the days of my life; I will do as He leads; and I will completely rely on His power as I do so."*

# Day 21

## Know the Truth!

*Genesis 3:1, "Now the serpent was more cunning than any beast of the field which the Lord God had made. And he said to the woman, 'Has God indeed said, 'You shall not eat of every tree of the garden?'"*

The devil consistently attempts to make people question the validity of God's character and Word. The phrase, *"Has God indeed said,"* began the downward spiral of doubt in the mind and heart of Eve. Once there is the slightest questioning of God's will on one issue, every other instruction begins to hold less ground in our lives, including our impression of His good character and faithfulness towards us. If Eve held onto her personal revelation of the steadfast character and will of God for their lives she would have dismissed the devil on his first attempt to lead her astray. Instead, his cunning twist of the truth with statements like, *"you won't die"*, and *"your eyes will be opened"* and *"you'll become like God"*, led her to believe a lie that would cost them dearly. Adam and Eve already possessed eternal life with God. They were able to enjoy unbroken fellowship with Him where no truth was hidden from them. They were already made in the image and likeness of God and were empowered and commissioned to have dominion and replenish the earth. They were given authority over all things, including the devil. Never let the devil deceive you concerning the truth of who you are in Christ and all you have been given as you live in Him. All that Adam and Eve lost has been restored to us through the finished work of the cross - know the truth, stand your ground and live strong in Him!

# Day 22

## Topple the Devil's Kingdom

*Acts 17:6 (NKJV), "But when they did not find them, they dragged Jason and some brethren to the rulers of the city, crying out, 'These who have turned the world upside down have come here too.'"*

As children of God, we have been empowered by the Holy Spirit to be true ambassadors of Christ! The more truth we learn and believe from the Word of God, the more formidable we become to the enemy's kingdom and the status quo of this world's systems. The work of the Holy Spirit in our lives produces a light that no darkness can overshadow or consume. As you declare the truth of God over circumstances with faith and confidence, know that the authority you have been given will see unseen forces shift and change will come. The kingdom of darkness suffers great defeat when we know, believe, and declare the truth and command light over darkness. Romans 8:19 declares, *"For the earnest expectation of the creation eagerly waits for the revealing of the sons of God."*

Since we carry Christ in us, we carry the answers to the problems that plague the world. Christ died for a people who would seek Him and His ways first and then walk in His authority and power to establish His kingdom on this earth. So, we lead all people to the Lord by loving, healing, and restoring their lives with the power of God, while coming against the evil principalities that have already been defeated by Jesus, our commander and chief. It's time to turn the world upside down as we restore the correct order and topple the devil's hold over people's lives.

# Day 23

## Resist the Devil

*James 4:7 (NKJV), "Therefore submit to God. Resist the devil and he will flee from you."*

Jesus declared that the devil had nothing in Him (John 14:30). He would not allow the enemy a single hold in His life. He immediately recognized a thought or idea that was in opposition to the truth of His Heavenly Father, resisted it, and replaced it with the correct one. As children of God and imitators of Christ, we are to follow Jesus' example. In Ephesians 4:27, Paul says, *"Leave no [such] room or foothold for the devil [give no opportunity to him]."* We are responsible to keep a guard on what we allow into our hearts and minds. 1 John 5:18 says, *"but he who has been born of God keeps himself, and the wicked one does not touch him."*

We can **keep ourselves** through the help of the Holy Spirit. The Word says He leads us into all truth! The more time we spend in the Word of God, the more the Holy Spirit reveals God's truth to us and makes it alive in us. This way we become extremely sensitive to what is of God, and what is not. 1 John 5:18 says, *"We know [absolutely] that anyone born of God does not [deliberately and knowingly] practice committing sin, but the One Who was begotten of God carefully watches over and protects him [Christ's divine presence within him preserves him against the evil], and the wicked one does not lay hold (get a grip) on him or touch [him]."* Hallelujah!

Yield to the Holy Spirit's warnings, resist the devil, and he will flee from you!

# Day 24

## Set the Oppressed Free

*Mark 5:6-7 (AMPC), "And when from a distance he saw Jesus, he ran and fell on his knees before Him in homage, and crying out with a loud voice, he said, 'What have You to do with me, Jesus, Son of the Most High God? [What is there in common between us?] I solemnly implore you by God, do not begin to torment me!'"*

The demon possessed man lived in absolute torment and agony. His bondage was so severe, even the thought of being free seemed impossible! Yet, at the sight of Jesus, the demon recognized His authority. He made the man fall on his knees before Jesus, in complete surrender to a power that was far greater than his. At this moment, the demoniac knew Jesus could save him. He had the power to accept and receive his deliverance.

Any person under Satan's rule has the power to choose to be free when they encounter the Presence of Jesus. It just takes a decision to surrender to His Lordship and accept His delivering power that will break every demonic oppression! Jesus has given us His power and authority over unclean spirits, to cast them out, and to heal all kinds of sickness and disease (Matthew 10:1, Mark 3:15). As we live full of His Word and full of His Holy Spirit, we will walk in the confidence of knowing we carry the love and power of God in us to set those who are oppressed free.

# Day 25

## Covenant Purpose

*Genesis 18:17,19 (AMPC), "And the Lord said, 'Shall I hide from Abraham [My friend and servant] what I am going to do, ⋯ For I have known (chosen, acknowledged) him [as My own], so that he may teach and command his children and the sons of his house after him to keep the way of the Lord and to do what is just and righteous, so that the Lord may bring Abraham what He has promised him.'"*

God reveals His covenant plans to His children and shows them their own part in them. God told Abraham He would bless and multiply him and lead him to a land He would show him. God called Jeremiah to be a prophet. He would lead him and put His words in his mouth. Samson's mother was to raise her child as a Nazirite, and never cut his hair. He would be used by God to deliver Israel from the 40year captivity of the Philistines. For us, who have been grafted into Christ, 1 Peter 2:9-10 declares that we are, *"a chosen people, a royal priesthood, a holy nation, God's special possession".* Acts 17:28 says, *"...in Him we live and move and have our being; ... For we are also His offspring."* We are not puppets at the mercy of a master puppeteer. We are given a free will to surrender our lives to the Lord, to know Him, and work together with Him completing a purpose that is far greater than we could accomplish independent of Him. God is not in the business of hiding His plans from us. He wants us to know, through experience, the great things He desires to do through us. As we draw near to Him, He reveals His heart to us, and His Spirit gives us the desire and ability to work with Him. In Psalm 25:14, David wrote, *"The friendship of the Lord is for those who fear Him, and He makes known to them His covenant."* Give God your willing and obedient heart, and you'll never look back in regret for doing so!

# Day 26

## Anointed for Purpose

*Luke 4:18 (NKJV), "The Spirit of the Lord is upon Me, because He has anointed Me To preach the gospel to the poor; He has sent Me to heal the brokenhearted, To proclaim liberty to the captives And recovery of sight to the blind, to set at liberty those who are oppressed;"*

Directly translated, the word *anoint* means *to rub or smear oil, or perfume upon an individual.* In both the Old and New Testaments, this oil would represent the Presence of the Holy Spirit. When the priests or kings were appointed by God, they would be anointed with oil, symbolizing God's Presence being poured upon them, enabling and empowering, and setting them apart for the Divine purpose they were called to function in. In Luke 4:18, Jesus was declaring that the power of the Holy Spirit upon His life was what would empower Him to perform what He was purposed to do on the earth. The truth is if Jesus needed the anointing of God to fulfil His purpose, then we undoubtably need it too. The anointing is the empowerment of the Holy Spirit, and the defining mark of God upon a believer. When we operate under the anointing of God, we work with God. His supernatural power accompanies our faith and efforts resulting in supernatural results that affirm we are sent by God to fulfil His purpose. If you have been baptized in the Holy Spirit, with the evidence of speaking in tongues, and choose to remain saturated in His power, then you are anointed and filled with the power of God to do His will. Today, allow the Lord to fill you afresh with His anointing oil. Listen to Him speak to your heart, and as you obey - signs and wonders will follow.

# Day 27

## The Evidence of Your Faith

*Genesis 26:14 (NKJV), "...for he had possessions of flocks and possessions of herds and a great number of servants. So the Philistines envied him."*

God has anointed you to be envied and not pitied. Just like it did for Isaac, the world must be able to look at your life and see the evidence of your faith in God. Faith without evidence is not true faith. Think about it, God has put everything in place to ensure your success and increase. Even when circumstances appear to be opposite to what you are believing for, if we refuse to give up believing and confessing God's promises from the conviction of our hearts, we will see those circumstances yield to the Word and change in our favor. Provided we are doing whatever the Word instructs us to do concerning the promise. Romans 8:28 says, *"And we know that all things work together for good to those who love God, to those who are the called according to His purpose."* If we love God, we are obeying His Word and are busy with what He has called us to do. This is when we can stand confidently, even in the face of stubborn circumstance and know things are going to change and work towards our favor! Focus your attention on loving the Lord and being busy doing His will – then, whatever promise you have applied faith to, will become your reality. Those around you will have no doubt that you are living in the evidence of your faith! Hallelujah!

# Day 28

## Christ Living in Me

***John 12:26 (NLT) "Anyone who wants to serve Me must follow Me, because My servants must be where I am. And the Father will honour anyone who serves Me."***

Jesus said, *"...My servants must be where I am."* When we accepted Jesus not only as our Savior, but also as our Lord, we made the decision to firmly follow Him. This means His ways, will and Spirit are given precedence over our own will. Believe it or not, this is not an impossibility, or a difficult "hoop to jump through'. We have God's Word, and His very Own Spirit living inside us to teach, guide, and lead us into all truth! And He doesn't do this with a firm hand of discipline either. If we open our hearts to the Lord, He will literally pour His love into us, causing our relationship with Him to flow with joy and peace! We become so in love with Him, and so impressed with His nature and His ways, that learning about Him and following Him becomes the absolute delight of our hearts! The result is always the same, we will prosper and succeed in every area of life, and whatever we ask of Him, we receive (Psalm 1:3, Joshua 1:8, John 15:7). As children of God, we are meant to be known as His followers, representatives, and His ambassadors. So, it goes without saying that our lives need to reflect our love to serve and follow the Lord. Our greatest goal is to echo the words of Paul, where our own will has been swallowed up in God's will, and we can confidently say, *"It's no longer I that live, but Christ Who lives in Me!".*

# Day 29

## Carry the Reality of Heaven

*2 Timothy 3:1,5 (NKJV) "But know this, that in the last days perilous times will come: For men will be... lovers of pleasure rather than lovers of God, having a form of godliness but denying its power. And from such people turn away!"*

2 Timothy 3:1-5 gives a descriptive list of the character decline we are to expect from people who have rejected Christ. As well as those who say they know Him yet refuse the work of the Holy Spirit in their lives and the transforming power of the Word. scripture tells us that they will have a form of godliness but reject the power that makes them Godly. They will act religious, but their words will be empty of the love and power of God, that is evident in those who know Him and belong to Him. Jesus came to save all people; He gave us the free will to choose to receive His saving grace. But the choice must be made all the same. You will find many leaders, in prevalent positions declare that all people are children of God, no matter their life-choices. Don't be caught up in their deceiving words that entice you to compromise. The Word clearly tells us that those who are led by the Spirit of God, they are the sons of God. In these last days, never be ashamed to stand out for the truth you know. Let the love and power of God speak for you as you carry the reality of heaven in you, to those who are looking for the truth.

# Day 30

## A Supernatural Display of His Goodness

*John 2:5 (NLT), "But His mother told the servants, 'Do whatever He tells you.'"*

The very first miracle Jesus performed, showing off the goodness of God, was at the wedding in Cana. It's most fitting to use the celebration of a wedding feast as the backdrop for our first lesson in working miracles! That's because every motive God has concerning invading our natural world with the supernatural is to bring people joy! When we follow the lead of the Holy Spirit and influence the world around us with His love and power, we must always remember that the fruit of joy is going to be evident in the lives of those we touch! The other significant truth we learn from this miraculous event is revealed in Mary's simple faith. We can draw great value from the instruction she gives to the servants: *"Do whatever He tells you to do."*

As we practice instant obedience to God's Word, we will see every result it promises to deliver! Jesus only did what His Father instructed Him to do, and it always resulted in a glorious success. A life set apart for the supernatural has everything to do with our faith in and obedience to God's Word. Practice listening to and obeying His voice as He speaks directly to your spirit. You will see how it will lead you to display God's goodness in a supernatural way!

# OCTOBER

# Day 01

## Tell it Like it is!

*John 9:25 (NLT), "'I don't know whether he is a sinner,' the man replied. 'But I know this: I was blind, and now I can see!'"*

A man born blind encountered Jesus and the impossible happened - he received his sight! Here was a man who lived his entire life without the ability to see the ones he loved, or the beauty of the world around him. This was his normal, it was something he, and everyone who knew him had settled for - he was blind from the day he took his first breath and would be blind until he breathed out his last. But then Jesus came into His life! How could he ever be the same again? But rather than celebrating this glorious miracle, the religious leaders interrogated him in a desperate attempt to cast doubt on the legitimacy of Jesus. Even in today's world there are still those obsessing over side-tracking miracle-holders with cross-questioning. If they could just poke a hole in the theory of God's will and power to see all people healed and set free, they could justify their own disillusionment. We would do well to learn from this man who refused to enter debate over his miracle! Just as he did, we must shrug off the cross-examination and sound out loud the truth and nothing but the truth. Clever debates and arguments will only distract you from living out your miracle with great joy. Let the evidence of God's abounding goodness in your life speak loudly and clearly as you tell it as it is!

# Day 02

## The BEST News Ever Told!

*Matthew 24:14, "And this gospel of the kingdom will be preached in all the world as a witness to all the nations, and then the end will come."*

The gospel of the kingdom is the BEST news this world could ever receive! Telling a prisoner who has been subject to misery, hopelessness, and agonizing mental and physical torment that he can be set free - is the BEST news he could ever receive! Well, this is the message of God's kingdom! Through sin, the devil literally held us captive in spiritual darkness with no hope for the future. We were completely at the mercy of his manipulation of circumstances, sickness, lack, fear, and every other mental and physical torment. Then, praise God, Jesus came into our world! He took every evil curse and sentence the devil had over us, and placed it upon Himself, as the ultimate sacrifice, in our place! He paid the ransom for our complete freedom with His Own blood! Then He rose again, from the dead, and was given the highest place of power and authority over all principalities and power! What's more, He has taken everyone who believes in Him and accepts His Lordship over their lives, and placed us right with Him, in that place of rule and authority! This means we get to live in victory over the devil and do exploits for God's kingdom forever! We can live free, healed, and prosperous - with a powerful, glorious purpose! Today, choose to be someone that tells others the BEST NEWS they will ever hear!

# Day 03

## Testify!

*1 Corinthians 1:30 (NKJ), "But of Him you are in Christ Jesus, who became for us wisdom from God—and righteousness and sanctification and redemption—..."*

As children of God, we are all called to be ambassadors of Christ! This may seem a little daunting, but thank the Lord, we are well able to live up to this call! How? Well, firstly by believing what the Word says we are! Romans 3:22 declares that we have been made the righteousness of God, through our faith in Christ Jesus. Towards the end of 1 Corinthians chapter 1, Paul explains how we cannot take any glory or credit for the position we now have in Christ Jesus. It is an astounding miracle that happened to us! The power of God literally re-created our spirits to be brand new - without even a trace of sin, or its consequence! Then the Holy Spirit came and took up residence in our re-created spirits! Now we have access to direct, un-broken fellowship with God. As we spend time acknowledging His Presence in us and renewing our minds to the wisdom of His Word, we open our hearts to receive fresh surges of His life and power, causing us to fill up, flood, and overflow with Himself! It's the life of Christ in us that enables us to live righteous, sanctified, redeemed lives - representing Him well, as His ambassadors here. So, draw near to Him and let His power that is at work in you display His goodness and bring Him glory!

# Day 04

## Here Comes Your Wave of Hope

*Hebrews 10:35 (NKJ), "Therefore do not cast away your confidence, which has great reward."*

Hope is a supernatural virtue that undergirds our faith and is never dependent on natural circumstances. It's what gives us a sure confidence to hold on and push forward amid every good fight of faith in our lives. That's because Godly hope is having a clear mental picture of what God's Word has promised us. It can create and maintain an earnest expectation within us to see what God has promised to become our reality. That's why the Bible says the Word of God produces a sure hope that becomes the anchor to our souls! Romans 4:18 says that Abraham chose to ignore the hopelessness of his natural body and placed his hope in God's promise for him to become the father of many nations! Romans 15:13 says the God of hope will fill us with all joy and peace as we choose to believe Him and will cause us to **abound** in hope by the power of the Holy Spirit. That word **abound** gives the picture of a wave coming over us and overtaking us. We can expect a surge of supernatural hope to wash over us and continue without fading in force or power as we fix our gaze on the truth of God's Word concerning us - until that promise becomes our physical reality.

# Day 05

## Every Opposition Defeated

*Deuteronomy 28:7 (NKJV), "The Lord will cause your enemies who rise against you to be defeated before your face; they shall come out against you one way and flee before you seven ways."*

Whatever situation you are facing today, know that as a faithful follower and lover of Jesus, you are not facing it alone. What's more, God is backing you with His power and has already secured your victory (John 16:33). As you come before the Lord, He will give you His strategy to come through triumphantly. That strategy always begins with you being in His Presence. When David was faced with danger and calamity, he would fall on his face before the Lord - seeking His Presence first. He knew this was where his help would come from. Hebrews 4:16 says, *"Let us therefore come boldly to the throne of grace, that we may obtain mercy and find grace to help in time of need."*

It's in God's Presence that His love and peace casts out all fear. Without that hounding fear, we can hear His voice clearly, be strengthened in our spirits, and receive the exact Word we need to build our faith upon and move forward in triumph. Never underestimate God's ability to move on your behalf as you stand in faith and declare His Word for your victory!

# Day 06

## Secured Victory

***Psalms 119:162, "I rejoice at Your word as one who finds great treasure."***

When the Word of God takes preference over all else in our lives, victory is secured! This doesn't mean we won't face trials and things that contradict God's promises. It does mean we have the treasure of His Word to know what His perfect will is for us so we can exercise our faith to contend for each promise. The Word shows us the authority we've been given to stand our ground in faith and command all things to come into line with the kingdom of God (Matthew 18:19).

The Word also explains our benefits of living under the New Covenant, in Christ: We don't live afraid of the devil and the curse of poverty, sickness, and separation from God's best for us. Instead, we stand in authority over the devil and all his works (Luke 9:1, 10:19). We see him flee as we live submitted to the Lord (James 4:7); and we know we have been made righteous through the blood of Jesus - so no weapon formed against us will prosper (Isaiah 54:17). All these wonderful truths, and many more besides, prove the Word of God to be one of the greatest treasures we will ever possess! It literally provides the keys to living in victory! As you give God's Word the honor it deserves in your life, it will bring you great joy, peace, and success as it teaches you your position in Christ, how to refuse fear, and live each day in overcoming faith!

# Day 07

## Faith to See People Set Free!

*Matthew 17:19-20a (AMPC), "Then the disciples came to Jesus and asked privately, 'Why could we not drive it out?'. He said to them, 'Because of the littleness of your faith [that is, your lack of firmly relying trust] ….'"*

In Matthew 17 we read of three disciples and Jesus returning from the mountain to find the remaining disciples in a hot dispute with Jewish scribes. The disciples tried to expel a dangerous demon that was victimizing a young boy, but the demon would not obey them. When the disciples asked Jesus why they couldn't cast it out, He told them it was their lack of faith. He explained that to do the work of God, they need to have absolute faith and trust in Him. We must remember that faith to operate in the power of God, in this case, to drive out demon spirits, works powerfully in the context of our relationship with Him.

Once we've committed our lives to His Lordship, we begin to partner with Him. We learn how to confidently trust and obey Him. As our faith grows, so does our capacity to hold and operate in His supernatural strength and power. The more we surrender to the fresh infilling of the Holy Spirt, and have His Word build faith inside us, we line up our thinking and behavior with His, and confidently follow His lead, in faith, to see people set free!

# Day 08

## Pruned for Good Success

*2 Timothy 4:3 (NLT): "For a time is coming when people will no longer listen to sound and wholesome teaching. They will follow their own desires and will look for teachers who will tell them whatever their itching ears want to hear."*

Whenever we find ourselves at a place where Scripture demands more of us – a deeper commitment, a finer character, more giving of ourselves to God's will above personal convenience – we're in a good place. It's the best time to lean in rather than avoid what we've read. Jesus said if we love Him we will keep His commands. This means taking the **whole truth** of the Word – in its entirety – even when it's uncomfortable. Our complete surrender to the truth of God's Word, invites His purifying fire to deal with those mindsets that hold us back from walking in the greater things He has for us. The hay, wood and stubble are burned away – to bring out what is of true value in us. Resolving to be diligent students and doers of the Word, through the personal tutorship of the Holy Spirit, will result in Him cutting off every hinderance to His perfect and glorious will for our lives. Proverbs 16:16 says, *"How much better it is to get skillful and godly Wisdom than gold! And to get understanding is to be chosen rather than silver."* Embrace the teaching and wisdom of the Word of God, in its entirety. Welcome its pruning in your life - it will lead you into righteousness, peace, and the joy of the Holy Ghost - while making your way prosperous and giving you good success!

# Day 9

## Violent Faith

*1 Timothy 6:12 (NKJV), "Fight the good fight of faith, lay hold on eternal life, to which you were also called and have confessed the good confession in the presence of many witnesses."*

Faith is a force, but it's also forceful. Every child of God must come to recognize that our adversary, the devil, is not a gentleman. According to John 10:10, his agenda is clear. He is bent on killing, stealing, and destroying any good thing in our lives. Now, the finished work of the cross sealed his defeat and broke his power over us to harm us, but he is a criminal by nature, and will continue to take what he wants until he is stopped by those who use their authority to stand up to him. That would be us! That's why the Bible tells us to be vigilant and aware of his nature and tactics, and to stand our ground in faith, in the authority Jesus has given us (1 Peter 5:8-9). It instructs us to withstand the devil; to be firm in faith against his onset—rooted, established, strong, immovable, and determined!

The truth is this, what you do not confront you can never conquer. Matthew 11:12 says, *"And from the days of John the Baptist until now the kingdom of heaven suffers violence, and the violent take it by force."* We must be people who possess violent faith! Not a slither of hope in the storms of life, but a violent force that empowers us to rise above every challenge, declare the will of the Lord, and enforce the devil's defeat. It's time to lay hold of all God has promised you and entrusted you to do for His kingdom - fight the good fight of faith and let the devil suffer the violent force of its power.

# Day 10

## Unashamed to Stand

*John 12:42-43 (NLT), "Many people did believe in Him, however, including some of the Jewish leaders. But they wouldn't admit it for fear that the Pharisees would expel them from the synagogue. For they loved human praise more than the praise of God."*

In John 12, Jesus was performing many signs, wonders and miracles. Even the religious leaders believed in the works He was doing! These leaders had witnessed with their own eyes the proof that Jesus was doing the work of God, and yet they still chose to speak against Him and confess their unbelief in Him. Their fear of being cast out and expelled from their position in society and the synagogue was greater than their fear of rejecting the Son of God. They were more driven by their ambition to keep face and be popular than pleasing God. When we refuse to conduct our lives from an eternal perspective - weighing carefully what we choose to stand for considering the truth we know - we set ourselves up for destruction. As believers, we most certainly will be held accountable for what side of the truth we publicly stand for. The Bible has strong standards and principles that are right and lead to the prosperity of our spirits, souls, and bodies. They are always relevant for all generations and every area of life. The world's standards will always oppose the truth and righteous ways of God's kingdom. For the righteous, this means making a stand for no compromise, especially when it's not popular, or even dangerous. But there is great reward for those who know their God, love His ways, and stand, unashamedly for His truth.

# Day 11

## Keep on Believing!

*Mark 5:36 (AMPC), "Overhearing but ignoring what they said, Jesus said to the ruler of the synagogue, 'Do not be seized with alarm and struck with fear; only keep on believing.'"*

In this life there may be times where things suddenly happen and seem to knock the wind out our sails and turn our world upside down! This is what happened to the ruler of the synagogue in Mark chapter 5. He had rushed to Jesus, convinced He had the power to heal his dying daughter. After Jesus said He would come to his home to heal her, a messenger interrupted them and delivered the dreaded news that it was too late - his daughter was dead. Jesus fully aware of the tremendous blow this devastating news had on the ruler, made a point to help him regain the faith-filled focus he previously had. Even when it appears to be impossible, our faith in God can overcome **every** obstacle that stands in the way of us receiving the fulfilment of His promise. We can picture Jesus looking intently into the eyes of that alarmed father, and saying the words that literally snapped him out of despair, *"Do not be seized with alarm and struck with fear; only keep on believing."* Then Jesus went with him to his home and raised his daughter from the dead! Regardless of how impossible it seems - choose to ignore the unbelieving threats, focus your faith on God's Word and you will see His promise fulfilled!

# Day 12

## Fresh Fire

***Leviticus 6:12 (NKJV),** "And the fire on the altar shall be kept burning on it; it shall not be put out. And the priest shall burn wood on it every morning and lay the burnt offering in order on it; and he shall burn on it the fat of the peace offerings."*

The fire upon the alter was lit supernaturally by God, but it was to be maintained by the priests every single day. There was to be fresh wood added, so the fire never faltered and went out. In context of the New Testament believer, a spiritual fire from God is ignited in the spirit-man when we become born-again. When we receive the baptism of the Holy Spirit, that fire is accelerated! Then, from day to day, each believer has the responsibility to maintain and keep that spiritual fire burning. The fresh wood needed to keep that fire blazing, is the fresh, living Word of God we receive into our hearts and minds. It's also the daily surrender to the Holy Spirit, and the infilling of His power. That power infuses our spirits with supernatural strength! It also kindles the love, passion, and desire for us to know God more, walk in His ways, and carry His power to others. We must be a people who burn with fresh fire in our hearts! Today, settle in your heart that you will daily feed on the Word of God, and drink deeply from the power of His Holy Spirit. As you do, the fire in your spirit will never die out, but remain strong and vital for Him.

# Day 13

## The Reward of Generosity!

*Proverbs 11:25 (NKJV), "The generous soul will be made rich, and he who waters will also be watered himself."*

Paul instructed the church at Philippi to esteem others better than themselves (Philippians 2:3). The Scriptures have many common threads of truth running through them. One being the principle of unselfishly considering others above ourselves. Something to remember concerning the teachings of the Word, is that willful obedience to it always results in great reward. One translation of Proverbs 11:25 says *"those who refresh others will themselves be refreshed".* When we are trusting the Lord for a breakthrough in a particular area, it's easy to become so self-focused, we overlook the pressing needs of others around us. However, many times our breakthrough is manifest the moment we place the needs of others before our own. Faith works by love, so make a point of walking in love towards others and being generous - while you're believing for your own breakthrough. You will be amazed at the goodness of God that's released right back into your life as you act in selfless generosity towards others.

# Day 14

## Place a Demand on God's Power

*Mark 5:28-29 (AMPC), "For she kept saying, 'If I only touch His garments, I shall be restored to health.' And immediately her flow of blood was dried up at the source, and [suddenly] she felt in her body that she was healed of her [distressing] ailment."*

What is impossible with man, is possible for God. We often place too much faith in science and the limited knowledge of man. If we would only place more faith in God and His Word, our lives would probably look quite different. We can certainly learn from the woman in Mark 5. After exhausting her finances and efforts on the best, earthly opinions, and expertise she had access to, she fixed her attention on Jesus. She knew she needed more than what any doctor or remedy could offer her and was convinced it would come from Him. So, she kept confessing her healing would come the moment she touched His garment. Her steadfast faith came from hearing the reports of Jesus, and grew stronger inside her, until it became revelation truth in her heart. This woman understood Jesus had authority over her ailment, and that He carried the power within Him to heal her. It was her faith that placed a demand on His power the moment she reached out and touched Him. As a result, she received everything she had purposed in her heart. Like that woman, we must allow the truth of the Word we hear to dwell richly inside us. We must also be careful to only confess that truth, and nothing else. This way our faith will place a demand on the power of God, just as hers did, and we will see what we have set our hearts on become our reality too.

# Day 15

## Grow in Wisdom and Favor

*Isaiah 11:2 (NLT), "And the Spirit of the Lord will rest on Him— the Spirit of wisdom and understanding, the Spirit of counsel and might, the Spirit of knowledge and the fear of the Lord."*

The prophet Isaiah prophesied that Jesus would walk with the Spirit of the Lord resting on Him. We know this is what caused Him to grow in wisdom and stature, and favor with God and man (Luke 2:40). The Bible teaches on the many benefits of Godly wisdom. It says wisdom will protect us, guard us, make us great, honor us, shower on us beauty and grace, lead us in straight paths, propel us, and grant us a long, good life (Proverbs 4). All these things are certainly desirable!

The Bible says Jesus grew in wisdom, so we know we can do that too. In fact, James 1:5 tells us all we need to do is ask for wisdom and God will freely give it to us! The first place we can find wisdom is from God's Word! As we spend time in the Word, we can trust the Holy Spirit to make that word come alive in us. Its truth will be made plain to us, and as we apply its principles, just like Jesus - we will begin to grow in favor with God and man, reflecting His glory everywhere we go.

# Day 16

## Go Look Again!

*1 Kings 18:43 (NKJV), "'Go up now, look toward the sea.'. So he went up and looked, and said, 'There is nothing.'. And seven times he said, 'Go again.'".*

Friend don't give up on six when the breakthrough is coming on seven! In the above scripture God sends Elijah to declare to King Ahab that after a long period of drought, rain is on its way. This happened to be right after a glorious show-down between the prophets of Baal and Elijah, as to whose God truly lived. The contest ended with a killing frenzy, where Elijah, under the hand of God, single handily slaughtered every one of the 400 prophets. Now that the evil manipulators were literally removed from the high places over Israel, God would break the terrible drought and bring relief to the land and His people, despite their unfaithful hearts towards Him. Even though there was no physical sign of rain, God had given Elijah a Word, and he refused to acknowledge anything that was contrary to it. On the 7th command for his servant to report for a sign of rain, he finally reported a cloud, the size of a man's hand. Regardless of the size of the sign - Elijah was satisfied! He knew God's Word would produce what He said! What followed afterward was a torrential downpour of rain! It's time for God's people to place their unmovable faith in His Word again! It's a fight of faith that we are in, and we must lay hold of God's Word and refuse to be moved until we see it produce what it promises in our lives. Whatever you've been believing God for, don't give up, GO LOOK AGAIN until that breakthrough has become your reality.

# Day 17

## Purpose Greater than Ourselves

*Matthew 10:38 (AMPC), "And he who does not take up his cross and follow Me [cleave steadfastly to Me, conforming wholly to My example in living and, if need be, in dying also] is not worthy of Me."*

To take up our cross and follow Jesus has everything to do with living in and for Him, and not ourselves. Just like Him, we are here for a purpose that is greater than ourselves. So, we lay everything down, including our pride and popularity, to fulfil the assignment we were created to do. In Philippians 3:10, Paul speaks about this determined purpose: to know the Person of Jesus more; to know the power of His resurrection; and to share in His sufferings. All of which would cause us to be completely transformed into the likeness of Jesus. The sufferings Jesus and Paul are referring to have nothing to do with punishment for sin, nor anything Jesus overcame on the cross. That was a burden only He was worthy to die for. Rather, the suffering we all need to go through is resisting the kingdom of darkness that oppose everything Jesus paid for to see us live in. 1 Peter 5:8-10 speaks of this very truth. We are warned to be extremely vigilant concerning our adversary, the devil, and his intention to destroy every good thing God has done. We are to constantly resist him, stand our ground in faith, and push back the kingdom of darkness in the authority Jesus has given us, despite the persecution it will entail. It means laying down our own agendas, popularity, and will to the Lord, and living completely for Him and His cause! This suffering includes constantly dying to our old sinful nature, and embracing the new, renewed life we have in Jesus - a daily battle that requires everything of us. Then we are well able to enforce the devil's defeat on this earth and release the love and power of God over people's lives wherever we go.

# Day 18

## God Always Honors His Word

*John 11:42 (AMPC), "Yes, I know You always hear and listen to Me, but I have said this on account of and for the benefit of the people standing around, so that they may believe that You did send Me [that You have made Me Your Messenger]."*

From His prayer in John 11, we can assume that Jesus already had a discussion with His Father concerning Lazarus, and received His answer the first time he received the news he was ill (John 11:4). Which would make sense of His obvious frustration when those closest to Him didn't take Him at His Word and were angry and hurt when He didn't personally show up in their time frame (John 11:37-38). Jesus said He was calling Lazarus forth on the account of those standing around Him - so they would finally recognize that He was from God, in communion with God, and only spoke what He heard God say. When Jesus said Lazarus would be just fine the first time He heard of his illness, He wasn't being polite and kind, He was literally saying what His Father told Him would happen. Surely by now His friends would have recognized this about Him, and not given up faith, even when their brother had died. They had seen Jesus raise the dead before, and they had His Word that Lazarus would be well again. When God gives us a Word, no matter how contrary to that word the circumstances seem to be - we cannot lose hope and stop believing. God will always honor His Word concerning us.

# Day 19

## The Blessing of The Righteous

*Micah 2:7 (AMPC), "O house of Jacob, shall it be said, Is the Spirit of the Lord restricted, impatient, and shortened? Or are these [prophesied plagues] His doings? Do not My words do good to him who walks uprightly?"*

There is a condition attached to experiencing the goodness of God's Word in and through your life. Micah wrote that God's words will only do good to those who walk uprightly. The Word of God will not profit those who are walking contrary to it. Many people wonder why they aren't seeing the proof of the promises of God's Word come to pass in their lives. Yet most of the time the problem lies with their disobedience to the Word. The Bible says in Hebrews 4:2 that the Word of God did not profit those who heard it, because it was not mixed with faith. It's not just reading and hearing the Word that gives us access to its benefits, it's the diligent application of the Word in faith that opens our lives to its blessings. If we want to unlock the riches of God's favor, then we must live in a way that honors the Lord - in all things. There's no sense in limiting the flow of God's blessing in our lives by choosing selective obedience. Ephesians 3:20 says that the Lord can carry out His purpose far above all that we dare ask or think! As long as we choose to surrender all of ourselves to Him and walk uprightly before Him.

# Day 20

## Honor God's Word

*1 Timothy 6:17 (AMPC), "As for the rich in this world, charge them not to be proud and arrogant and contemptuous of others, nor to set their hopes on uncertain riches, but on God, Who richly and ceaselessly provides us with everything for [our] enjoyment."*

Everything that exists, that is good, God created. He has filled it all with Himself, sustaining it with His power (1 Corinthians 8:6, Colossians 1:16). There is no-one greater than He is, no other Name higher than His own. Yet, Psalm 138:2 says He has exalted His Word above His Name. Just how dependable must His Word be? In John 15, Jesus said that if we would make it our business to abide in Him and have His Word remain in us, to mold and transform us, we could expect 2 distinct results. Firstly, we will bear much fruit, and secondly, whatever we ask will be done for us. There's nothing insignificant about those results! Results brought on all because of our attitude towards the Word of God!

There's more: 1 Timothy 6:17 teaches us that when we place our hope in God, we will find ourselves living in His unending provision, furnished with everything for our enjoyment. Today, as you become aware of how much God values His Word being alive inside of you, choose to embrace and treasure it with the honor it deserves. You will never be ashamed for trusting in it and will see a cycle of rich and ceaseless provision set in motion in your life.

# Day 21

## Ready for Our Bridegroom

*Matthew 25:1 – 4 (NLT), "Then the Kingdom of Heaven will be like ten bridesmaids who took their lamps and went to meet the bridegroom. Five of them were foolish, and five were wise. The five who were foolish didn't take enough olive oil for their lamps, but the other five were wise enough to take along extra oil."*

This Parable Jesus taught ended with the five wise bridesmaids entering the wedding feast, while the five foolish ones were locked out because they were unprepared for the groom's return. In Matthew 5:14-16, we are told that Christ living in us reflects a light burning so bright that we are the light of the world. It says this light reflects our moral excellence, and good deeds, and it glorifies our Heavenly Father. What is responsible for keeping this light burning is the oil of the Holy Spirit. For the light of Christ to be reflected in and through our lives, we must be continuously filled with the fresh oil from Heaven.

Jesus calls the Holy Spirit a precious gift from heaven! His Presence inside our spirits fuels us for life! He is the oil that causes us to live godly lives that bring glory to the Father. He is the oil that keeps our passion and hunger for God's Word to transform us into the image of Jesus! His oil refreshes and strengthens and empowers us to live supernatural lives while here on earth. Our attention to keep our hearts open to receive His fresh infilling keeps us living vitally connected to Jesus, where we walk in our authority over the devil, and carry God's goodness to people wherever we go. When our oil levels remain full, our fire keeps burning, and we remain positioned, ready for our bridegroom.

# Day 22

## Come up the Mountain!

*Exodus 24:12 (NKJV), "Then the Lord said to Moses, 'Come up to Me on the mountain and be there; and I will give you tablets of stone, and the law and commandments which I have written, that you may teach them.'"*

For us to truly be effective for the Kingdom of God in this hour, we must prioritize the Presence of God in our lives. The Lord told Moses to meet Him up on the mountain. The word of God instructs us to come to a place where we can meet with Him, it's called *The Secret Place*. Even though we are aware of His Presence living inside us, we need to deliberately set time aside to visit with Him, outside of distractions. It's in this place that He reveals His heart and will to us. He also imparts His wisdom, love, and supernatural, empowering grace. In the end, our effectiveness for the kingdom is determined by the closeness we have with the Lord. We will have true impact in this world when we prioritize intimacy with the Lord. The same way He called Moses up the mountain, the Lord is calling you. Understand, because of the finished work of the cross, you can boldly draw near to Him today, and every day, to receive whatever you need, and all that He has for you (Hebrews 4:16).

# Day 23

## Whole Heart

*Jeremiah 24:7 (NKJV), "Then I will give them a heart to know Me, that I am the Lord; and they shall be My people, and I will be their God, for they shall return to Me with their whole heart."*

Every true believer has a passion and love for God and His people. Part of the devil's strategy against the church is to weaken and make light of this. King Solomon said it best, *"Keep and guard your heart with all vigilance and above all that you guard, for out of it flow the springs of life."* (Proverbs 4:23).

When your heart delights in the Lord, above all other things - you can be sure of His undivided attention and favor! Psalm 91:14-16 promises that He will always answer us, deliver us from all trouble, honour us, and satisfy us with a good, long life - because we have set our love upon Him. Give God your heart today, let your eyes delight in His ways, as you spend time in His Word. Its truth will keep your heart and mind pure of all unclean and negative thoughts. As a result, and your life will be established, and every area filled with pleasant treasure and riches (Proverbs 24:3-4).

# Day 24

## Stand for His Glory

*1 Peter 4:14 (AMPC), "If you are censured and suffer abuse [because you bear] the name of Christ, blessed [are you-happy, fortunate, to be envied, with life-joy, and satisfaction in God's favor and salvation, regardless of your outward condition], because the Spirit of glory, the Spirit of God, is resting upon you. On their part He is blasphemed, but on your part He is glorified."*

According to the Word, the times we are living in now, will only become more wicked. But for the righteous, our paths will only grow brighter and brighter (Proverbs 4:18). God sent Jesus to destroy the work of the devil and his power over us. Jesus triumphantly overcame the devil and his evil reign in this world for us (John 16:33). Then He gave us the authority and power to enforce the devils defeat on this earth as we stand in the faith and victory He won for us. Because of Jesus, we can live vitally connected to our Heavenly Father, through His Precious Holy Spirit living in us. We have been given access into the throne room of heaven while our bodies are here on earth, to reign as kings in life through Jesus (Romans 5:17). No matter how dark the work of the devil appears to be around you, know who you are in Christ Jesus, and the purpose He has given you. Fear God enough to not be swayed by persecution while you stand strong to glorify Him. When we care about God more than anything else on this earth - we are empowered by the Spirit of glory Himself. He rests upon us and causes us to abide in the fullness of His Presence and power.

# Day 25

## Showcase His Goodness

*Acts 14:16 - 17 (NLT), "In the past He permitted all the nations to go their own ways, but He never left them without evidence of Himself and His goodness. For instance, He sends you rain and good crops and gives you food and joyful hearts."*

Paul and Barnabas were preaching the good news of the Gospel in Greece with such power that many Jews and Gentiles converted to Christianity. In one town, Paul commanded a lame man to rise and walk, because he could see the man believed the good news of Jesus. The moment the miracle occurred the people flocked to Paul and Barnabas and called them by the names of their Greek gods. They started bringing them offerings and worshipping them. This upset the two missionaries so much that they tore their clothing and shouted to the crowd to stop their foolishness. They told the people that even though they had worshipped their gods for generations, they were not real. There was only One true God that had in the past *permitted all the nations to go their own ways, but He never left them without evidence of Himself and His goodness.* It was this true God that they had come to tell them about, and it was by His power that these miracles were happening - not their own. Today, let a confidence rise inside of you as you realize that same God lives within you, and can fill you with His power, just as He did for Paul and Barnabas. You and I are His vessels to display His goodness to the world. Start believing God to showcase His love and power through you again and again!

# Day 26

## Living Water

***Revelation 21:6 (NLT), "... It is finished! I am the Alpha and the Omega—the Beginning and the End. To all who are thirsty I will give freely from the springs of the water of life."***

In the natural, when we are unwell, we tend to lose our appetite for food. Just the same, in the realm of the spirit, a good indication of something being 'off' in our relationship with the Lord, is a loss of appetite for the things of the Spirit. And yet, when it comes to our spiritual appetites, it is possible to be full and hungry at the same time! That's because as we fill up on God's Presence and His Word, we begin longing for more of the same. When we drink deeply from the truth of God's Word, we are in truth, drinking from Jesus Himself; taking in the Living Water that nourishes, refreshes, and satisfies our souls. This always leaves us thirsting for more! The trouble comes when we begin drinking from the opinions and reasoning of the world, instead of the Word. We may feel gratified for a moment but before long we are left feeling dissatisfied and disillusioned. In Matthew 5:6, Jesus said, *"Blessed are those who hunger and thirst for righteousness for they shall be completely satisfied."* That's because spiritual hunger and thirst drives us directly to the Word, which fills us with supernatural life, peace, and joy while producing the force of faith within us. A sure recipe for continuous victory! Today, choose to drink deeply from the living water, you'll never be disappointed for doing so!

# Day 27

## Hosting the Glory

*Isaiah 60:2 (NKJV), "For behold, the darkness shall cover the earth, and deep darkness the people; but the Lord will arise over you, and His glory will be seen upon you."*

Every born-again, Holy Spirit baptized child of God has the capacity to host the glory of God. We are most certainly living in the days where the kingdom of darkness is ruling and dominating the hearts of people across the earth. But, the prophecy declares that the Lord will arise over His people, and His glory will be seen upon them! It's the glory that distinguishes those who are of God amongst those who are not. It causes the former to shine with His hope, goodness, and power. Like moths are drawn to the light, those who are lost, broken and full of fear will be drawn to that glory, and find peace, freedom, and safety. But the glory of God will not settle on just anybody. For us to become a people that host the glory, we must walk before the Lord with pure hearts, always putting His will and ways above our own. And we must cultivate a deep hunger and thirst for His manifest Presence and Word. When these become evident in our lives, the glory of the Lord settles upon us in a powerful way. We must become people who host the glory of the Lord, while there is still time for the world to receive a Savior and defy the darkness that threatens their lives.

# Day 28

## Save Your Soul

*James 1:21 (NKJV), "Therefore lay aside all filthiness and overflow of wickedness, and receive with meekness the implanted word, which is able to save your souls."*

As believers in Christ, the Word of God defines exactly who we are. That's why we are instructed to receive the truth of the Word with meekness. This means to be completely submissive to its teachings, welcoming them into our lives and allowing them to transform us into the image of Jesus. There are believers who are inwardly changed by their spirits becoming born-again, but their old thinking patterns have become a bad habit. They still hold onto those incorrect mindsets and negative attitudes. In other words, the way they think and act are not consistent with the clean, new condition of their inner man. That's because they have not treasured the Word of God with meekness. They haven't allowed their minds to be renewed to its truth and as a result, their souls will never prosper. If their souls don't prosper, their bodies will follow suit. Even though their spirits are born-again, they will never walk in the freedom, peace, and blessing of the Lord - until they surrender their minds to the authority and power of the Word. (3 John 1:2). We must never lose our hunger and desire for the truth of God's Word to dominate every area of our lives, it will continuously transform us from 1 degree of glory to the next and has the power to save our souls! (2 Corinthians 3:18).

# Day 29

## The Presence of the Holy Spirit

*1 John 2:27 (NKJV), "But the anointing which you have received from Him abides in you, and you do not need that anyone teach you; but as the same anointing teaches you concerning all things, and is true, and is not a lie, and just as it has taught you, you will abide in Him."*

Many people believe the Holy Spirit to be a quiet, unobtrusive part of the Godhead. He is often explained to be more of a spiritual power or influence, than a person with a personality, an intellect, a will, and emotions that we can personally experience. The Bible teaches us that He can be grieved, and quenched by our actions and attitudes, as well as be excited and motivated to increase His work and manifest Presence in our lives. When we see the Holy Spirit as a person, we are able to hear Him lead and teach us and are able to yield and surrender to His will. He is the One who explains, reminds us of, and convicts us of God's Word. When we treat Him with honor and sincere love, we don't have to look for power - He simply gives it to us. The Bible describes the Holy Spirit as a loving friend, and an ever-present helper and comforter (1 Corinthians 2:10-13). He is the One who connects us with the Father and makes Jesus real to us (John 15:12). He also quickens our physical bodies with supernatural power, and is constantly at work imparting and infusing God's divine nature in us - making us holy. The Holy Spirit's power flows through us to cast out demons and heal the sick. The Holy Spirit is the anointing that abides, He is how God dwells in and with us, and the measure to which we can experience Him depends on our hunger for Him. Become aware of His wonderful Presence in you, and yield to His leading today.

# Day 30

## Tongues of Fire

***Acts 2:3 (NLT) "Then, what looked like flames or tongues of fire appeared and settled on each of them."***

When a fire is ignited, it's not long before people nearby become aware of its presence. They smell the smoke, hear the crackle of the flames, feel the heat, and see the blaze. When the Holy Spirit came upon the believers, in the book of Acts, tongues of fire appeared above their heads! The Bible says people throughout the city recognized something powerful was happening in that upper room! When a believer is baptized in the Holy Spirit, we are baptized with His spiritual fire!

It's a purifying fire that burns away every negative attitude and bondage the devil has on us and fuels a passion and hunger for more of God's Word and Presence in our lives. It rekindles a fervent love for God and a boldness to tell others about Him! There is no mistaking someone who is burning with the fire of God inside them - they think, talk, and act differently. And their passion and joy are contagious! Just as a natural fire must be tended to keep it burning and not go out, our internal, spiritual fire must be fanned into flame too. As we keep ourselves involved in the things of God, daily fellowship with Him in His Word, and pray in our heavenly tongue, that fire will keep ablaze inside us. This way the world will recognize we carry something sent to us from Heaven! Allow the fire of God to continually burn inside you, drawing others to His love and power.

# Day 31

## Your Stronghold

*2 Samuel 5:17 (NLT) "When the Philistines heard that David had been anointed king of Israel, they mobilized all their forces to capture him. But David was told they were coming, so he went into the stronghold."*

God's assignment on a life is time sensitive. When we step into God's destiny for our lives, the whole of hell hears, and will do it's best to oppose us. That's why it's so important for every believer to understand the authority we have in Christ Jesus, and how to operate in it. God's Word is the stronghold of our lives. It holds the truth of who we are in Him and gives us the practical wisdom and faith to overcome every tactic of the enemy. No matter what fiery dart the enemy directs at us, when we know what God's Word has to say on a matter, we can hold up the shield of faith and stop that dart in its tracks. For instance, when the enemy manipulates a circumstance and brings negative news to your attention to discourage you and fill your mind with doubt and fear - the Holy Spirit will remind you of the truth of God's Word on the matter. That Word will come alive with power inside you and give you an injection of faith-filled courage. You immediately reject every fear-filled thought and replace it with God's opinion instead. Then, as you declare that Word from the conviction of your heart - everything must yield to that Word - and victory is secured! Let God's Word become your stronghold today as you overcome the enemy and move forward in your destiny!

# NOVEMBER

# Day 01

## None of These Things Move Me!

*Acts 20:24 (NKJV), "But none of these things move me; nor do I count my life dear to myself, so that I may finish my race with joy, and the ministry which I received from the Lord Jesus, to testify to the gospel of the grace of God"*

What a glorious hour we live in! What a time to see the greatest harvest come into the Kingdom of God. We are alive to run the race Jesus has set before us, and to run this race well, it takes faith in the person Jesus and the power that resides in His Name. Paul had a clear revelation of the power and authority carried in Jesus' Name. That's why he literally shrugged off every threat and persecution for preaching in that Name wherever he went. There is no power that exists to compare with the power that resides in the Name of Jesus, and Jesus gave us the legal right to use it! In Mark 16:17-18, and Matthew 28:18-20, Jesus declares what the power of His Name will do when we use it in faith. Every evil force and bondage is broken and destroyed over people's lives when we speak the Name of Jesus. The devil is powerless against it. The Bible says Jesus came to seek and save those who are lost to the kingdom of darkness, to break them free from its power, and then give them a brand-new life and position seated with Him in heavenly places! A place far above all other rule and power, to reign as kings in life through Him (Ephesians 1:21, Romans 5:17). Hallelujah! When we grab a hold of this truth, like Paul, we will declare that no opposition moves us or deters us from carrying out our purpose for the kingdom of God in the Name of Jesus!

# Day 02

## Incomparable

*Jeremiah 10:24 (NKJV), "'But let him who glories glory in this, that he understands and knows Me, that I am the Lord, exercising lovingkindness, judgment, and righteousness in the earth. For in these I delight,' says the Lord."*

In Luke 10, the disciples were really delighted with the fact that evil spirits obeyed them. Jesus drew their attention to the truth that the only reason the demons obeyed them, was because of the disciples' relationship with Him. The apostle Paul understood the real treasure in life was not just the glorious benefits of working for the Lord and operating in His delegated authority, but personally knowing the Person of Jesus. When we encounter Jesus and experience the joy of being in His manifest Presence, we soon realize it's without comparison. He becomes the prize far above all prizes.

Knowing Jesus fuels the desire to know Him more, to live in His ways, and to follow Him for the rest of our lives. In the Old Testament, there were people who were able to know God and carry out great exploits for Him, but what they knew and experienced was far inferior to what we are allowed and invited to know and experience today! Everything worth knowing in life, and all things that hold true value are found and experienced from personally knowing the Person of Jesus. Draw close to Him today, you will find He will draw you into a life of pure love and power, incomparable to anything you have ever, or will ever know outside of knowing Him.

# Day 03

## Remain in Him

*1 John 2:28 (AMPC), "And now, little children, abide (live, remain permanently) in Him, so that when He is made visible, we may have and enjoy perfect confidence (boldness, assurance) and not be ashamed and shrink from Him at His coming."*

Truly abiding in Christ, by His Holy Spirit, will ensure we never drift away from Him. 1 Thessalonians 5:16-24 tells us how we can do this. It says we are to refuse the devil any foothold in our lives. We do this by 2 essential things, by constantly keeping ourselves in communion with the Lord and by receiving His Word into our hearts and minds. Of course, communion with the Lord would mean spending time with Him in prayer. But it also means shutting off all distractions and drinking deeply of the fresh infilling of His Holy Spirit. This is done by us simply focusing our full attention on Him and affectionally acknowledging His Presence in us. As we pour out our love on Him, we open our hearts to receive a fresh, overwhelming flow of His love and power in return. As we fully yield our thoughts, will, and emotions to Him in this time - we are strengthened by His mighty power in our inner man.

The second essential practice to keep the influence of the enemy out of our lives, is to constantly receive God's word into our hearts and minds. It's not enough to just read the Word, we must joyfully and gratefully allow it to transform us by the power of the Holy Spirit. We do this by not just agreeing with it, but wholeheartedly believing it. That's where the Spirit of God makes it alive inside us! Then, when we apply its principles to our lives we bear substantial fruit! The promise of the Lord is that in doing these two essential things, He will personally keep and preserve us until He returns!

# Day 04

## Reinforced

*Isaiah 40:31 (NLT), "But those who trust in the Lord will find new strength. They will soar high on wings like eagles. They will run and not grow weary. They will walk and not faint."*

Ephesians 3:16 says that the glory of God will empower and reinforce our inner man with strength through the Holy Spirit indwelling our spirit and personality. When we start to feel the pressures from the world around us, and the demands of life on us, our inner strength begins to wane. An easy way to detect someone's inner resolve progressively getting weaker is by the slight change in their personality. Instead of a bubbling joy and confident peace, there's a subtle agitation just under the surface, or a slight distance they keep towards others compared to normal. For some, the moment they recognize the deficiency of inner strength within themselves, they make the decision to spend more time in the glory of God, yielding to the Holy Spirit, allowing Him to fill, empower, and reinforce them with His power. For others, they decide to push those agitating feelings and anxious thoughts down, to ignore them and press on, pulling on whatever strength they have left. The problem is, once strength is depleted, unless it's reinforced, the effects become more severe affecting not just our personalities, but our physical health too. This is not God's will for us. He wants to see us prosper and be in health, even as our souls prosper (3 John 1:2). He wants to be the One who personally does this for us from the rich treasury of His glory. Make time to drink deeply in the Presence of the Lord - let Him fill and refresh you as He reinforces you with His mighty strength today.

# Day 05

## Fire-lighter for Revival

*Joel 2:28-29 (NLT), "Then, after doing all those things, I will pour out my Spirit upon all people. Your sons and daughters will prophesy. Your old men will dream dreams, and your young men will see visions. In those days I will pour out my Spirit even on servants—men and women alike."*

Revival is God's spirit moving deeply in the hearts and minds of men, refreshing and rekindling the awareness of His Presence within them for the advancement of His Kingdom. Once it breaks out, it spreads like wildfire and marks whole regions for God! The great revivals and spiritual awakenings in the past are remembered for the way they radically impacted society in whole nations! People, in their masses, turned their hearts to God with such earnest passion that their lifestyles dramatically changed, influencing their families, communities and cities. In every case, this spiritual inferno began with a single heart hungry for and surrendered to the Spirit of God. God's gift to us is the outpouring of His Precious Holy Spirit. Jesus paid the price for us to be able to receive Him in full measure in our lives. The Bible says we can be bodies wholly filled and flooded with the richest measure of His personality and power when we choose to acknowledge and respond to Him. Recognize God's Holy Spirit has already been poured out on us. He already dwells in the fullness of His power and love inside us. Begin to burn with a hunger and passion for more! The more we burn, the more the fire within us grows until it starts to jump onto those around us - infecting them with that hunger and passion too. Before long, whole communities are alight with the fire of revival - burning bright on all who stand in its wake! Awake to God's Presence inside you and become the fire-lighter for revival today!

# Day 06

## God Revealed

***Genesis 1:1 (ESV), "In the beginning, God created the heavens and the earth."***

GOD is the beginning of all things! Everything good started from Him and is filled with Him sustained by His power. Look at how 1 Corinthians 8:6 confirms this truth, *"Yet for us there is [only] one God, the Father, Who is the Source of all things and for Whom we [have life], and one Lord, Jesus Christ, through and by Whom are all things and through and by Whom we [ourselves exist]."* Colossians 1:16 says the same, *"For it was in Him that all things were created, in heaven and on earth, things seen and things unseen, whether thrones, dominions, rulers, or authorities; all things were created and exist through Him [by His service, intervention] and in and for Him."*

There is no-one greater than God, no other Name higher or more excellent! It goes without saying that a God so mighty and powerful must be known by everything and everyone He has created! Romans 1:19 - 20 says that God has shown Himself to all men in their inner consciousness. It says that since the creation of the world His invisible nature and attributes have been made clear in all He has created! So, no one is excused from not knowing about Him. What is truly thrilling, is that He wants us to not just know *about* Him - He wants us to personally know Him! In John 17: 3, Jesus said to have eternal life is to personally know God. Open your heart to Him today as you spend time getting to know your GREAT God, and His WONDERFUL heart towards you!

# Day 07

## Expect His Power

*Acts 14:3 (NLT), "But the apostles stayed there a long time, preaching boldly about the grace of the Lord. And the Lord proved their message was true by giving them power to do miraculous signs and wonders."*

Paul and Barnabas were preaching the Gospel in the synagogues throughout Greece. The crowds grew as the people joyfully accepted the news of grace into their hearts. The trouble came when the Jewish, religious leaders grew jealous of the crowds that were being drawn to hear the good news, so they stirred up great opposition against Paul and Barnabas. In response, Paul simply and boldly declared that God had sent them to tell the good news of salvation to the Jews first, but since they rejected it, they would turn to the Gentiles instead. When the Gentiles heard this news, they were ecstatic and received the Gospel with great joy! But once again, great opposition came from the unbelieving Jews. This time, instead of leaving town, Paul and Barnabas stayed longer, preaching boldly. The Lord confirmed their message by empowering them to do great signs and miracles. No matter the opposition to the truth about Jesus you tell those around you - when the Lord prompts you to stay - you can be confident He is with you and will back you with His power! Never shrink back into silence when the Lord tells you to testify, instead, expect signs, wonders and miracles to follow as you speak of His goodness each day!

# Day 08

## Be the Salt!

*Matthew 5:13 (NKJV), "You are the salt of the earth; but if the salt loses its flavour, how shall it be seasoned? It is then good for nothing but to be thrown out and trampled underfoot by men."*

Salt adds flavor to flavorless food, it enhances its taste. Jesus said that we are the salt of the earth. Just as salt enhances the taste of food, we enhance the lives of those on this earth, by what they 'taste' through the way we speak and behave. In the time Jesus was teaching this, salt was a very costly commodity. It wasn't just used to add flavor, it would also be used to preserve food. The reason it was so costly was largely due to the refinement process of producing salt that useful. When salt came out of the ground, or marshes it was mixed with all kinds of impurities. They had to go through an arduous process to separate the impurities from the salt before it became pure and useful. Salt that had not been properly refined would be compromised and lose its flavor and usefulness. Jesus warns believers of losing our flavor and usefulness for His kingdom when we live compromised lives. Sin not only puts out the fire of God in our lives, it compromises our walk of purity and removes our "saltiness". The world is attracted to believers who speak and behave differently when faced with the same challenges and threats. In times of danger, confusion, and fear those walking close to the Lord, with His Presence overflowing in and from them - add great value to this world. Stay vitally connected to the Lord, allowing His Word and Spirit to continually sanctify you, and you will be the salt of the earth He made you to be - vital and useful to Him.

# Day 09

## Know Him and Live Free!

*1 John 2:3-4, "Now by this we know that we know Him, if we keep His commandments. He who says, 'I know Him,' and does not keep His commandments, is a liar, and the truth is not in him."*

The Bible says the person who really knows God, will keep His Word. If you find it difficult to break free of the habits of your old sinful nature, or to come out from under the oppression of fear and discouragement. You will feel powerless to obey God's Word. The truth is, the moment we get a hold of the revelation of the finished work of the cross, we will know who Jesus is, and experience living the new life of freedom and victory we have in Him. It's a life completely free from the power of sin and full of the life and power of God to live in Him and His ways! Galatians 2:20 says that when Jesus died on that cross, our old, sinful nature went to the cross with Him. It literally died with Jesus! We died to every bondage, every sin, every torment. Every work of the devil lost its hold and power over us when we were crucified with Christ! Hallelujah! Then, when Jesus rose again, He rose with us in Him! It doesn't just end there! The Bible says Jesus was given the place of the highest honor, above all rule and power, and given the name that is above every other name - in heaven, on earth, and bellow the earth! And who do you think He took with Him to this place of victory? He took you and me! So, the life we now live here, we live by faith IN Jesus! He has literally taken occupation of our spirits, filled us with His resurrection life and power and is living in and through us! Get to know your real identity in Christ and walking in His ways will become second nature to you.

# Day 10

## He Carefully Watches over You

*Exodus 9:26 (NLT), "The only place without hail was the region of Goshen, where the people of Israel lived."*

After God instructed Moses to lead His people out of Egypt, we read of a series of events that unfolded each time Moses and Aaron approached Pharaoh for the release of the Israelite people. Since Pharaoh's heart was hardened, Egypt was struck with 10 plagues which brought disaster and devastation across the nation. Accompanying the plague of hail were fierce winds and storms but not one piece of hail was found in Goshen, where God's people lived. Even though disaster was happening around them, it did not touch them! Today, know that your covenant with God positions you in a place of protection, provision, and peace! In this world, there is devastation all around us, but have your faith stirred by this – even though it is happening around you, it does not have to touch you and your family! As you abide in Jesus and remain fixed and rooted in His Word, being careful to walk in His Ways by the power of His indwelling Holy Spirit, you will be safe and secure. Never lose faith in your covenant God, He will never forsake you but will carefully watch over you and honor His Word concerning you (1 Peter 5:7, Psalm 55:22).

# Day 11

## Rest in Him

*Psalm 16:1 (AMPC), "Keep and protect me, O God, for in You I have found refuge, and in You do I put my trust and hide myself."*

In Acts 17, Paul was preaching in Thessalonica. He and his team were laying the foundation work for the first church in that area. The Christians that lived there were faced with such persecution from all sides. Not just the pagan priests, but very hostile Jews were furious at them for seeing their followers converting to Christianity. The spiritual, religious, and political environment was so intense, and the persecution of the believers was rife. They desperately needed relief from their stress to quieten their hearts and minds and see things from God's perspective again. That's why Paul told them in 2 Thessalonians 1:7, to come aside for a little while and rest, so they can receive a fresh revelation of the Lord being with them and protecting them. This would give them new strength to go on.

When we begin to feel overwhelmed by the pressure around us, we need to take Paul's advice. Take time to separate yourself from the stress and trouble you're facing by coming into the presence of God. Let His Word refresh your soul, and give you a clear perspective of His will, protection, and provision for you. Allow His Spirit to strengthen your inner man as He reminds you of His truth. Then you'll be reinforced and ready to go on in His strength and His peace. His joy in your heart will cause you to face each challenge triumphantly in His grace, because you have chosen to make the time to rest in Him.

# Day 12

## Keep Your Post

*Nehemiah 6:3 (NLT), "So I replied by sending this message to them: "I am engaged in a great work, so I can't come. Why should I stop working to come and meet with you?"*

A child of God that is focused and faithful is a significant threat to the devil. In these last days, the Bible tells us many will turn away from the Lord. Those who were once burning hot for Him will become cold and depart from the faith. However, there will be a remnant of people who will remain committed to Christ and His call. These are intentional in purpose and undistracted by the ploys of the enemy. Nehemiah knew the urgency to get the wall around Jerusalem built. He was diligently engaged in this great work. But two men, inspired by the devil to distract and murder him, came on the scene. Nehemiah was a man of God and no fool. He simply refused to leave his post on the wall to speak with them. Understand, the devil knows the urgency of the hour and the power of the message God has placed on your heart for others. Refuse to be distracted by him and keep your heart focused on the work the Lord has assigned you to. Like Nehemiah, remain faithful and fixed, and you will defy the enemy while you fulfil God's purpose and get the job done!

# Day 13

## Powerful Prayer

*James 5:16 (AMPC), "...The earnest (heartfelt, continued) prayer of a righteous man makes tremendous power available [dynamic in its working]."*

Those in the early church recognized the importance of prayer. Throughout the Book of Acts we see how Peter, as well as the other apostles, appointed seven men to oversee the daily distribution of food. They did this so they were able to give themselves *"to prayer and to the ministry of the word"* (Acts 6:4). If we look at the life of Christ, we see He often withdrew to the wilderness to pray. It was because of His steadfast devotion to be in close, intimate contact with the Father that He was able to perform His works. We must recognize that the source of the continual flow of power available for us to operate in, to do the work of the Lord, lies in our regular, intimate communion with Him and His Word. Just as Jesus, the apostles in the early church, and other great men and women of God recognized the power earnest, sincere prayer makes available; we need to acknowledge its importance in our lives too. Our personal, intimate connection with the Lord moves us from a place of being a hireling in His kingdom, to a son and daughter, working in un-broken fellowship, and partnership with Him. If we are prayer-less currently, we will be both unfulfilled and powerless in all we do.

# Day 14

## Living Proof

*1 John 2:6 (AMPC), "Whoever says he abides in Him ought [as a personal debt] to walk and conduct himself in the same way in which He walked and conducted Himself."*

Anyone who says they abide in Christ, must live in a way that resembles His Presence in their lives. The Bible tells of some significant changes that take place in a person who has surrendered to the Lordship of Jesus Christ! 2 Corinthians 5:17 says the nature of our inner man becomes completely new! Our old nature, with its sinful desires and selfish motives has gone, replaced by a new, clean, perfect nature of Jesus! 1 Corinthians 6:17-20 says we have become one spirit with Jesus! We are now His dwelling place, hallelujah, His Spirit has literally taken occupation and possession of our inner man. Now it's no longer we who call the shots, Jesus does!

So, we live trusting and believing in Him to show us how to think, speak, and behave after His ways and personality (Galatians 2:20). If this is all true, and we say that we are abiding in Jesus and His life-giving word; then it's impossible to not have evidence of this change in the way we conduct ourselves. The love and affection Jesus displayed for His Father was evident in everything He did. His chief desire was to please Him as He represented Him well. Jesus lived in victory over the devil and sin, and He joyfully brought healing and wholeness through His acts of love and compassion everywhere He went. It's time to let the new nature we have been given dominate the way we live - providing proof of the change inside us!

# Day 15

## Refuse Compromise

*Isaiah 7:4 (AMPC), "...And say to him, 'Take heed and be quiet; fear not, neither be fainthearted because of these two stumps of smoking firebrands...'"*

Ahaz was a wicked king of Judah. He allowed compromise into his kingdom and welcomed the worship of other gods. He had just received word that the king of Syria, and the king of Israel had made an alliance and were marching towards Judah. They wanted to attack Jerusalem, defeat the capital of Judah, then depose of Ahaz. King Ahaz and his people were terrified. God sent Isaiah to tell Ahaz to not be afraid of the threats of the two kings. The attack would fail, and He would spare Jerusalem. If Ahaz would turn to the Lord and put his trust in Him alone - he and Jerusalem would be spared. However, if he didn't trust in the Lord, he and his reign would not be blessed and established. Unfortunately, Ahaz didn't trust in the Lord. He placed his trust in an alliance with the king of Assyria instead. In the end, Jerusalem was spared, but Ahaz and his reign came to an end. Ahaz's compromised life caused him to become thoroughly corrupt. He entered an ungodly alliance for "good" reasons, and it ended in his demise. When we allow compromise in our walk with the Lord, we choose a slippery slope that easily leads to us walking out of His blessing and favor. We should learn from Ahaz's mistake. We must keep our hearts fixed on the Lord, and wholeheartedly follow Him. Refuse the temptation of compromise so you can remain established and blessed in the goodness of God.

# Day 16

## Words that Attract the Right Attention

*Malachi 3:16 (ESV), "Then those who feared the Lord spoke with one another. The Lord paid attention and heard them, and a book of remembrance was written before Him of those who feared the Lord and esteemed His name."*

There is much to be said about the power of words – words that are encouraging and uplifting to the hearer; words that speak of the goodness of the Lord and build faith! It's these kinds of words, rooted in faith, that please God. That's because words inspired by faith, speak His language - they give Him something to respond to, something concrete to work with. We know God always honors His Word, and watches over it to perform it! The reverse is also true - speaking negative words, whether out of fear or anger, even in jest, gives our enemy, the devil, free reign over whatever we are speaking negatively about. Which is precisely why we must speak words aligned with faith, not just in our prayers, but in our daily conversations too, because they will always go to work and produce good! Understanding that God uses words for building what is of Him in every situation, keeps us intentional regarding what we say. Let's take special care to draw the correct attention with our words today! As we do, we will be counted among those who fear the LORD with words that are noteworthy in Heaven as we produce life and peace everywhere we go.

# Day 17

## God Rewards Diligence

*Hebrews 11:6 (AMPC), "But without faith it is impossible to please and be satisfactory to Him. For whoever would come near to God must [necessarily] believe that God exists and that He is the rewarder of those who earnestly and diligently seek Him [out]."*

Many believers set their minds to walk closer to the Lord. They have great intentions to spend valuable time in prayer and in His Word, only to give up when they become distracted with other things. The truth is, God promises a great reward for those who choose to remain completely committed to their promise to diligently seek Him and His will for their everyday lives. In the Greek translation of this verse in Hebrews, the phrase *diligently seek*, means *to zealously seek for something with all your heart*. It takes commitment and diligence to achieve anything worthwhile, and a pursuit to know God more is certainly that! If you're battling to keep your commitment to spending daily, quality time with the Lord in His Word - ask the Holy Spirit to renew your hunger and passion to do so! Philippians 2:13 says the Holy Spirit will energize us and create in us the power and desire both to will and to work for His good pleasure! He will reward your efforts by revealing glorious things about the Lord you would *never* experience outside of your diligent pursuit to know Him more.

# Day 18

## Root Yourself in Him

*Colossians 2:6-7 (NLT), "Let your roots grow down into Him, and let your lives be built on Him. Then your faith will grow strong in the truth you were taught, and you will overflow with thankfulness."*

When you plant a seed in the ground, the roots that shoot down are at first thin and small, in proportion to the developing seedling. Then, as those roots absorb the water and nutrients from the soil, they supply the plant on top of the soil with what is needed to produce the necessary energy to cause the entire plant to flourish and grow strong. The deeper and stronger the roots, the more established and fruitful the plant becomes. Now, when the seed is planted in fertile soil and is regularly watered, the development of that plant is expedited, and the fruit produced is healthy and bountiful! Scripture often likens this natural process of established growth and fruitfulness to our own spiritual growth. The most fertile ground we could ever develop our spiritual roots in, is the Person of Jesus. As we open our hearts to know Him more and establish our identity in Him - we will grow strong and true, and our lives will yield an abundance of excellent fruit! Fruit that resembles Him in every way. Jesus is the Word, and we have been given the Precious Holy Spirit to teach us and lead us into the truth of who Jesus is in us, and who we are in Him. The richer this truth is received into our hearts and minds - the richer our fruit will be. Let your roots continually grow down into Jesus, build your life on Him, and you will overflow with thankfulness at what He produces in you!

# Day 19

## Empowered to Go!

*Acts 1:8 (NLT), "But you will receive power when the Holy Spirit comes upon you. And you will be my witnesses, telling people about me everywhere – in Jerusalem, throughout Judea, in Samaria, and to the ends of the earth."*

After Jesus was filled with the Holy Spirit, He ministered in great power and authority (Luke 3:22). The Bible records how He went from town-to-town preaching about the Kingdom of God, demonstrating and proving His message with signs, wonders and miracles everywhere He went. While He was ministering on earth, He was training his disciples to continue His ministry after His death, resurrection, and ascension. The most important part of His final instruction to them, before He went to be with His Father, was that they were to wait for the promised Holy Spirit (Joel 2:28). Jesus wanted them to understand He was not sending them into the world to do the work alone, or by their own authority. He would still be present in them, empowering them by His Spirit. This way they would have the authority to do what He did and say what He said. When the Holy Spirit filled them on the day of Pentecost, none of them were ever the same, they had been empowered for life and ministry. Just as the Holy Spirit empowered them to live free of sin, and full of the life and power of God to demonstrate His kingdom to people wherever they went, we have been given the same commission and empowerment! Open your heart to receive the baptism of the Holy Spirit and continue to yield to His infilling of love and power each day. Then you will carry the very Presence of Jesus to people everywhere you go! Go in His Name, His authority, and His power!

# Day 20

## Our Explosive Treasure

***Ephesians 6:10 (NLT), "Be strong in the Lord and in the power of His might."***

At the time of our salvation, the Bible explains how the Holy Spirit recreates our spirit-man, and then takes occupation of it! Then, when we receive the baptism of the Holy Spirit, the flow of His life and power in us is activated to flow like a mighty river in and through us! This power strengthens us in our inner man to withstand every attack from the enemy and move forward in things of God! The word *power* used in this verse is translated *dunamis* in Greek. It's described as an explosive, demonstrative power. It's same power Jesus operated in when He healed the sick, cast out demons, opened blind eyes, and rose people from the dead! This *dumanis* power is designed to be placed into a vessel out of which it can flow. We have been created to be those vessels that carry this divine power. When God recreated our spirits, He made them fit and strong enough to house the full measure of God's power inside us! That's why 2 Corinthians 4:7 says, *"But we have this treasure in earthen vessels, that the excellence of the power may be of God and not of us."* When we recognize and acknowledge that we have a reservoir of God's own unstoppable power inside of us - we will be able to tap into that explosive power and be strengthened to stand strong in the Lord and push on to victory in all He has called us to!

# Day 21

## Resurrection Power in You!

*Romans 8:11 (AMPC), "But if the Spirit of Him who raised Jesus from the dead dwells in you, He who raised Christ from the dead will also give life to your mortal bodies through His Spirit who dwells in you."*

Life runs at a fast pace for most of us! Besides the millions of things to get done, there's the pressure to get them done on time! When we are constantly on the go, it's easy to get so caught up in the busyness we don't even realize the strength beginning to drain from our physical bodies and emotions. One of the devil's greatest tactics is to wait for us to be tired and weak so that we become susceptible to his lies. That's when he attacks our emotions and tries to discourage us with thoughts of failure and inadequacy. That's why it's essential for us to keep tapping into that reservoir of extra, supernatural strength that's inside of us. Romans 8:11 says the Holy Spirit within us literally infuses us with the same resurrection life He used to raise Jesus from the dead! That life super-charges our spirit-man, brings peace and joy to our emotions, and rejuvenates our physical bodies too! If you will yield to the Holy Spirit, who lives in you, He will refresh you with a brand-new surge of His resurrection power - as He reminds you of the truth of God's Word! God's truth will re-charge and re-set your soul, and strengthen your physical body to get up, push forward and excel in everything that you need to accomplish - and you'll do it with great joy too! Tap into the resurrection power today!

# Day 22

## God's Will Above Our Own

*Genesis 13:14-15 (NLT), "Look as far as you can see in every direction—north and south, east and west. I am giving all this land, as far as you can see, to you and your descendants as a permanent possession."*

Abram and his nephew Lot had to separate ways to avoid conflict between their growing families and livestock. Abram graciously allowed Lot to select the land he wanted to occupy, before selecting his own. Out of his own will, Lot lifted his eyes and selected the rich, fertile lands along the Jordan valley, in the spiritually depraved region of Sodom. Then God visited Abram and instructed him to lift his eyes to view the land. Unlike Lot, Abram was learning to trust the Lord and depend on His will for direction, provision, and protection. He didn't make a choice dependent on his own interests; he reserved that right for the Lord.

Genesis 13:10 tells us Abram only "lifts his eyes" to view the land at the command of the Lord. His decision to place God's will above his own resulted in the Lord blessing him, even greater than what was first promised! The original promise was that God would give Abram and his descendants all the land he could see. Now, He adds to that promise and says it will be theirs forever! When we settle in our hearts to choose God's will above our own, and trust Him in that decision - He will not only honor His promises to us, He will add His favor and blessing to everything concerning us - far above what we could dream and imagine!

# Day 23

## His Extravagant Goodness

*Psalm 84:11(TPT), "For the Lord God is brighter than the brilliance of a sunrise! Wrapping Himself around me like a shield, He is so generous with His gifts of grace and glory. Those who walk along His paths with integrity will never lack one thing they need, for He provides it all!"*

As children of God, we have been redeemed from the curse, and have found our new identity in Jesus! Because of His death and resurrection, we can partake of the riches of our glorious inheritance now! When we understand our old, selfish, sinful life died and was buried with Jesus, we will stop identifying ourselves with it! We won't allow our thoughts and conversations to align with negative feelings and past failures! Instead, we will make a moment-by-moment choice to align ourselves with what the Word says our new nature is! The Apostle Paul believed this so strongly that he said his own identity and won't even exist anymore - he was dead to it! Instead, he chose to let Jesus rule over everything he thought about, dominate every conversation he engaged in, and have influence over everything he did. The Bible promises that when we chose to live like this, we will never lack any good thing. Choosing to see ourselves from His perspective and live in the new nature He has given us, causes us to walk in the reality of His extravagant goodness, provision, and protection every single day!

# Day 24

## Eyes of Faith

*2 Corinthians 5:7 (TPT), "For we live by faith, not by what we see with our eyes."*

Jesus made it clear that to know and understand things of the spirit, we need to perceive things from our spirits, and not our natural intellect. In fact, just understanding God's word through our mental capacity alone will rob us from really experiencing its power! The moment we became born-again, our spirits were made alive by the Spirit of God. That means we were given the ability to perceive things that reach beyond this natural world. God's Own Spirit reveals His truth, from the scriptures, directly to our spirits. As we read and meditate on God's word, the Holy Spirit causes it to come alive inside us! We see its truth through the eyes of our spirit-man, which is far superior to just seeing it through our mental capacity to understand. This is the way we are expected to live - perceiving things through eyes of faith, not through our natural senses which limits God's power in our lives. Practice seeing things through your eyes of faith so you can live in the fullness of life God has for you!

# Day 25

## Identity Change

*Ephesians 1:4 (NKJ), "...He hath chosen us in Him before the foundation of the world, that we should be holy and without blame before Him in love:"*

God is in the business of changing identities! Even if we think there are parts of our nature that are too stubborn to change, the Holy Spirit has the power to remake us from the inside out - if we will just get in agreement with Him! Ephesians 2:10 tells us that we are God's own handiwork! We are His project of choice! And the plans He has for us are so good! They involve living the good life, full of good works which He prearranged and made ready for us to live! This new identity became ours the moment we became born-again. 2 Corinthians 5:17 says we became ingrafted in Christ. Our old, sinful, flawed nature DIED with Jesus on that cross! Now a fresh and new one has been recreated by God Himself inside us! Provision for this new life was made before we were saved, it became our possession when we became born-again, and it becomes our reality as we walk in the light of the Word! 2 Corinthians 3:18 explains what happens when we look intently into the Word and feed on its truth. It literally begins to transform us from the inside out as we receive revelation knowledge of what it says. Let the Holy Spirit show you your new identity in Christ, as He builds from the inside out - renewing your thinking and attitudes. You will be forever changed by taking on your new identity in Him!

# Day 26

## Dead Man Walking

***Philippians 3:11(AMPC), "That if possible I may attain to the [spiritual and moral] resurrection [that lifts me] out from among the dead [even while in the body]."***

Paul received the revelation of exactly what happens to every believer the moment we surrender to the Lordship of Jesus Christ. In the spirit realm, our old, sinful, selfish nature is nailed to the cross with Jesus. There was nothing easy, or pleasant on that cross for Jesus. *"That cross of old Roman times knew no compromise;...He was alive when they hung Him on that cross and completely dead when they took Him down six hours later."* (A.W. Tozer - The Radical Cross).

The cruelty of the cross was severe and final. When that cross brought Christ's life to an end, it also crucified, and ended our first life, the old nature we had before we knew Jesus. When that life died, so did every legal hold and accusation the devil had over us! Then, the same resurrection power that raised Jesus from the dead, raised us too! That new life surged into our spirits, creating a brand-new nature that resembles the resurrected, victorious Jesus! Paul often refers to the need for us to continuously walk in the revelation that we can experience the power of the resurrection life of Jesus when we share in His sufferings, which are His death on the cross! We simply can't have one without the other! There is absolutely nothing about our old nature that should be allowed to live again in us! Not if we are going to live in the fullness of life, power, authority, and victory Jesus paid for us to have. Decide today you are dead to your old life - and fully alive in Jesus - Who loves you and gave Himself for you!

# Day 27

## One Word From God!

*Judges 6:12 (AMPC), "And the Angel of the Lord appeared to him and said to him, The Lord is with you, you mighty man of [fearless] courage."*

At the time the angel visited Gideon, he was in hiding. He was beating wheat in an underground wine press, out of sight of the Midianites. The Bible explains Gideon's mindset as gloomy and depressed. Every time he tried to do something to provide for his family, or people, the enemy would destroy it all. He was probably on the verge of becoming bitter towards the Lord, complaining about Him rejecting His people. Gideon had lost hope of any redemption out of his situation. He had lost faith in the God who redeemed his ancestors from Egypt, which is what makes the angel's address to Gideon almost laughable. He called Gideon a mighty man of fearless courage! There was simply no evidence of this in Gideon's life! And yet God's Word was all that was needed to shake Gideon out of his degenerative mindset and infuse new hope and faith into Him. Romans 4:17 says, *"... God gives life to the dead and speaks of the nonexistent things that [He has foretold and promised] as if they [already] existed."* Hallelujah!

If you are feeling discouraged and hopeless about your circumstances, and inadequate to bring any change, then it's time to pick up God's Word and be shaken out of that incorrect, negative mindset! All it takes is one Word from God to come alive in your heart to produce the faith needed to break free of defeat and set you on the path of victory! Take God at His Word today, believe what He says and let faith move you to fulfil your destiny in Him!

# Day 28

## Knowing Jesus

*1 John 5:20 (AMPC), "And we know that the Son of God has come and has given us an understanding, that we may know Him who is true; and we are in Him who is true, in His Son Jesus Christ. This is the true God and eternal life."*

In Matthew 16, after the disciples had spent so much time with Jesus, watching and studying Him closely, He finally asked them who they thought He was. Simon Peter responded from what He had seen and knew in His heart to be true: *"You are the Christ, the Son of the Living God."* Simon Peter identified who Jesus really was from taking in everything He saw, heard, and felt in His experiences with Him. Jesus told Peter that his perception wasn't based on just what he had observed through his physical senses - but from the Spirit of God revealing the truth to him. What Peter had gained and understood from knowing Jesus, resulted in his identity being changed! Jesus told him he would no longer be someone who was indecisive or wavering in his convictions. He would be known as Peter the Rock! Having a clear revelation of who Jesus really is - is the foundation He will always build His church on!

Directly after this, Peter was given the keys of the kingdom - to walk in the same authority Jesus did, to see God's kingdom advance on the earth. As we pursue knowing the Person of Jesus, through the Holy Spirit revealing Him to us in His Word, like Peter, we will have the sure confidence and conviction to walk in His authority and see His kingdom advance each day, as we live in Him.

# Day 29

## Authority over Disease

*Matthew 8:3 (AMPC), "And He reached out His hand and touched him, saying, I am willing; be cleansed by being cured. And instantly his leprosy was cured and cleansed."*

As Jesus came down the mountain from preaching, a man with leprosy approached Him. This man was very close to violating the Old Testament law that enforced lepers to keep their distance from uninfected people, because of how contagious the disease was. The leper declared that he knew Jesus possessed the power and authority to cleanse and cure him. The question wasn't if Jesus *could* do it, it was if He was *willing* to do it. Of course, Jesus was willing, not just because it was in His compassionate nature to do so, but because His purpose was to demonstrate the power and love of God. Jesus could have healed the man by just speaking the Word, instead, He seemingly violated the law by reaching out and touching the man. This was a forbidden act, because anyone who touched a leper would in turn be infected and made unclean. But Jesus demonstrated that the power He carried destroyed the disease on contact! He wasn't defying the law; He was fulfilling it! He was demonstrating how our belief and trust in Him draws a power so extreme that even infectious diseases are powerless in comparison. We carry this same power and authority since Jesus lives in us! Let faith arise in you as you become the one to infect people with the power and life of God, instead of being fearful of being infected by what you have the power to destroy!

# Day 30

## Never Ashamed!

***Acts 7:56 (AMPC), "And he said, Look! I see the heavens opened, and the Son of man standing at God's right hand!"***

Before declaring these words, Stephen had enraged his accusers by arguing so well that Jesus is the Messiah. They couldn't refute what he said. The only way to silence him was to falsely accuse him and sentence him to death. Stephen exposed the Sanhedrin's stubborn refusal to recognize this truth, after proving to them, from the scriptures, that the Jesus they killed fulfilled every prophecy about Himself. They simply couldn't indulge such a public confession and acknowledgement that Jesus really was exactly who He said He was - and died at their hand for saying it. Then, what sealed Stephen's fate was telling them what he saw when he gazed into heaven and saw Jesus standing at the right hand of the Father. The Sanhedrin were enraged they shouted, put their hands over their ears and rushed upon him all at once! They dragged him out of the city and stoned him to death. But Stephen was so caught up in the glory of seeing the One he so boldly proclaimed - he only cared to ask for his accusers to be forgiven before stepping into the arms of Jesus. Many scholars believe Stephen saw Jesus standing at the right hand of the Father instead of sitting, as the scriptures record, because He was deeply moved by Stephen's witness and stood as his advocate in return (Matthew 10:32). Never be ashamed, or afraid to proclaim the truth about Jesus that you know to be true. Just as you confess Him before men, He will in turn, confess you are His before His Father in heaven.

# DECEMBER

# Day 01

## Identify with the Word

*Luke 2:52 (AMPC), "And Jesus increased in wisdom (in broad and full understanding) and in stature and years, and in favor with God and man."*

This world is filled with people who are trying desperately to *'find themselves'*. The market is saturated with 'self-discovery' materials and courses. 'Life-coaching' has become a booming occupation, offering people some sort of clarity on who they are, so they can be steered in the right direction for their lives. The truth is, there is only one place we will receive our identity and purpose - the Word of God. The Bible says before Jesus came to this earth, He emptied Himself of His deity power, and in humility, studied the scriptures to find out who He was and what His purpose was. Of course, He knew inherently that He was the Son of God - but from the age of about 11 or 12, He spent much of His time in the synagogues, studying the scriptures and learning from the men who had studied them too. Then the day came where He was handed the book of Isaiah, and as He read, He discovered exactly who He was, and what purpose He was to fulfil: *"The Spirit of the Lord [is] upon Me, because He has anointed Me [the Anointed One, the Messiah] to preach the good news (the Gospel) to the poor; He has sent Me to announce release to the captives and recovery of sight to the blind, to send forth as delivered those who are oppressed [who are downtrodden, bruised, crushed, and broken down by calamity]"* (Luke 4:18). As you spend time in God's Word, the Holy Spirit will reveal everything you need to know about who you are in Christ, and the purpose He created you to fulfil by His power that is at work in and through you.

# Day 02

## Meditate on This!

***2 Corinthians 5:17 (AMPC), "Therefore if any person is [ingrafted] in Christ (the Messiah) he is a new creation (a new creature altogether); the old [previous moral and spiritual condition] has passed away. Behold, the fresh and new has come!"***

Since our salvation experience has made us completely new in Christ - we must base our identity on what God's Word says we are. When we meditate on the truth it says about us - we will begin to re-program our minds to align with the new nature of our spirit-man. This is so powerful, because our thoughts directly influence our emotions and attitudes, which in turn affect behavior, our health, and our life choices! Here are some truths concerning your new nature that you can meditate on and trust the Holy Spirit to make alive in you, so you can experience them becoming your reality. Your life is hidden in Christ! (Colossians 3:1-3). Since your old nature died with Christ, sin, and its power over you was nailed to that cross too! So, you no longer serve sin! (Romans 6:4-6). Now your new life is raised up with the victorious Christ, and you are seated with Him in heavenly places - where you already have the victory over anything you will ever face in this life! (Ephesians 2:4-6). So, you keep your mind focused on things that are true, according to the Word of God - things that are full of faith and not fear (Philippians 4:8). Refuse to entertain grumbling, murmuring, and complaining speech and only speak words that are uplifting, wholesome, and full of faith! (Colossians 4:6, Titus 2:8). This is the way to success and prosperity - and being exactly who God created you to be! (Psalm 1:1-3).

# Day 03

## Dominate Over Sin!

**Hebrews 10:17-18 (NKJ), "'Their sins and their lawless deeds I will remember no more.' Now where there is remission of these, there is no longer an offering for sin."**

Many Christians don't have a personal revelation of what their New Birth means. They don't understand what the finished work of the cross has done for them. They believe in the forgiveness of sins, but they don't understand remission of sins. What does that mean? When we became born again our sins were not just forgiven, they were cancelled or blotted out. According to God's point of view - there is simply no trace of them left! No stain to remind Him of any wrongdoing! No handicap holding us back from living in the fullness of life and victory in Christ Jesus! While we only believe in the forgiveness of sin, and not the remission of it - we will remain in the position where the devil will dominate us for the rest of our lives. Why? Because we don't recognize the full truth of what happened to us at our salvation. Not only were our sins and any remembrance of them destroyed; our nature to sin died too! We have become a new creation, our new nature in Christ is the same as His Own nature! Just like Him, we love righteousness and hate wickedness. The Bible says we have literally **become** the righteousness of God in Christ Jesus! The moment we understand this is our new identity - we immediately recognize which thoughts and speech are not in line with our new nature and bring them into line with God's truth! This is how we begin to dominate over sin, bringing every thought and motive into submission to God's truth before we play into the devil's hand. This is what living the life of victory looks like!

# Day 04

## Spiritually Discerned

*1 Corinthians 2:14 (NKJ), "But the natural man does not receive the things of the Spirit of God, for they are foolishness to him; nor can he know them, because they are spiritually discerned."*

The Bible tells us we were created in the image and likeness of God. We are living spirits that are housed in physical bodies, and have a soul comprising of our intellect, will and emotions. E.W. Kenyon wrote that before sin, man's spirit was the dominant force, and after sin his mind became dominant. That's because sin dethroned the spirit and crowned the intellect. Despite this, man still craves the touch of a living God. He is drawn to the supernatural because of his internal longing to be satisfied by God and see His manifest power - even when he doesn't realize it. The answer to this craving is found in 3 supernatural events: The new birth, the indwelling presence of the Holy Spirit, and the Name of Jesus! The empowering grace of God restores the spirit of man to its place of dominance, and when the child of God recognizes that the realm of the spirit is his normal home, he begins to live in the realm of the supernatural without effort! Mr. Kenyon wrote that communion with God will be a normal experience, that faith in His miracle-working power will become a natural way of life! Sin has made us workers, but God's empowering grace has made us trusters! Yield to the Spirit of God and trust Him to reveal the privileges you have in Christ - things that have been revealed in His Word, but which we have failed to see because we tried to comprehend them with human reasoning, instead of our discerning spirits.

# Day 05

## God Always Confirms His Word

*1 Kings 18:24 (NLT), "'Then call on the name of your god, and I will call on the name of the Lord. The god who answers by setting fire to the wood is the true God!' And all the people agreed."*

We read in the Book of 1 Kings about a contest that took place on Mount Carmel. God instructed the Prophet Elijah to have King Ahab gather the people of Israel, along with the prophets of Baal and Asherah. Then Elijah was to challenge the people as to how long they would waver between the false gods and the One true God. He declared that this was the day they would need to decide which they would serve. The contest between God and the false gods was on! Whichever was true would answer by fire - a supernatural demonstration to confirm their authenticity - which is exactly what happened! While no response came from Baal or Asherah, the Lord God caused a roaring fire to consume the burnt sacrifice, and the wood and the stones and the dust, and it licked up the water that was in the trench. Elijah had obeyed the word of the Lord Who in turn confirmed His word with a mighty demonstration of power (1 Kings 18:36-38). As we work in partnership with our covenant God, we should constantly remind ourselves that He will always confirm His word with the demonstration of supernatural power (Mark 16:20; 1 Corinthians 2:4). Faith filled obedience will be met with His supernatural working in our lives. We serve a God who is not limited by the natural things of this world and is always ready and willing to not only hear our prayers, but to answer them in power! Place your full confidence in your God Who always confirms His word supernaturally!

# Day 06

## Choose the Spirit of Faith

*2 Corinthians 4:13 (NKJV), "And since we have the same spirit of faith, according to what is written, 'I believed and therefore I spoke,' we also believe and therefore speak,"*

There are two key spirits that are in operation on the earth today, the spirit of fear (linked to the devil) and the spirit of faith (linked to God). While we are here on earth one of these two will dominate our souls. It's vital for us to decide which one we will surrender to and operate in. The reality is that just as much as faith activates and releases the power of God, fear activates and releases the power of the devil in our lives. The Bible tells us God has NOT given us a spirit of fear, but a spirit of power, love, and a sound mind. It's important to know this because many of God's children succumb to the spirit of fear because they don't know how to resist it. Never forget that what we don't actively resist will have the right to remain in our lives. The will of God for us is to resist the spirit of fear and embrace the spirit of faith at all costs.

As we allow the Holy Spirit to enlighten His Word to us, He will reveal its wisdom and release its peace and life to work inside us. The Word of Faith we receive into our hearts gives rise to and releases the Spirit of faith within us, to dominate our lives and lead us into triumph! Today, choose to follow the Spirit of faith, resist fear, and live in the victory God has secured for you!

# Day 07

## Pray in the Holy Ghost

*1 Corinthians 14:4 (NKJV), "He who speaks in a tongue edifies himself, but he who prophesies edifies the church."*

The Bible says that when we pray in the Spirit, we edify ourselves. The word edify means to uplift or to encourage. Even when we don't know how or what to pray for a particular problem - praying in our heavenly language releases the perfect will of God into that circumstance to bring about the victory! The moment we feel the release of joy and peace come up from our spirit-man, we know the battle is over and God's Word, released from our spirits has enforced the devil's defeat and released the atmosphere of heaven. Kenneth E. Hagin once said, *"Praying in the Spirit charges your spirit like a battery charger charges a battery"*. Trials and tribulations will come because of our decision to follow Christ, but since we have His victorious Spirit living inside us, all we need to do is tap into that power and release it over our lives and whatever issue we are dealing with. Proverbs 24:10 says that if we faint in the day of adversity, it's because our strength is small. Our strength is small when we neglect to charge ourselves up in the Spirit to rise higher and higher like an edifice - dominating every opposing agenda of the devil - by praying in the Holy Ghost (Jude 1:20). This is how we remain strong in the day of adversity, being supernaturally empowered to stand steadfast during any trial, and overcome victoriously!

# Day 08

## Abiding Destroys the Power of Sin

*1 John 3:6 (ESV), "No one who abides in Him keeps on sinning; no one who keeps on sinning has either seen Him or known Him."*

When we have a true encounter with the Presence of Jesus we are significantly changed. In just a moment His Spirit cuts away those things in our lives that hold us back from experiencing the fullness of His blessing and the freedom to live victoriously over sin. The way we sustain the power of that encounter is by having daily encounters with God's Word. As we welcome the word into our hearts, the Holy Spirit releases supernatural faith and peace inside us, which dominates our thoughts and keeps us in a place of victory over sin. This is where nothing contrary to God can be found within us because we are literally abiding in Jesus, and His Word is abiding in us. The Bible says that those who entertain sinful lifestyles and keep on sinning have never really seen God or known Him. It's impossible to abide in Jesus and have a taste for sin. If we really are abiding in Him we will not allow offence to take root inside us because God's love will be dominating our lives. We will never acquire a taste for sin while we are delighting ourselves in Him. Our hearts will be full of joyful thankfulness when we abide in Jesus. We become sensitive and attentive to His leading and deliberately walk in love with others because our confidence is securely found in Christ. Decide to abide in Jesus every day, His love and power will cause you to soar in victory over sin and destroy its wicked agenda concerning you forever!

# Day 09

## What You Already Possess

*Hebrews 13:5 (ESV), "Keep your life free from love of money, and be content with what you have, for He has said, 'I will never leave you nor forsake you.'"*

In a world economy that functions with the currency of money, what would, *"keep your life free from love of money"* even mean? The latter part of this verse gives us a key – just as Jesus did when He taught about how to not let the cares of this world overwhelm us in Matthew 6:25-34. He brings to our attention the truth that **we have** a loving Heavenly Father who knows what we need and is more than willing and able to not only meet those needs but bless us even beyond meeting them. He delights in the prosperity of His children and is never glorified through our lack. After all, Jesus dealt with the curse of poverty through the finished work of the cross. So, He has no problem with His children possessing money, what concerns Him is money possessing us. He wants us to have our chief focus on *what* we already possess – we have GOD! We have His Word, which teaches us His way of being and doing right, and it *never* fails! Our security is not to be found in possessions which can come and go, it must primarily hinge on the One who teaches us to be cheerful givers in order to receive. Before the day's work even begins, give thanks to the Lord for being your source and that His power to meet your needs and see you prosper is completely at your disposal as you obey the principles in His Word.

# Day 10

## Stop Your Grumbling

*1 Corinthians 10:9-10 (ESV), "We must not put Christ to the test, as some of them did and were destroyed by serpents, nor grumble, as some of them did and were destroyed by the Destroyer."*

While the children of Israel journeyed through the wilderness, despite the Lord's provision and protection, they were ungrateful and started grumbling (Numbers 21:4-5). Their constant complaining against the Lord and Moses tried God's patience and the Bible says they were bitten by fiery serpents. Their negative attitude brought destruction on them. When we begin to grumble and complain we become ungrateful and open the door to the Destroyer to harass us. That is why we should maintain a heart of thankfulness and gratitude, even during tough times, by constantly acknowledging every good thing we have in Christ Jesus! (Philemon 1:6). This way we keep our hearts and minds focused on the victory and limitless power He has given us to reign as kings in life! (Romans 5:17). Don't slip into the same trap of complaining that the Israelites fell into. We snare ourselves with the words of our mouths when we begin to complain. Later on, in Numbers 14:28, the children of Israel complained against the Lord again, refusing to keep their hearts focused on His goodness and kindness towards them. Their faithless grumbling prevented them from entering the promised land - instead they got exactly what they spoke over themselves (Numbers 14:28). When times seem tough - abound in thanksgiving! Your praise will draw the goodness of God to you as a moth to the flame! He inhabits the praises of His people - but grumbling gives way to the destroyer.

# Day 11

## Perfect, Established and Strengthened

*1 Peter 5:10 (NKJV), "But may the God of all grace, who called us to His eternal glory by Christ Jesus, after you have suffered a while, perfect, establish, strengthen, and settle you."*

This is a powerful promise from God for every believer. The only phrase that doesn't seem to fit well is the one that says, *"after you have suffered a while".* What did Peter mean when he wrote about us suffering? Well, when we read the verses preceding verse 10, we understand what sufferings he was referring to. 1 Peter 5:8-9 says, *"Be sober, be vigilant; because your adversary the devil walks about like a roaring lion, seeking whom he may devour. Resist him, steadfast in the faith, knowing that the same sufferings are experienced by your brotherhood in the world."* We live in a fallen world and have a very real adversary who is bent on trying to deceive and destroy the church of Jesus Christ. Making a stand for righteousness will certainly invite rejection and persecution from all sides. However, through the finished work of the cross, the devil has been defeated and stripped of his power to harm us. So even if he throws his best punch, we have been given the authority to stand firm in faith and use the Name of Jesus to enforce the devils defeat. In 2 Corinthians 4:8-9 Paul said, *"We are hard-pressed on every side, yet not crushed; we are perplexed, but not in despair; persecuted, but not forsaken; struck down, but not destroyed!"* When we choose to hide ourselves in Christ by fully abiding in Him and having His Word abide in us - we will always overcome anything the devil throws our way. Learning to resist him and to stand securely in faith will cause us to be made perfect, established, and strengthened for victory in Christ Jesus!

# Day 12

## Choose Your Position

*1 Kings 18:39 (NLT) "And when all the people saw it, they fell face down on the ground and cried out, "The Lord—He is God! Yes, the Lord is God!"*

The position we hold while on this earth matters! I am not talking about a title, or the position we may hold in a career, I am talking about our position as children of God! The Bible says Jesus is seated far above all things, and that He has given us this same position while we are living on earth! Since we represent our God and His Kingdom, the position we choose to stand in will determine what we experience in life. We can choose victory over defeat. We can choose health over sickness. We can choose prosperity over poverty. Since Jesus already paid the price on the cross for all of these things, our responsibility is to step into His fullness and walk it out on earth! Just as it happened in 1 Kings 18, all those who worshiped false gods witnessed firsthand the sovereignty of God. The same God that Elijah served is the God we serve today – He has not changed. Just as those who did not believe in Him fell to the ground and acknowledged, *"The Lord is God!"*, as we stand our ground in faith and take up the position of authority we have been given over the devil, people all around will notice that God is alive! We are His representatives here on earth, bringing all glory and honor to His name through the life we live. Today, choose to position yourself in Him and you will always live above and walk out the evidence of His promises!

# Day 13

## The Power of Association

***Mark 2:5 (NKJV), "When Jesus saw their faith, He said to the paralytic, "Son, your sins are forgiven you."***

Here's a thought-provoking statement: "If you are walking with 5 fools there will soon be 6 fools!" There is power in association. Who you associate yourself with is vital for the effective fulfilment of your destiny. The reality is that there are people to walk with and people to walk away from. The above scripture demonstrates the power of association. A paralytic had 4 friends who ripped a roof open and lowered him before Jesus. What's powerful about this story is that the faith that got the paralytic man healed was not his own, but the faith of his friends! The Bible records, "*seeing their faith...*". A man was healed because of the faith found in the people he associated himself with! The people you associate with will either be a blessing or a curse. They will either build you up or break you down. Today, be very intentional about who you choose to associate with. There are people to walk with and then there are people to walk away from.

# Day 14

## No Lack

*Philippians 4:19 (NKJV), "And my God shall supply all your need according to His riches in glory by Christ Jesus."*

David writes that he has never seen the righteous forsaken nor their children begging for bread. We serve a God that amply supplies all our needs, in fact one of His names is *"Jehovah Jireh"*, meaning *"The LORD will provide"*. The rich young ruler made the mistake of thinking he would be in lack if he sold everything and followed Christ. Yet Jesus said that those who have left their land, house and family for His sake would receive a hundredfold in return - in this lifetime, despite persecution (Matthew 10:29-30). That means even when we are persecuted for His sake we will be fruitful! All that God requires of us is our trust and obedience. As we seek His Kingdom first, everything we need will be added to us. God promises to meet your needs as you stay focused on Him.

Rest assured that as you keep your eyes fixed on Him, and fully trust Him to keep His Word concerning you - as you walk in faith-filled obedience - everything you will ever need will be added to you!

# Day 15

## Remain In Christ

*Ephesians 6:14 (NLT), "Stand your ground, putting on the belt of truth and the body armour of God's righteousness."*

We have been made the righteousness of God in Christ Jesus! That means while we are in Christ, we will remain in right standing with God. How do we remain in Christ and right standing with God? The above text tells us: *"Stand your ground, putting on the belt of truth."* To put on the belt of truth, is to secure ourselves in the Word of God. Deciding to be steadfast in the scriptures, anchoring ourselves in God's perspective is what keeps us in line with His will. Giving ourselves to the Word draws the Holy Spirit to come alongside us and lead us into all truth. He brings to remembrance all those precious promises and supernatural wisdom we fed ourselves on when we diligently spent time in His Word. He literally whispers the exact word we need at the exact time we need it to strengthen our faith and position us for victory. Even so, this is a choice we must make, a conviction we must hold – to have the word of God dwell richly inside us. This is how we abide in Christ and remain in right standing with God. If we choose to not do this, we will return to a life of slavery to sin and be overcome with its devices. The Word says it is better we had not known the way to righteousness, than to know it and reject it (2 Peter 2:21). Standing in righteousness is living a holy life. Holiness comes because of close intimacy with the Lord and His Word. Remain steadfast **in** Christ and you will overcome the world!

# Day 16

## Consider Wisely

***Proverbs 4:26-27 (NKJV), "Ponder the path of your feet, and let all your ways be established. Do not turn to the right or the left; Remove your foot from evil."***

Just like the Apostles of the early church, God has a specific, unique assignment for each of us to walk in. Ephesians 2:10 says, *"...we are God's [own] handiwork (His workmanship), recreated in Christ Jesus, [born anew] that we may do those good works which God predestined (planned beforehand) for us [taking paths which He prepared ahead of time], that we should walk in them [living the good life which He prearranged and made ready for us to live]."* While God has laid out the exact direction for our lives, we have the responsibility to choose to walk in it. It doesn't just happen by chance or unintentionally. We are told to carefully consider the path we are walking on, constantly assessing if it aligns with the assignment God has for our lives. Remember personal ease and comfort is no indication of whether you are on the right path or not. Obeying God is never going to be easy for our flesh. In truth, walking in His will is where our flesh is crucified so that our old nature doesn't stand in the way of us being submissive to the leading of God's Spirit. We have an enemy whose greatest fear is to see us walk out the good path the Lord specifically planned for us to walk in. He knows that when we are in God's perfect will for our lives it will result in God's kingdom advancing and his own kingdom retreating. Dr. Rodney Howard-Browne wrote this statement, "No matter how the enemy plots against you, you must be persuaded that everything you say and do comes out of obedience to the leading of the Holy Spirit. Always do what He says, nothing more, nothing less, and nothing else." Consider the path you are on today because your destiny depends on it.

# Day 17

## Immersed in the Word

*1 Timothy 4:15 (ESV), "Practice these things, immerse yourself in them, so that all may see your progress."*

One of the things Paul exhorted Timothy to immerse himself in was the public and private reading of scripture that would exhort, teach and instill doctrine (1 Timothy 4:13). Then, as he was diligent to cultivate and mediate on these truths, he would increase in every way and his progress would be evident to all. Timothy's steadfast devotion to the Word was essential for his success. Proverbs 4:4-13 list some invaluable qualities imparted to us when we give ourselves to meditating on and embracing the wisdom of God's Word. The benefits of loving and highly prizing the word of God in our lives are far too valuable to set aside or ignore! The word that is alive inside us will keep, defend, protect, and guard us. It will exalt, promote, and bring us honor. It will crown us with gracefulness, beauty, and glory! It will add years to our lives and our steps will not be hampered because it will clear and open the path before us; and it will cause us to run in our purpose without stumbling! Choose to daily immerse yourself in the word so your progress along with these wonderful qualities will be evident to all!

# Day 18

## Have the Faith of God

***Mark 11:22 (NKJ), "So Jesus answered and said to them, 'Have faith in God.'"***

Some translations of this text read, *"Have the faith of God"*, or *"Have the God kind of faith"*. The Bible records many instances where Jesus recognized either the abundance of faith, or the lack of faith in people. Each time He recognized substantial faith, the person would be healed or received whatever they were believing for. The God we serve is moved by compassion and always responds to our faith. He created faith to be the currency of His kingdom. Because of its nature, faith is a powerful commodity that always produces results, without fail! It is never uncertain or doubtful, and it never hesitates because it's based on a confident knowing! A confidence strongly founded on the Word of God. When we unwaveringly believe what the word says concerning who God is, and who we are in Christ, we will have no difficulty believing for any of His promises concerning us. The book of Philemon says that our faith is made effective when we constantly acknowledge every good thing we have in Christ Jesus! The more we read and meditate on these truths, the more they become established inside of us and our faith becomes unshakable! That's where the God kind of faith begins to operate and produce in our lives; where we know we will receive what we ask for in Jesus Name!

# Day 19

## The Gift of Adoption

*Galatians 4:4-5 (ESV), "But when the fullness of time had come, God sent forth His Son, born of woman, born under the law, to redeem those who were under the law, so that we might receive adoption as sons."*

This Christmas season is a time to reflect on the absolute goodness of God and His Father-heart towards us. Look at the people around you. Notice how they are caught up in the rush of this festive season, trying to find fulfilment, but instead finding despair. See what's really in their hearts – look beyond the façade of extravagant decorations and lavish parties. *People are orphaned.* Many lack the revelation of God's abundant and unconditional love for them. There are people all around us who live in a Godless, purposeless, unfulfilled reality! The glorious truth is that the Father sent His Son to be born into the world He created, so that He would redeem and deliver us from being eternally separated from Him and reconcile us to Himself! Jesus willingly gave Himself up and exchanged His life for ours! The moment we accept Jesus Christ as the Lord of our lives, every part of our old nature that shackled us to a hopeless existence without God, died with Jesus on that cross! Jesus who was righteous took on our sin nature and it was crucified with Him! Then, the Spirit of God raised Jesus up and we were raised with Him into a brand-new life and nature! We have been given the greatest gift ever - adoption as **Sons and Daughters of God**! The greatest gift *we* can give is to introduce others to Jesus and the wonderful life of adoption we have in Him. Whichever way the Lord prompts you, present Jesus to those around you and watch how His gift of adoption transforms their lives this Christmas.

# Day 20

## God's Inexpressible Gift

*2 Corinthians 9:15 (ESV), "Thanks be to God for His inexpressible gift!"*

In the context of the above verse, Paul the Apostle was stirring up the church to give generously into God's kingdom work, encouraging them to see their generosity as a personal ministry unto the Lord. He said their generous giving would produce generosity in others. This is significant because generosity produces joy in both the one giving, and the one receiving! Paul ends off this chapter by proclaiming: *"Thanks be to God for His inexpressible gift!"* Any gift we give can be measured or expressed by a value attached to it; however, the gift that comes from God is *inexpressible*! His gift to us is His Precious Holy Spirit! It is His very Own nature living inside of us! This season, when you look upon the nativity scene, don't just see the Savior of the world as a baby. Perceive the reality that your King came from glory and humbled Himself to become His very creation – to show us the way back to the Father. Jesus, in His glorious love, made it possible for us to receive the inexpressible gift of the Holy Spirit who enables us to live in an inseparable relationship with God. God's great generosity towards us caused a joy to well up inside Jesus to endure that cross as He *gave* Himself; and that same generosity produces joy in all who *receive* Him! This Christmas, with great joy, carry the testimony of God's inexpressible gift operating in and through you, as you showcase His generosity!

# Day 21

## He Dwells in Us!

*John 1:14 (ESV), "And the Word became flesh and dwelt among us, and we have seen His glory, glory as of the only Son from the Father, full of grace and truth."*

In the days of Moses in the wilderness, the first Tabernacle of God was constructed and many encounters with God took place inside this tent of meeting. It was where God spoke with Moses, *face to face* (Exodus 33:11). Then, in King Solomon's time, the priests ministered unto the Lord in such a way, that they were unable to complete their duties and lay face down on the floor because God's Glory filled the tabernacle. Later, the Jewish people had a tabernacle where they would meet with God on the basis of a sacrifice for atonement of sins. For as long as they could remember, there was always something they had to do, somewhere they had to go, a sacrifice they were expected to present to be close to their God. But when Jesus came, He fulfilled the law. He did all that was required for us to not only meet with God, but for His Presence to dwell in us permanently. We no longer need a place of meeting with a list of requirements to fulfil before we can meet with Him. The Spirit of God dwells within us and He reveals Himself to us as we delight ourselves in His Word. This Christmas, celebrate the privilege we have of God's presence dwelling within us - filling us with love, peace, and joy to share with those around us!

# Day 22

## Uncluttered Heart

*Matthew 1:21 (NKJV), "And she will bring forth a Son, and you shall call His name Jesus, for He will save His people from their sins."*

Christmas is a special time set aside for us to celebrate the most extraordinary event in history. It is a time of joy where we remember how Bethlehem's manger became the link that bound a lost world to a loving God. From that manger came a Man who not only taught us a new way of life but brought us into a new relationship with our Creator- God. Christmas celebrates the truth that our God is interested in the affairs of people and that He loves us so much that He was willing to give His Son for our redemption. It's quite easy to be distracted during this season. It's easy to be drawn into all the festivities that are void of the true reason for this season. Let's become even more intentional to spend quality time with the Lord in prayer, and His Word. Let's remain sensitive to the voice of His Holy Spirit. If you feel as though you're already becoming overwhelmed by the trappings of the season, stop for a moment, steal yourself away, and thank the Lord for giving everything of Himself to leave the glory of heaven to come into our world to make Himself clearly know to us. Say from your heart, *"Lord Jesus, as I remember Your birth, cleanse my heart that it might be an uncluttered, sanctified gift for You today."*

# Day 23

## Redeemed by a Covenant of Peace

*Isaiah 9:6 (NKJV), "For unto us a Child is born, unto us a Son is given; and the government will be upon His shoulder. And His name will be called Wonderful, Counsellor, Mighty God, Everlasting Father, Prince of Peace."*

Isaiah prophesied a coming deliverer who would lead God's people into a life of joy, peace, and a right relationship with God. This prophecy came at a time when two northern tribes of Israel were hit hard by an Assyrian invasion, devastating the land, bringing great suffering to the people. There was a desperate need for a Messiah to remedy the situation. Isaiah's prophecy described the character of the expected Messiah. The prophecy maintained that in the darkness of Israel's distress, the Child being born would be a great light to the people, and His kingdom would never come to an end. Today, we as believers, live in the reality of this prophecy. We have been redeemed from our enemy the devil and all the suffering he inflicts. We have received our Messiah and entered His everlasting covenant of peace - where in Him, there is nothing missing, nothing lacking, and nothing broken! As we celebrate Christmas, understanding that we are living in the fulfilment of Isaiah's prophecy, we must remember our responsibility to carry Him to the world around us, so they can be reconciled back to God and be set free from the bondage and tyranny of the devil's destructive reign in their lives. Ask the Holy Spirit to lead you to those who are ready to receive the good news of Jesus - the One who has come to take away their oppression forever!

# Day 24

## The Greatest Gift

*John 3:16 (NKJV), "For God so loved the world that He gave His only begotten Son, that whoever believes in Him should not perish but have everlasting life."*

The greatest gift that has ever been given to mankind cannot be found wrapped *under* a tree somewhere, it was found *nailed to* a tree over 2000 years ago. The greatest gift that ever was given, that ever is, and that will ever be given - is the gift of Jesus Christ. The above scripture is probably one of the most known scriptures in the Bible. It's known by believers and unbelievers alike. That God loved the world so much that He gave His Only Son for us! The gift of Jesus is the evidence of Father God's love for us. He sent His only Son to die fully aware that many would reject Him. Even knowing that, He still sent Jesus for those who would receive Him and become His own. This powerful truth is what sets us apart in this hour. We chose to respond to God's love and receive the greatest gift ever. Because of Jesus, our spirits are alive with the hope of glory inside of us. Today, choose to be so grateful for Jesus. He is the greatest gift we could ever receive. We can share this glorious gift with others. There are people we pass every day that need to hear this glorious Good News of Jesus. We keep Christ at the center of Christmas by telling others about the greatest gift ever given.

# Day 25

## Jesus - Heard, Seen, and Touched

*1 John 1:1(NKJ), "That which was from the beginning, which we have heard, which we have seen with our eyes, which we have looked upon, and our hands have handled, concerning the Word of life..."*

Today it's important to recall the purpose of why we celebrate Christmas. It is so easy to take what we have in Jesus for granted. 1 John 1:2 says that eternal life which was with the Father was manifested to us! What does this mean? Well, the word "manifest" means to make clear and obvious to the eye. So, John was saying that Jesus, the Son of God, who is eternal life and existed with the Father in heaven - was born on this earth and manifested in the flesh - for us to know, see and touch! Hallelujah! 1 Timothy 3:16 says, *"And without controversy great is the mystery of godliness: God was manifested in the flesh, justified in the Spirit, seen by angels, preached among the Gentiles, believed on in the world, and received up in glory."* Jesus came to earth to show us what eternal life with the Father looks like! And once He demonstrated that glorious truth, He personally made a way for us to live in that reality, while we are living here on earth! The finished work of the cross took away the sin barrier that prevented us from personally knowing God and being filled with His Presence in our lives. He also destroyed the work of the devil, which was not only to bring about the separation, but fill this earth with devastation. Jesus gave us back our authority over the devil! In His Name we can cast out devils, live in divine protection, and see the sick healed! (Mark 16:17-18). This is why we celebrate this glorious Day! It was the day God manifest Himself through His Son and made it possible for us to always enjoy hearing His voice, seeing Him move in our lives, and touching the glorious manifestation of His Presence! Merry Christmas!

# Day 26

## Jesus - The Word

*John 17:14 (NLT) "I have given them Your word. And the world hates them because they do not belong to the world, just as I do not belong to the world."*

There is so much power in the Word of God. Why? Because Jesus is the Word made flesh (John 1:14). John 1:1-5 tells us that *"In the beginning the Word already existed. The Word was with God, and the Word was God."* God's Word is the very expression of who He is; it reveals truth to us that is vital for our overcoming the world and walking in glorious victory in this life! As His children, to know, believe, and live by what is written in the word will bring us life, peace, and power! As we read His Word a few things become very evident to us, who our God is, who we are in Jesus Christ, what we can have in this life, and what is possible when we put our faith in Him! Isn't it such a wonderful truth to know, that the Word of God is alive and powerful, ready to fill us with the richness and truth of Heaven. But it is up to us to pick it up, get its truth on the inside of us, meditate on it and allow it to become our reality. Remember, Jesus is the Word; He is our perfect example of the life we can live as His representatives. We really can live above the circumstances and things of this world because we are in covenant with the God of Heaven who desires to give us all that is written in His Word! Today, choose to fully step out and live a life in His Word.

# Day 27

## Dedication that Brings Prosperity

*Acts 2:42 (NKJV), "And they continued steadfastly in the apostles' doctrine and fellowship, in the breaking of bread, and in prayers."*

Did you know that our level of dedication to the Word of God reveals our level of dedication to Him? We truly believe that God's Word, alive inside us, is the key to a life that's marked by true success and prosperity. Ephesians 2:10 says that God prearranged good works for us to walk in; and 2 Timothy 3:16-17 says it's God's Word that fully equips us for these good works! The early Church displayed sheer dedication to God's word, especially during the most difficult of circumstances. The Bible says they continued steadfastly in the apostles' teachings. When our lives are fully reliant on, and steadfastly dedicated to the Word of God being imparted to us, and lived through us - we will live in the reality of all it promises. Know this, it's impossible to obey the Word of God faithfully and not prosper in life. God's Word always produces increase and expansion when it's received and applied by faith and obedience. Today decide to embrace a lifestyle that is marked by a fervent dedication to God's Word, and watch the fruit that follows.

# Day 28

## Commitment Marked by Holiness, Peace, and Joy!

*Psalm 119:11 (NKJV), "Your word I have hidden in my heart, That I might not sin against You."*

Geographers rely on maps and graphs to locate areas not yet found. By the same token, we have the Word of God as our guide. There is no guidebook suitable to lead us in the kingdom of God way, except for the Bible. Moreover, we have a first-class, personal guide and teacher who is committed to lead us step by step into every truth the Word lays out for us. He reveals each glorious mystery to our hearts and quickens it to us - making it alive with the power to do exactly what it says to do! Philippians 2:13 says, *"for it is God who works in you both to will and to do for His good pleasure."*

As you begin each day, let the Holy Spirit be your guide in the Word. While you meditate on its truth, you will find it protects your heart from bitterness and fear, shields your mind from all temptations to sin, and makes your way prosperous. A life committed to God's Word, by His Holy Spirit, is marked by holiness, peace and joy, causing us to continually move forward from one degree of faith and glory to the next!

# Day 29

## Divine Revelation

*Matthew 16:17 (NKJV), "Jesus answered and said to him, 'Blessed are you, Simon Bar-Jonah, for flesh and blood has not revealed this to you, but My Father who is in heaven.'"*

Divine revelation is what moves us from living a life of almost enough, to a life of more than enough. We're not just referring to finances. For any area of our lives to reflect the abundance of life Jesus said He came to give us, we must live by divine revelation. This is where mere intellectual knowledge of the Word is replaced by a deep, inner knowledge of the Word - through experience! The Pharisees and Sadducees knew the scripture on an intellectual level only. That's how they missed recognizing who Jesus really was. When the Holy Spirit makes the Word come alive in us - He supernaturally reveals its truth to us in a way that we encounter Jesus in His Word. He literally opens the eyes of our hearts to perceive the Spirit of the One who authored it and have fellowship with Him in it. As the words become revelation to us, our hearts leap with joy and our minds and bodies are flooded with a glorious peace and hope! Jesus told the religious leaders that they search the scriptures because they think they lead to eternal life, but the scriptures point to Him. It's possible to know the Bible yet miss the author. The Holy Spirit is the source of all revelation. If you want to possess revelation, you must know the Holy Spirit and be devoted to spending quality time in the Word. There is nothing preventing any born-again, child of God from experiencing this reality. Put off every delay and set your heart to receive divine revelation today.

# Day 30

## Abundance in Him

*John 10:10 (ESV) "The thief comes only to steal and kill and destroy. I came that they may have life and have it abundantly."*

The Kingdom of Heaven is a Kingdom of abundance! This abundance refers to walking in all Jesus paid the price for us to walk in. Divine health, freedom from fear and the power of sin, and a life full of victory! This is true abundance that makes our lives rich with the blessing that comes from knowing Jesus and experiencing all He did for us! It is something the world can never give us, and praise God, it can never be taken away from us either! This is our covenant with God - living in His wonderful purpose while walking in the fullness of joy - knowing all is well with us and our families! John 10:10 in the New Living Translation says *"...My purpose is to give them a rich and satisfying life."* Hallelujah, we have access to a rich and satisfying life in Christ Jesus!

As we seek Him first and daily yield to His Spirit, every need will be met, and every blessing will be provided (Matthew 6:33). God will bless us with material and physical provision if we refuse to neglect the most important thing – putting Him and His Kingdom first! Out of this everything else flows. *He* empowers us to live an abundant, rich, and satisfying life!

# Day 31

## Transformed by The Spirit

***1 Samuel 10:6 (ESV), "Then the Spirit of the LORD will rush upon you, and you will prophesy with them and be turned into another man."***

In the Book of Acts Jesus promised the disciples that they would receive power when the Holy Spirit came upon them (Acts 1:8). Samuel promised Saul that when the Spirit of God came upon him, he would be turned into another man (1 Sam 10:6). The Spirit of God can use any vessel, whether small or great, for His glory. All He requires is a willing, obedient heart. The Bible says God has chosen the foolish things of this world and the things that are weak to confound the wise and the strong (1 Cor 1:28-29). Throughout scripture we see the mighty, transforming power of the Spirit of God touch and transform ordinary, even broken in spirit, people to become strong and courageous and do great exploits for His kingdom. We see how He transformed David, a shepherd boy, into a mighty king. We see how He transformed Gideon, a weak and timid farmer, into a mighty man of valor. We see how He transformed the disciples from ordinary fishermen into bold fishers of men. Don't think for a moment that the Lord can't do the same for you.

The Spirit of God, without exception, can and will transform and empower anyone yielded to Him. All He requires is your willing obedience! Yield yourself to Him today and watch the glorious transformation begin!

Printed in Great Britain
by Amazon